GED

PREPARATION FOR THE
HIGH SCHOOL EQUIVALENCY EXAMINATION

SCIENCE
NEW GED TEST 3

ROBERT MITCHELL

Project Editor
Julie Landau

CONTEMPORARY
BOOKS, INC.
CHICAGO ▪ NEW YORK

Library of Congress Cataloging-in-Publication Data

Mitchell, Robert P.
    GED, preparation for the high school equivalency
examination, Science, new GED test 3.

    Cover title: Contemporary's GED, preparation for the
high school equivalency examination. Science, new GED
test 3.
    1. Science—Examinations, questions, etc.   2. General
educational development tests.   3. High school
equivalency examination.   I. Landau, Julie.   II. Title.
III. Title: Contemporary's GED, preparation for the high
school equivalency examination. Science, new GED test 3.
Q182.M52   1987   507'.6   87-13429
ISBN 0-8092-5036-5

Published by Contemporary Books, Inc.
180 North Michigan Avenue, Chicago, Illinois 60601
Manufactured in the United States of America
International Standard Book Number: 0-8092-5036-5

Published simultaneously in Canada by
Fitzhenry & Whiteside
91 Granton Drive
Richmond Hill, Ontario L4B 2N5
Canada

Editorial Director	*Illustrators*
Caren Van Slyke	Clifford Hayes
	Miguel Ibarra
Editorial	Rosemary Morrissey-Herzberg
Sarah Schmidt	
Christine Benton	*Art & Production*
J. D. Fairbanks	Sue Springston
Mark Boone	Arvid Carlson
	Lois Koehler
Production Editor	
Patricia Reid	*Typography*
	Lisa A. Waitrovich
Art Director and Cover Design	
Georgene G. Sainati	Cover photo © Image Bank

CONTENTS

TO THE STUDENT

Introducing the Science Test

Part of preparing for a test is working through the doubts and questions that you have. Perhaps it has been a long time since you took an important test. Maybe you are not sure what is required to pass the GED Science Test, or you are nervous about the test-taking situation.

This book has been designed so that you can succeed on the test. It will provide you with instruction in the skills you need to pass the test, background information on key science concepts, and plenty of GED-type practice. If you work carefully through this book, you should do well. The material on pages xi–xii will give you advice on how to use this book.

What Kind of Test Is This?

The GED Science Test consists of multiple-choice questions. These questions require you to know some of the basic science concepts that will be covered in this book. However, the test emphasizes your ability to think about these concepts. You will not have to recall an isolated fact or date as on some tests. Rather, you will read a passage or look at an illustration and answer questions based on it. To answer successfully, you will need to:

- have an understanding of basic science concepts

- be able to interpret illustrations and reading passages

- be able to show that you can:
  - understand what you read
  - apply information to a new situation
  - analyze relationships among ideas
  - make judgments about the material presented

Actually, you already do all of these different kinds of thinking in daily life. In this book, we will help you apply these skills to science materials.

What Does the Test Look Like?

There are 66 multiple-choice questions, and you will be given 95 minutes to complete the test. About two-thirds of the questions will be based on reading passages of up to 250 words each, and one-third will be based on diagrams, charts, or graphs. To get an idea of what the test is like, look at the practice test at the end of this book. This practice test is based on the real GED Test.

What's on the Test?

The GED Science Test can be broken down into the content areas it covers and the skills it tests.

These subjects make up the content of the test:

Life Sciences   50%
  • Biology

Physical Sciences   50%
  • Earth Science
  • Chemistry
  • Physics

These essential science concepts are covered in Chapters 5–9 of this book. However, keep in mind that a given question may draw from a number of these subjects. It's hard to discuss society or people without touching on a number of topics. For example, a question on air pollution may draw from material covered in both biology and chemistry.

Also, remember that you are being tested on your ability to think about certain ideas and concepts. You will be asked to do more than just find an answer that was given in a passage.

Thinking skills that you will be tested on include:

Understanding Ideas   20%
Applying Ideas   30%
Analyzing Ideas   30%
Evaluating Ideas   20%

Chapters 1–4 of this book focus on these thinking skills, and all of the activities and questions in this book will help you answer these types of questions. However, when you answer a question, you shouldn't be concerned about which thinking skill is being tested. The chart above is intended simply to show you how the GED Science Test may differ from other tests you have taken.

The Five GED Tests

The following section answers some of the questions asked most frequently about the GED tests.

Q: WHAT DOES *GED* STAND FOR?

A: *GED* stands for the Tests of General Educational Development. The GED is a national examination developed by the GED Testing Service of the American Council on Education. The credential received for passing the test is widely recognized by colleges, training schools, and employers as equivalent to a high school diploma.

While the GED measures skills and knowledge normally acquired in four years of high school, much that you have learned informally or through other types of training can help you pass the test.

The GED test is available in English, French, and Spanish, on audio-cassette, in Braille, and in large print.

 WHAT SHOULD I KNOW TO PASS THE TEST?

The test consists of five examinations in the areas of writing skills, social studies, science, literature and the arts, and mathematics. The chart below outlines the main content areas, the breakdown of questions, and the time allowed per test.

THE GED TESTS

Test	Minutes	Questions	Percentage
Writing Skills			
Part I	75	55	Sentence Structure 35% Usage 35% Mechanics 30%
Part II	45	1 topic	
Social Studies	85	64	History 25% Economics 20% Political Science 20% Geography 15%* Behavioral Science 20%
Science	95	66	Biology 50% Physical Sciences 50%
Literature and the Arts	65	45	Popular Literature 50% Classical Literature 25% Commentary 25%
Mathematics	90	56	Arithmetic 50% Algebra 30% Geometry 20%

In Canada, 20% of the test is based on geography and 15% on behavioral science.

On all five tests, you are expected to demonstrate the ability to think about many issues. You are also tested on knowledge and skills you have acquired from life experiences, television, radio, books and newspapers, consumer products, and advertising. In addition to the above information, keep these facts in mind:

1. Three of the five tests—literature and the arts, science, and social studies—require that you answer questions based on reading or interpreting

cartoons, diagrams, maps, charts, and graphs in these content areas. Developing strong reading and thinking skills is the key to succeeding on these tests.

2. The writing skills test requires you to be able to detect and correct errors in sentence structure, grammar, punctuation, and spelling. You will also have to write a composition of approximately 200 words on a topic familiar to most adults.

3. The math test consists mainly of word problems to be solved. Therefore, you must be able to combine your ability to perform computations with problem-solving skills.

Someone once said that an education is what remains after you've forgotten everything else. In many ways, this is what the GED measures.

Q: CAN I TAKE THE TEST?

A: Each year, more than 700,000 people take the GED test. In the United States, Canada, and many territories, people who have not graduated from high school and who meet specific eligibility requirements (age, residency, etc.) may take the test. Since eligibility requirements vary, it would be useful to contact your local GED testing center or the director of adult education in your state, province, or territory for specific information.

Q: WHAT IS A PASSING SCORE ON THE GED?

A: Again, this varies from area to area. To find out what you need to pass the test, contact your local GED testing center. However, you must keep two scores in mind. One score represents the minimum score you must get on each test. For example, if your state requires minimum scores of 40, you must get at least 40 points on every test. Additionally, you must meet the requirements of a minimum average score on all five tests. For example, if your state requires a minimum average score of 45, you must get a total of 225 points to pass. The two scores together, the minimum score and the minimum average score, determine whether you pass or fail the GED.

To understand this better, look at the scores of three people who took the test in a state that requires a minimum score of 40 and a minimum average score of 45 (225 total). Tom and Sarah did not pass, but Ana did. See if you can tell why.

	Tom	Sarah	Ana
Test 1	44	42	43
Test 2	43	43	48
Test 3	38	42	47
Test 4	50	40	52
Test 5	50	40	49
	225	207	239

Tom made the total of 225 points but fell below the minimum score on Test 3. Sarah passed each test but failed to get the 225 points needed; just passing the individual tests was not enough. Ana passed all the tests and exceeded the minimum average score. Generally, to receive a GED credential, you must correctly answer half or a little more than half of the questions on each test.

Q: WHAT HAPPENS IF I DON'T PASS THE TEST?

A: You are allowed to retake some or all of the tests. Again, the regulations governing the number of times that you may retake the tests and the time you must wait before retaking them are set by your state, province, or territory. Some states require you to take a review class or to study on your own for a certain amount of time before taking the test again.

Q: HOW CAN I BEST PREPARE FOR THE TEST?

A: Many libraries, community colleges, adult education centers, churches, and other institutions offer GED preparation classes. Some television stations broadcast classes to prepare people for the test. If you cannot find a GED preparation class locally, contact the director of adult education in your state, province, or territory.

Q: I NEED TO STUDY FOR THE OTHER TESTS. ARE THERE OTHER MATERIALS AVAILABLE?

A: Contemporary Books publishes a wide range of materials to help you prepare for the tests. These books are designed for home study or class use. Contemporary's GED preparation books are available through schools and bookstores and directly from the publisher, at Contemporary Books, 180 N. Michigan Ave., Chicago, IL 60601.

Now let's focus on some useful test-taking tips. As you read this section, you should feel more confident about your ability to succeed on the science test.

Test-Taking Tips

1. **Prepare physically.** Get plenty of rest and eat a well-balanced meal before the test so that you will have energy and will be able to think clearly. Last-minute cramming will probably not help as much as a relaxed and rested mind.

2. **Arrive early.** Be at the testing center at least fifteen to twenty minutes before the starting time. Make sure you have time to find the room and to get situated. Keep in mind that many testing centers refuse to admit latecomers.

3. **Think positively.** Tell yourself you will do well. If you have studied and prepared for the test, you should succeed.

4. **Relax during the test.** Take half a minute several times during the test to stretch and breathe deeply, especially if you are feeling anxious or confused.

5. **Read the test directions carefully.** Be sure you understand how to answer the questions. If you have any questions about the test or about filling in the answer form, ask before the test begins.

6. **Know the time limit for each test.** The science test has a time limit of 95 minutes.

   Some testing centers allow extra time, while others do not. You may be able to find out the policy of your testing center before you take the test, but always work according to the official time limit. If you have extra time, go back and check your answers.

   For this 66-question test, you should allow a maximum of one-and-a-half minutes per question. However, this is not a hard and fast rule. Use it only as a guide to keep yourself within the time limit.

7. **Have a strategy for answering questions.** You should read through the reading passages or look over the pictorial materials once and then answer the questions that follow. Read each question two or three times to make sure you understand it. It is best to refer back to the passage or illustration in order to confirm your answer choice. Don't try to depend on your memory of what you have just read or seen. Some people like to guide their reading by skimming the questions before reading a passage. Use the method that works best for you.

8. **Don't spend a lot of time on difficult questions.** If you're not sure of an answer, go on to the next question. Answer easier questions first and then go back to the harder questions. However, when you skip a question, be sure that you have skipped the same number on your answer sheet. Although skipping difficult questions is a good strategy for making the most of your time, it is very easy to get confused and throw off your whole answer key.

   Lightly mark the margin of your answer sheet next to the numbers of the questions you did not answer so that you know what to go back to. To prevent confusion when your test is graded, be sure to erase these marks completely after you answer the questions.

9. **Answer every question on the test.** If you're not sure of an answer, take an educated guess. When you leave a question unanswered, you will *always* lose points, but you can gain points if you make a correct guess.

   If you must guess, try to eliminate one or more answers that you are sure are not correct. Then choose from the remaining answers. Remember, you greatly increase your chances if you can eliminate one or two answers before guessing. Of course, guessing should be used only when all else has failed.

10. **Clearly fill in the circle for each answer choice.** If you erase something, erase it completely. Be sure that you give only one answer per question; otherwise, no answer will count.

11. **Practice test-taking.** Use the exercises, reviews, and especially the posttest in this book to better understand your test-taking habits and weaknesses. Use them to practice different strategies such as skimming questions first or skipping hard questions until the end. Knowing your own personal test-taking style is important to success on the GED.

HOW TO USE THIS BOOK

Congratulations on your decision to continue your education. This may not be an easy step in your life, but it can be a richly rewarding one. Not only will you be admired by friends and relatives, but you can achieve the personal goals that education makes possible. These goals may include personal satisfaction, passing the GED or other test, getting a better job, and possible further education.

This book will introduce you to the types of questions you will find on the GED Science Test. To answer some test questions, you may need to be aware of a few basic scientific ideas that you have heard or read about previously. Many of these are related to scientific issues that affect society as a whole. If you read newspapers, magazines, or books, or if you watch science news on television, you learn about many of these issues. If you do not read very much or pay much attention to science news, now is a good time to start. You will improve your science knowledge, and you will set an excellent pattern for lifelong learning.

1. As your first step in this book, it is a good idea to take the pretest. This will give you a preview of GED Science Test questions, and it will help you identify those areas in which you need the most work. You can use the chart at the end of the pretest to pinpoint the types of questions you answered incorrectly and to determine the skills on which you need special work. You may decide to concentrate on specific areas or to work through the entire book. However, working through the whole book is the best way to prepare yourself for the actual test.

2. This book has a number of features designed to make the task of test preparation easier, as well as more effective and enjoyable. These features include:

   - four introductory chapters that isolate the four thinking skills—comprehension, application, analysis, and evaluation—and provide you with plenty of practice in applying these skills; this section includes a broad sampling of passages and graphics from all five subject areas covered on the science test; these chapters are indicated by the symbol

   - skill builders (in the four introductory chapters only) that are concise hints for reinforcing science reading skills and concepts; these are indicated by the symbol

- content chapters that cover the essential science concepts that you need to know; these chapters are indicated by the symbol

- questions from the four levels of thinking skills in a format similar to the GED test

- high-interest reading passages that deal with science issues presently affecting society

- a variety of exercise types to maintain reader interest

- writing activities based on thought-provoking issues that provide an opportunity to practice critical thinking and writing skills for the essay portion of the GED Writing Skills Test; these are indicated by the symbol

- over 300 practice questions for strengthening science reading and thinking skills

- an answer key, coded by skill level, that explains the correct answers for the exercises; if you make a mistake, you can learn from it by reading the explanation and then reviewing the question to analyze the error

3. After you have worked through the five subject areas—plant and animal biology, human biology, earth science, chemistry, and physics—you should take the posttest. The posttest is a simulated GED test that presents questions in the format, level of difficulty, and percentages found on the actual test. The posttest will help you determine whether you are ready for the test and, if not, what areas of the book you would be wise to review. The posttest evaluation chart is especially helpful in making this decision.

SCIENCE PRETEST

Directions: Before beginning to work on this book, take the pretest. The purpose of this test is to help you determine which skills you need to develop in order to pass the Science Test.

The Science Pretest consists of 30 multiple-choice questions. All of the questions are based on charts, graphs, diagrams, and reading passages.

Answer each question as carefully as possible, choosing the best of five answer choices and blackening in the grid. If you find a question too difficult, do not waste time on it. Work ahead and come back to it later when you can think it through carefully.

When you have completed the test, check your work with the answers and explanations at the end of the section.

Use the Evaluation Charts on page 11 to determine which areas you need to review the most. For the best possible preparation for the Science Test, however, we advise you to work through this entire book.

Pretest Answer Grid

1 ① ② ③ ④ ⑤	11 ① ② ③ ④ ⑤	21 ① ② ③ ④ ⑤
2 ① ② ③ ④ ⑤	12 ① ② ③ ④ ⑤	22 ① ② ③ ④ ⑤
3 ① ② ③ ④ ⑤	13 ① ② ③ ④ ⑤	23 ① ② ③ ④ ⑤
4 ① ② ③ ④ ⑤	14 ① ② ③ ④ ⑤	24 ① ② ③ ④ ⑤
5 ① ② ③ ④ ⑤	15 ① ② ③ ④ ⑤	25 ① ② ③ ④ ⑤
6 ① ② ③ ④ ⑤	16 ① ② ③ ④ ⑤	26 ① ② ③ ④ ⑤
7 ① ② ③ ④ ⑤	17 ① ② ③ ④ ⑤	27 ① ② ③ ④ ⑤
8 ① ② ③ ④ ⑤	18 ① ② ③ ④ ⑤	28 ① ② ③ ④ ⑤
9 ① ② ③ ④ ⑤	19 ① ② ③ ④ ⑤	29 ① ② ③ ④ ⑤
10 ① ② ③ ④ ⑤	20 ① ② ③ ④ ⑤	30 ① ② ③ ④ ⑤

Questions 1–3 refer to the following information.

Commercially prepared food that is sold in the United States often contains one or more types of food additives. Preservatives are chemicals that are placed in food to retard spoilage by bacteria. Artificial coloring is placed in food to change its color, while artificial flavoring and sweeteners are added to improve taste.

In recent years, medical researchers have discovered that certain kinds of food additives, when they are eaten in very large amounts, can cause cancer in laboratory animals. However, scientists have not been able to prove that small amounts of these additives are harmful to people. Yet, even without medical evidence of danger to consumers, some companies now sell foods that contain no preservatives, artificial coloring, or artificial flavoring.

1. Which of the following is *not* mentioned in the passage as a reason that additives are placed in food?

   (1)   to retard spoilage
   (2)   to improve its taste
   (3)   to lower its cost
   (4)   to change its color
   (5)   to slow down the growth of bacteria

2. What assumption is made by food companies that sell food that is advertised as being 100 percent natural (containing no artificial additives)?

   (1)   Food additives do not cause cancer.
   (2)   Out of concern for their health, many customers will buy only food that is 100 percent natural.
   (3)   Many customers feed their pets scraps of food, and 100 percent natural food will be safer for these pets.
   (4)   Food that is 100 percent natural contains fewer calories than food in which additives have been placed.
   (5)   Food that is 100 percent natural has a better appearance than food in which additives have been placed.

3. Saccharin, a chemical substance 500 times sweeter than ordinary sugar, is used in the United States as a sugar substitute in many foods and beverages. In 1978, following the discovery that saccharin increases the incidence of bladder cancer in rats, the U.S. Food and Drug Administration began requiring that all products that contain saccharin carry a warning label.

   Which of the following studies could provide the most convincing evidence supporting the hypothesis that saccharin increases the risk of bladder cancer in humans?

   (1)   a study of the eating habits of a group of people in the United States who do not have bladder cancer
   (2)   a study of the eating habits of a group of bladder cancer patients in a country where saccharin is not used
   (3)   a study of the effects of saccharin on the health of rabbits and monkeys
   (4)   a study of the eating habits of a group of bladder cancer patients in the United States
   (5)   a study of the exercise and sleeping habits of a group of bladder cancer patients in the United States

Questions 4 and 5 refer to the graph below.

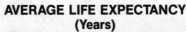

AVERAGE LIFE EXPECTANCY
(Years)

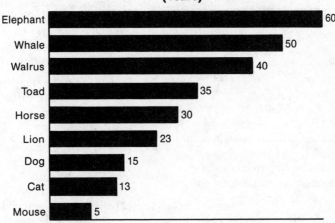

Elephant	60
Whale	50
Walrus	40
Toad	35
Horse	30
Lion	23
Dog	15
Cat	13
Mouse	5

4. A general rule for four-legged animals is that the larger an animal is, the longer its life expectancy will be. As you can see from the bar graph above, an exception to this rule is the

(1) walrus
(2) toad
(3) horse
(4) dog
(5) mouse

5. How many years longer is the average life expectancy of a whale than the average life expectancy of a dog?

(1) 13 years
(2) 24 years
(3) 35 years
(4) 50 years
(5) 63 years

Questions 6 and 7 are based on the following passage.

Sharks, the most feared of the large fish, are almost always predators that feed on other marine animals, from small fish such as sea bass and salmon to marine mammals such as elephant seals and whales. Shaped like a torpedo, a shark moves swiftly through the water and captures and rips its prey with rows of razor-sharp teeth. To aid in its endless search for food, a shark is equipped with a keen sense of smell, particularly for blood, and it can detect uneven vibrations in the water caused by an injured animal's swimming.

6. The torpedo-like shape of a shark gives the shark the survival advantage of

(1) strength
(2) speed
(3) flexibility
(4) keen vision
(5) tough skin

7. One type of shark, the great white shark, is known for its tendency to attack swimmers and even small fishing boats. Suppose that you want to know whether the great white shark is in danger of becoming extinct. It would be *most useful* to know the estimated number of

(1) teeth in the mouth of a great white shark
(2) swimmers killed by great white sharks each year
(3) types of sharks that are already extinct
(4) great white sharks alive today compared to their numbers 20 years ago
(5) diseases that affect great white sharks

Question 8 refers to the chart below.

Calorie Needs per Day	
Very active man	4,500
Inactive man	3,000
Very active woman	3,000
Inactive woman	2,500
Teenage boy	3,200
Teenage girl	2,800
Children 1–6	1,200–1,600

8. Which of the following statements is best supported by information presented in the chart above?

   (1) Teenagers need more calories each day than young children because teenagers get more daily exercise.
   (2) On the average, men are physically larger than women.
   (3) Adults need more calories each day than children or teenagers.
   (4) It is more difficult for a man to lose weight than it is for a woman.
   (5) The daily calorie need of an adult increases as activity level increases.

9. At room temperature, hydrogen gas mixes freely with oxygen gas. Without a source of heat, the gases do not chemically react or change in any way. However, a flame or an electric spark will cause this quiet mixture of gases to explode violently. A room that is full of this mixture can be blown apart if accidentally ignited!

   In a large industrial supply shop, what is the best rule regarding the storage of hydrogen and oxygen gas cylinders (containers of gas)?

   (1) Hydrogen gas cylinders should not be stored next to oxygen gas cylinders unless a danger sign is posted nearby.
   (2) Hydrogen gas cylinders should be stored at least six feet away from oxygen gas cylinders.
   (3) Smoking should be permitted around hydrogen gas cylinders only when no oxygen gas cylinders are nearby.
   (4) Hydrogen gas cylinders should be stored in a separate room, and preferably in a separate building, from where oxygen gas cylinders are stored.
   (5) Hydrogen gas cylinders should be stored with oxygen gas cylinders in a room that has steel-reinforced concrete walls.

Question 10 refers to the illustration below.

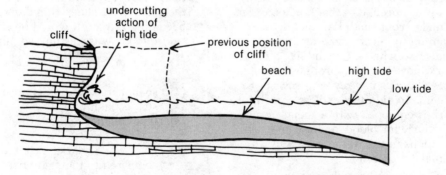

10. One result of the action of the high-tide waves on the cliff illustrated above is

    (1) a decrease in the height of the cliff
    (2) a decrease in the amount of beach
    (3) an increase in the height of the cliff
    (4) an increase in the amount of beach
    (5) an increase in the height of the high tide

Questions 11 and 12 are based on the following passage.

You may have heard a weather reporter talk about a temperature inversion and the dangers of air pollution that accompany it. To understand what a temperature inversion is, you must first know that, when weather conditions are normal, air temperature decreases with increasing altitude. In other words, the higher up you go, the colder it is. During an inversion, the opposite is true: the air is warmer as altitude increases.

A temperature inversion occurs when a layer of warm air passes over a layer of cooler air next to the ground. The layer of cooler air, which may be several hundred feet thick, traps air pollutants and holds them close to the ground. The layer of warm air above prevents the pollutants from dispersing at a higher altitude as they normally would. This situation is especially dangerous in and around large cities where pollution from automobile exhausts and industrial smoke can be at a health-threatening level even when atmospheric conditions are normal.

11. A city that is experiencing a temperature inversion is most likely to be bothered by

    (1) snow
    (2) hot weather
    (3) air pollution
    (4) water pollution
    (5) congested traffic

12. During a temperature inversion in and around a heavily polluted large city, what is the best advice that the mayor can give to the city's residents?

    (1) Don't drive your car unless absolutely necessary.
    (2) Wear warm clothes when you leave the house.
    (3) Stay home from work until the inversion is over.
    (4) Leave the city for a few days.
    (5) Write letters to the weather bureau and complain.

Questions 13 and 14 refer to the following information.

An important principle in biology is that each living thing is adapted (physically suited) to survive best in the conditions present in its home environment. As illustrated below, one adaptation shown by birds is foot structure.

FOOT STRUCTURE VARIATIONS OF COMMON BIRDS

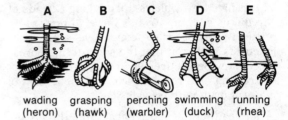

wading (heron) grasping (hawk) perching (warbler) swimming (duck) running (rhea)

13. Which two drawings above would be of most interest to someone studying birds that get their food from rivers and lakes?

    (1) A and C
    (2) A and D
    (3) B and E
    (4) C and E
    (5) D and E

14. The drawings above would have the *least* relevance to a person interested in

    (1) the walking abilities of birds
    (2) the dietary habits of birds
    (3) illustrations of wildlife
    (4) the climbing ability of birds
    (5) the soaring ability of birds

Questions 15–18 refer to the following passage.

Chemists working in medical research have developed quite a number of pain-relieving drugs. They have also recently discovered that the human body produces its own pain-relievers. Evidence shows that these natural painkillers, chemicals called *endorphins*, are produced by the body in response to the stress of tiring exercise. Chemists believe that endorphins are probably responsible for "runner's high," a feeling of calm and absence of pain experienced by athletes during long periods of strenuous running. What's more, although medical evidence is not conclusive, some chemists point out that the short-term depression many people feel when they must give up exercising on a regular basis may be a form of natural drug withdrawal!

After reading the above paragraph, three students made the following statements.

A. Even though endorphins are natural body chemicals, endorphin withdrawal is a serious drug problem.
B. Endorphins are types of chemicals produced by the body in response to strenuous exercise.
C. The reason I'm moody today is that I'm experiencing endorphin withdrawal from all the exercise I got last week.

15. Which of the above statements is a correct restatement of information given in the passage?

(1) A only
(2) B only
(3) C only
(4) A and B only
(5) B and C only

16. Which of the above statements is a hypothesis (a possible explanation of an observed fact or condition)?

(1) A only
(2) B only
(3) C only
(4) A and B only
(5) B and C only

17. Which of the following is the most reasonable prediction that can be made based on the information given in the passage?

(1) Further research will show that there is no such thing as endorphin withdrawal.
(2) The adverse side effects of all pain-relieving drugs will someday be eliminated.
(3) Learning to control a person's endorphin level may someday give doctors a new method of relieving pain.
(4) Chemists will someday discover that endorphins are present only in the bodies of people who are drug abusers.
(5) Further research will show that taking aspirin also causes the body to produce endorphins.

18. Considering what is now known about endorphins, for what symptom would synthetic endorphins *most likely* be recommended if they someday become a safe medicinal drug?

(1) chest pain due to a cold
(2) a headache due to a hangover
(3) an upset stomach
(4) a broken bone
(5) overall body soreness due to hard physical labor

Questions 19–21 refer to the following passage.

A storm cloud is much like a giant electricity generator. When the cloud forms, electric charges within the cloud separate. Positive charge accumulates near the top of the cloud, and negative charge accumulates near the bottom. As the cloud passes overhead, the negatively charged lower part of the cloud causes a large positive charge to appear on the ground below. Because positive charge is strongly attracted to negative charge, this ground charge follows the cloud like a shadow. Both the negative charge in the cloud and the positive charge on the ground increase as the storm cloud grows.

Before lightning strikes the earth, the air between the cloud and the ground acts as an insulator and does not allow electricity to pass through it. However, when the electrical force pulling the cloud's negative charge toward the earth's positive charge becomes strong enough, it overcomes the resistance of the air. When this happens, lightning occurs: negative charge rushes down from the cloud to meet the positive ground charge.

When lightning strikes the earth, it takes the path of least resistance. This path is most often just the shortest distance from the cloud to anything touching the ground. That's why lightning frequently strikes the highest point of an area, usually a tall tree, a high tower, or a skyscraper. People have also been struck, often when walking in an open area such as a field or when boating on a lake. In fact, the National Center for Health Statistics reports that about 125 Americans are killed by lightning each year, and more than 500 are injured.

Although lightning can't be prevented, there are ways to protect tall buildings from its destructive power. The most common way is with a lightning rod, a sharply pointed rod that runs from the highest point of the building down into the ground. The lightning rod is made of material like copper that conducts electricity rather than resisting it. If lightning strikes the rod, the electricity safely flows to the ground without damaging the building or harming the people inside.

19. For what reason is a lightning rod placed on a tall building?
    (1) to help prevent lightning storms from occurring in the sky over the building
    (2) to prevent lightning from striking near the building
    (3) to protect the building from lightning by providing a high-resistance, safe electrical path to ground
    (4) to protect the building from lightning by providing a low-resistance, safe electrical path to ground
    (5) to prevent cloud-to-earth lightning bolts and cause cloud-to-cloud bolts instead

20. When lightning strikes an object like a tree, the object is heated as electricity passes through it.

    Which of the following could be caused by lightning?
    (1) a heat wave
    (2) positive electrical charges accumulating on the ground
    (3) negative electrical charges accumulating in a cloud
    (4) a forest fire in a hot, dry area
    (5) the separation of electrical charges within a cloud

21. Imagine that you're unexpectedly caught in a violent lightning storm while hiking in the countryside, thirteen miles away from your car. Of the options listed below, what is the safest course of action?
    (1) Hike back to your car as quickly as possible.
    (2) Go to the lowest point of an open area and lie down, preferably in a ditch or depression.
    (3) Climb up a tree in order to get out of contact with the ground.
    (4) Go to the highest point of an open area and wait for the storm to pass.
    (5) Seek shelter next to the highest tree you can find.

Questions 22–25 are based on the following information.

Behavior is an organism's response to a stimulus. (A stimulus is anything that causes a living thing to act or to react in any way.) Below are five types of behavior demonstrated by vertebrate animals (animals with backbones). Three are types of inborn behavior, and two are types of learned behavior.

Inborn behavior:
(1) **Reflex:** a reflex is an automatic response—usually a simple act that is done quickly—to an unexpected stimulus
(2) **Instinct:** an unlearned pattern of complex activity that an animal naturally undertakes as part of its life cycle
(3) **Self-preservation:** a reaction shown by an animal for the purpose of escaping life-threatening danger or for protecting itself from harm

Learned behavior:
(4) **Conditioned response:** a learned activity that an animal displays in response to a stimulus but not as a result of a decision-making process
(5) **Intelligent behavior:** a complex activity involving judgment and decision making that an animal chooses to undertake

22. Each time Jenny claps her hands, her dog Scruffy rolls over and barks. Scruffy is demonstrating behavior best classified as

(1) reflex
(2) instinct
(3) self-preservation
(4) conditioned response
(5) intelligent behavior

23. When the cat came out the front door, the mouse on the steps ran for its life and ducked into its home in the woodpile. The mouse's running can best be called an act of

(1) reflex
(2) instinct
(3) self-preservation
(4) conditioned response
(5) intelligent behavior

24. After six years of smoking more than one pack a day, Arne finally decided it was time to quit, and he gave up cigarettes. Arne's decision is an example of

(1) reflex
(2) instinct
(3) self-preservation
(4) conditioned response
(5) intelligent behavior

25. During mating, the Adelie penguin of Antarctica builds a nest out of pebbles and the bones of its ancestors. This nest-building behavior is an example of

(1) reflex
(2) instinct
(3) self-preservation
(4) conditioned response
(5) intelligent behavior

26. Heat and light are forms of energy that almost always occur together. Usually, a consumer product is designed primarily to provide either heat or light energy, not both. For example, after you strike a match, both heat and light are given off, but the main purpose of a match is to make something start burning. You would use a match to light a darkened room only if there were no other source of light available.

For which *two* products below would heat be considered the *least* useful form of energy produced?

A. a cigarette lighter
B. a desk lamp
C. an electric oven
D. a candle

(1) A and C
(2) A and D
(3) B and C
(4) B and D
(5) C and D

Questions 27 and 28 refer to the illustration below.

**LUNAR ECLIPSE
(ECLIPSE OF THE MOON)**

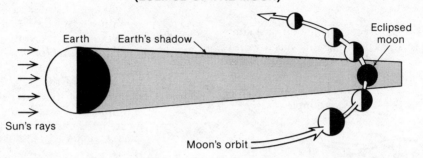

27. According to the illustration above, an eclipse of the moon occurs

    (1) only once a month
    (2) only once a year
    (3) only when the Earth is directly between the sun and the moon
    (4) only when the moon is directly between the Earth and the sun
    (5) only when the weather is clear on Earth and no clouds block the sunlight

28. Knowing that moonlight is reflected sunlight, what can you conclude happens during an eclipse of the moon?

    (1) For a few minutes, the moon turns dark and seems to disappear from the sky.
    (2) For a few minutes, the bright daytime sun turns dark and seems to disappear from the sky.
    (3) The moon, which otherwise is only partly visible as a crescent, slowly becomes a full moon for a few minutes.
    (4) The moon, which otherwise is not visible at all during that evening, slowly appears overhead as a full moon.
    (5) The otherwise bright daytime sun becomes much dimmer, similar to when it's hidden behind a cloud layer.

Questions 29 and 30 refer to the following information.

The volume of an odd-shaped object such as a small ceramic statue can be measured by the immersion method, the steps of which are given below.

STEP 1. Get a measuring cup or a similar container that has a volume scale along its side. Fill the container partly full of water and record its volume.

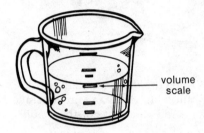

volume scale

STEP 2. Place the statue in the water and notice that the water level rises in the container.

STEP 3. Record the new volume level reached by the surface of the water. This volume is the combined volume of the water and the statue.

STEP 4. Subtract the volume measured in step 1 from the volume measured in step 3. The difference between these two volumes is equal to the volume of the statue.

29. Which of the following must be assumed if the volume of the statue is to be measured accurately using the immersion method?

(1) The volume of the statue is less than the volume of water in the container.

(2) The volume of the statue is greater than the volume of water in the container.

(3) The weight of the statue is equal to the weight of the water in the container.

(4) As step 2 is carried out, the water level does not rise above the top of the statue.

(5) As step 3 is carried out, the statue is totally covered by water.

30. Which of the following would lead to the greatest source of error when using the immersion method to measure the volume of clay actually used in making the statue?

(1) the use of a liquid other than water for the volume measurements

(2) the unknown fact that the statue is hollow inside

(3) a change in water temperature during the time the volume measurements were made

(4) the spillage of water while the statue was being removed from the container

(5) the unknown fact that a mistake had been made in an earlier measurement of the statue's weight

ANSWERS AND EXPLANATIONS
START ON PAGE 12.

Use the charts below to determine the reading skills areas in which you need to do the most work. The reading skills, covered on pages 14–91, are absolutely essential for success on the GED Science Test. Circle any items that you got wrong and pay particular attention to the areas where you missed half or more of the questions.

Pretest Reading Skills Chart

Skill Area	Item Number	Review Pages	Number Correct
Comprehension	1, 2, **4**, **5**, 6, 11, 15, 19, **27**	14–30	_____ /9
Application	12, 18, 22, 23, 24, 25	31–41	_____ /6
Analysis	**8**, 9, **10**, 16, 17, 20, 21, 26, 28	42–67	_____ /9
Evaluation	3, 7, **13**, **14**, **29**, **30**	68–91	_____ /6

The numbers in boldface are questions based on graphics. For the questions based on graphics that you missed, review the skill pages in which graphics are found.

Now look at the chart below and circle the same numbers for the items that you circled in the chart above. This will give you additional information about the science content areas in which you need the most work.

Pretest Content Areas Chart

Skill Area	Item Number	Review Pages	Number Correct
Plant and Animal Biology	4, 5, 6, 7, 13, 14, 22, 23, 25	92–121	_____ /9
Human Biology	1, 2, 3, 8, 24	122–51	_____ /5
Earth Science	10, 11, 12, 27, 28	152–83	_____ /5
Chemistry	9, 15, 16, 17, 18	184–220	_____ /5
Physics	19, 20, 21, 26, 29, 30	221–57	_____ /6

PRETEST ANSWER KEY

1. **(3)** Cost is the only factor listed that is not mentioned in the passage.

2. **(2)** Food companies correctly assume that there is a growing number of health-conscious people in the U.S. who do not want additives in their food. These companies produce 100 percent natural food to appeal to this market.

3. **(4)** The best evidence can be obtained by studying the eating habits of bladder cancer patients because they have the disease in question. Choice (2) is not a good choice because these patients have not consumed saccharin.

4. **(2)** The toad is the exception because it has a longer life expectancy than the mouse, cat, dog, lion, or horse, all of which are likely to be larger.

5. **(3)** The difference in life expectancy is 50 years–15 years = 35 years.

6. **(2)** According to the passage, the torpedo-like shape of a shark is related to the shark's ability to move swiftly.

7. **(4)** Long-term population change determines whether an animal is in danger of becoming extinct (choice 4). Choices (1) and (2) are not relevant. Choice (5) is wrong; all the sharks might be killed by one disease, or they might be killed by hunters rather than diseases.

8. **(5)** Although choices (1) and (2) may also be true, only choice (5) is supported directly by information from the chart.

9. **(4)** Because of the explosive nature of these two gases, the best rule is to store them as far away from each other as is reasonably possible. It would be unwise to take any risk of having them explode.

10. **(4)** As the cliff is undercut and worn away, the width of the beach increases. Neither the height of the cliff nor the height of the high tide is affected by wave action.

11. **(3)** During a temperature inversion, the air temperature is cooler but not necessarily cold, eliminating choice (1). As the passage states, air pollution is the main concern.

12. **(1)** Since some of the air pollution comes from automobile exhausts, city residents should be advised to leave their cars at home. Choices (3) and (4) are too drastic, and choice (5) wouldn't help.

13. **(2)** The birds most apt to get their food from rivers and lakes are birds adapted for wading or swimming.

14. **(5)** Of the listed choices, (5) is the person whose interest is least likely to involve foot shape, structure, or function.

15. **(2)** Statement A is an opinion. Only statement B accurately restates the information in the passage.

16. **(3)** Only statement C offers an explanation for a condition (moodiness).

17. **(3)** Choice (3) is a reasonable prediction based on the currently known effects of endorphins. Choices (2), (4), and (5) are not supported by information given in the passage. Choice (1) disagrees with evidence about endorphins that's already available.

18. **(5)** The discomfort of overall body soreness is similar to the discomfort felt in strenuous exercise, the cause of natural endorphin release.

19. **(4)** Lightning can't be controlled, but, as the passage states, buildings can be made safe through the use of a lightning rod, a low-resistance electrical path to the ground.

20. **(4)** When a bolt of lightning heats a tree in a hot, dry area, the result can be a forest fire. Choices (2), (3), and (5) are all causes of lightning, not effects.

21. **(2)** During a lightning storm you do not want to be in a tree, next to a tree, or near a high point in an open area. Choice (2) is the safest of the listed places.

22. **(4)** A dog is taught tricks over a long period of time. Rolling over on command is a learned, practiced behavior: a conditioned response.

23. **(3)** By running, the mouse is saving its own life, an example of self-preservation.

24. **(5)** The conscious decision by a human being to give up a dangerous activity is a good example of intelligent behavior.

25. **(2)** Nest building is an unlearned activity that is a natural part of a penguin's life cycle.

26. **(4)** The cigarette lighter and oven are both designed to be sources of heat. The lamp and candle are designed mainly to produce light, although both produce heat as well.

27. **(3)** An eclipse of the moon occurs only when the moon passes in the shadow of the Earth. An eclipse can happen only when the Earth is directly between the sun and the moon.

28. **(1)** When it moves into the Earth's shadow, the moon is no longer struck by sunlight, and it seems to turn dark and disappear from view.

29. **(5)** The total volume of the statue can be measured only if the entire statue is under water when step 3 is carried out. Choices (1), (2), and (3) are irrelevant. If choice (4) were true, the experiment would be flawed.

30. **(2)** None of the choices except (2) would lead to an error in measuring the clay's volume. If the statue is hollow, the actual volume of clay may be much less than the volume of the statue itself.

WHY STUDY SCIENCE?

Future generations may well point to the twentieth century and proclaim it to be the most remarkable century in history. During the past hundred years, almost all of the scientific advances known to society have been made. Discoveries in biology and chemistry have led to vast improvements in health care and consumer products. Discoveries in the earth sciences and physics have helped place astronauts on the moon and put landing craft on other planets. From each field of science has come a new understanding about the nature of life on Earth and about the nature of the universe itself.

Science reading skills are important in order for you to share in this new knowledge: both in the excitement it offers and in the often difficult decision-making that it requires. On the news, you hear of "test-tube babies," "genetic engineering," "radioactive waste," "intelligent computers," and so on. How you respond to such developments will help determine the way you and your children live in the future.

By strengthening your science skills, you give yourself some control over the direction that each new development takes. First, you increase your understanding of what's happening. You no longer feel like an outsider when you hear about scientific progress. Second, you become better able to make decisions regarding the use of each new service or consumer product resulting from scientific research. One place to influence the direction of science is at the ballot box. Armed with more information, you will be better able to decide how to vote on science-related issues.

1
COMPREHENDING SCIENCE MATERIALS

The word **comprehend** means to "understand." For example, when you comprehend or understand the game of soccer, you are able to watch the game and know what's going on. And, if you're watching with a friend who has never seen the game before, you are able to explain its rules. As you can see, comprehension means that you understand the general idea and have a good grasp of details. Comprehension in science is a measure of three abilities:

- the ability to summarize ideas
- the ability to restate information
- the ability to identify implications

Summarizing the Main Idea and Locating Details

To **summarize the main idea** is to express briefly an author's key thought. You can summarize the sentences of a paragraph, or you can summarize several paragraphs of a longer passage. In each case, you sum up, in just a few words, the main point the author is trying to make. For example, you may have just read a long article on research done on vaccines for common wintertime respiratory infections. Though a lot of details are given, the key thought you'll remember is that "there is still no way to prevent the common cold!"

A Main Idea May Be Expressed in a Single Sentence

In many passages, the author expresses the main idea, or key thought, as a single sentence. Other sentences provide details to support the main idea. In this type of passage, the author will most often place the key thought near the beginning or near the end. By putting the main idea near the beginning of the passage, the author draws the reader's immediate attention to it. If the main idea comes near the end, it can serve as a summary of all the information that has come before it.

Try finding the key thought in the paragraph below. Underline the sentence that best expresses the author's main point.

The action of ocean waves can change the shape of a shoreline. Waves can erode the shore, breaking up land masses near the water. Waves can also move the eroding dirt and rocks great distances down the shoreline. Beaches will be formed when waves move more rock fragments toward the shore than away from it. Cliffs are formed when waves move more rock fragments away from the shore than toward it.

Did you underline the first sentence? You should have, because the changing shape of the shoreline is the author's key point. Each of the other sentences gives an example of how this change takes place. Each example is a detail that supports the key point.

Now try underlining the main idea sentence of this paragraph:

Imagine taking a microscope and looking at the edge of a piece of paper in the hope of seeing a single atom! Using the world's most powerful microscope, you still couldn't see one clearly. In fact, if you could see one, you would find that it takes about 1 million atoms, placed side by side, to cross a distance as short as the width of the edge of the paper. Atoms are so small that even scientists must be content with studying large numbers of them at the same time, rather than trying to look at an single atom in the way that a doctor might look at a patient.

In the paragraph above, you should have underlined the final sentence. The author is making the point that atoms are very, very small. The first three sentences all emphasize this idea: the first sentence gets your interest, while the second and third sentences are details about the actual size of an atom.

A Main Idea May Not Be Expressed Directly

In some passages, a main idea may not be expressed in any one sentence. However, when this is the case, you can usually express the key thought as a one-sentence summary of several points made by the author.

Read the following passage and then write a sentence summing up the main idea.

> The first action your body takes when you eat food is to begin the process of digestion. Digestion takes place in the mouth, stomach, and intestines. During digestion, food is broken down into small molecules. These molecules pass into the bloodstream when they reach the intestines. The step following digestion is called absorption. During absorption, food molecules leave your blood and enter your cells. The final step, assimilation, takes place within the cells themselves. During assimilation, cells use the food molecules for body growth and maintenance.

Try writing a sentence that summarizes this passage: _____

_____

Your answer will probably be something like the following: "Digestion, absorption, and assimilation are the three steps used by the body in making use of the food you eat."

Notice that, because it is brief, a summary can't include many details. Instead, the summary expresses the main idea simply, using key words from the passage when possible.

Exercise 1

Directions: Read the passage below. Then circle the best answer to each question that follows.

> The possibility of life on the planets of distant stars has long been a favorite topic of science fiction writers and movie makers. Now this issue has drawn the serious interest of respected scientists.
>
> Using specially designed telescopes that are able to pick up very weak radio waves, astronomers are scanning the sky above us at every minute of each day and night. These radio telescopes can monitor over a million channels simultaneously as they search for any clue of a distant, advanced civilization broadcasting messages into space.
>
> No one can predict if we'll ever receive a signal sent by intelligent beings from elsewhere in the universe. But one thing is sure. If we do receive such a message, we'll be hearing thoughts from the past! Any incoming signal would have to have been sent into space hundreds, thousands, or even millions of years ago. This is because it takes radio waves this long to travel the incredible distances that separate Earth from other planets that may contain life.

1. The main idea expressed in the final paragraph is that

   (1) intelligent beings may live on other planets
   (2) a message received from space would have been sent into space long ago
   (3) large distances separate the Earth from stars elsewhere in the universe

2. The key thought of the passage is that

(1) science fiction writers and movie makers were the first people to popularize the idea that life may exist on other planets
(2) if distant civilizations were trying to contact us, they would use radio waves to send messages
(3) scientists are beginning to investigate seriously the possibility that life exists elsewhere in the universe

---

★ **GED PRACTICE** ★

Exercise 2

Directions: Read the passage below and answer the questions that follow.

Before you dump used motor oil on the ground or throw it in the garbage, think about your alternatives. You can take the oil to a recycling center, or you can give it to a service station that will have it recycled for you. To recycle means to reuse materials rather than throwing them away.

Recycling is the most environmentally sound thing you can do with old motor oil. When oil is not recycled, it is dumped on the ground or buried in a landfill, where it might well end up in your drinking water or food. What's more, dumped oil poses an immediate threat to the health of birds, small land animals, and plants. In spite of these dangers, only about 10 percent of all used oil is presently being recycled. The other 90 percent ends up in the ground.

If you change your own car oil, look around your community for a recycling service that may pick up the old oil at your home free of charge. If there isn't any, then take your old oil to a service station. Service station employees take the unwanted oil and store it until it can be picked up by a collection truck. The truck takes used oil to a refinery where it is refined once again just as if it had been freshly pumped from an oil well. After being restored to good condition, your old oil is ready to be sold again. This completes the recycling process. You've done your share to keep your environment clean, and you've helped preserve a limited natural resource.

1. Why does the author suggest taking old oil to a service station?

(1) Service stations do not charge much for oil changes.
(2) At a service station, you can buy new oil to replace the old.
(3) A service station will clean old oil and resell it.
(4) A service station will see that your old oil gets recycled at a refinery.
(5) A service station makes money by collecting and selling used oil.

2. Which of the following statements is the best summary of the author's main point?

   (1) Recycling old car oil will save you money in the long run because it will ensure that the oil in oil wells will last longer.

   (2) Because of problems with old oil, it would be better if people didn't change their car oil very often.

   (3) Recycling old car oil is an action you can take to help protect and preserve your environment.

   (4) Oil in drinking water and food is a serious health hazard throughout the United States.

   (5) Each community should assume the responsibility of building an oil recycling center.

ANSWERS AND EXPLANATIONS START ON PAGE 287.

Summarizing the Main Idea in Graphics

Graphics are used to present information visually, with pictures or numbers or both. The use of graphics makes it possible for an author to convey a lot of information in a compact way. And graphics make it easy for you to get a quick impression of this information without doing much reading.

The types of graphics we will work with in this book—and that are tested on the GED—are *graphs*, *tables*, *charts*, and *diagrams*. Each type of graphic is most useful for certain types of information. You'll see sample uses of each as you read through the next four chapters.

Many of the sections on graphics begin with a Skill Builder. The purpose of each Skill Builder is to introduce you to a certain type of graphic. The questions about the graphic will be based on the reading skill you've just learned. For example, you just learned how to find the main idea and details. The questions in the Skill Builder below will require you to summarize the main idea of a circle graph and locate details on it. In this way, you'll be learning to read different types of graphics while you're practicing your question-answering skills.

 ## Skill Builder
Reading Circle Graphs

A *circle graph* looks like a divided pie. Each "slice" or segment of the pie represents a part of a total amount. The total is represented by the whole circle. Most often, the amount of each segment is given as a percent, and the segments together add up to 100 percent. Because of their appearance, circle graphs are sometimes called *pie graphs* or *pie charts*.

Below is a circle graph. The title of this graph is "The Earth's Surface." Each segment has a name and a percent value. Looking at this graph, you can see that the Pacific Ocean covers 33 percent of the Earth's surface.

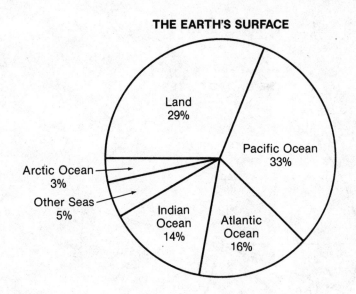

THE EARTH'S SURFACE

Try finding the following details on the graph above.

a. What percent of the Earth's surface is land? _____

b. What total percent of the Earth's surface is covered by the two largest oceans? _____

c. What total percent of the Earth's surface is covered by water? _____

The answer to a is 29 percent and is found by reading the segment labeled "land." The answer to b is 49 percent and is obtained by adding the percents for the Pacific Ocean (33 percent) and the Atlantic Ocean (16 percent). The answer to c is 71 percent and is found either by subtracting 29 percent (the amount of land) from 100 percent or by adding all the percents given for bodies of water: 33% + 16% + 14% + 3% + 5% = 71%.

By comparing the amount of surface covered by water with the amount of surface covered by land, what would you say would be a key point made by this circle graph?

_____

_____

The key point of the graph is that the surface of the Earth is covered mainly by water.

★ **GED PRACTICE** ★

Exercise 3

Directions: Questions 1 and 2 are based on the circle graph below.

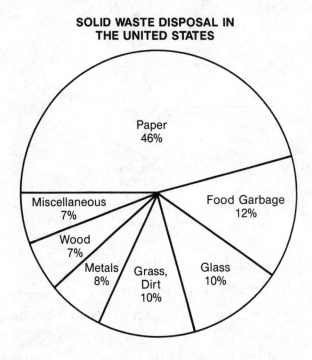

**SOLID WASTE DISPOSAL IN
THE UNITED STATES**

Paper
46%

Food Garbage
12%

Miscellaneous
7%

Wood
7%

Metals
8%

Grass,
Dirt
10%

Glass
10%

1. According to the graph, which material is the largest component of American garbage?

    (1) paper
    (2) glass
    (3) dirt
    (4) tin cans
    (5) pieces of wood

2. An author used this graph in an article about the value of recycling paper, metal, and glass products. Which of the following statements best summarizes a key point made by the graph and supports the author's argument?

    (1) The United States produces more garbage than any other country in the world.
    (2) Garbage can be conveniently classified into seven broad categories.
    (3) A full 64 percent of American garbage consists of material that could be recycled.
    (4) Recycling efforts are failing because of the amount of recyclable material that is found in garbage.
    (5) Due to the presence of a large amount of dirt in garbage, most things that are thrown away are not recyclable.

ANSWERS AND EXPLANATIONS START ON PAGE 287.

Restating Information

To *restate information* is to use different words and phrases to express the same idea. A restatement may not sound quite the same as the original statement, but it has the same meaning. Most often, you restate information in order to put it into words that are more familiar to you—words that make it easier for you to understand and remember what you're reading.

Here are two examples of restated information:

Original	**Restatement**
Excess fat and carbohydrate consumption can lead to obesity.	You'll get fat if you eat too many fats and carbohydrates.
Rocks from the moon's surface show features characteristic of rocks found on Earth.	Moon rocks are very similar to Earth rocks.

Now you try it. Using your own words, restate each sentence below.

Original	**Restatement**
a. Light reflected from the moon's surface indicates its spherical shape.	_____ _____
b. Touching the exposed electric wire, Jim's finger sensed the passage of a small amount of electricity, an experience that demonstrated the quick reaction of Jim's reflexes.	_____ _____

Answers will vary, but here are two possibilities:

a.   The moon looks round.
b.   Jim jumped when he got a shock.

Notice that each of these example answers restates information in a way more like the way you may talk or think. Yet, in each case, the information given is really about the same.

Exercise 4

Directions: Read the passage below and do the exercise that follows.

The two regions known as the Arctic and Antarctic are similar in that each lies at one of the Earth's two geographical poles. Yet, in many ways, these two ends of the Earth are very different from each other.

The Arctic, the region around the North Pole, is full of life. Over a hundred species of flowering plants grow there, as do many types of mosses and lichens. Many insects, birds, and mammals live there as well. The Arctic is also the home of about one million Eskimos and other peoples from North America, Europe, and Asia.

The Antarctic, the region around the South Pole, has much less life than the Arctic. Very few plants grow there because of the very harsh weather. In fact, the average monthly temperature is always below freezing, and winds of over a hundred miles per hour are common. These conditions make Antarctica a desert-like place that only penguins seem to love! Although these flightless birds make their home there, no mammals have done the same. The only exceptions are the few scientists who do research on this frozen continent and an occasional team of explorers.

Place a check mark before each statement below that is a restatement of information given in the passage. Be aware that a restatement may be a single sentence that combines information from more than one sentence in a passage. (Hint: Each statement below is a fact that you may already know. Be careful to check only those facts that are restatements of information presented above.)

_____ **1.** The Arctic is located at the North Pole and the Antarctic at the South Pole.

_____ **2.** The continent of Antarctica is as large as the United States and Canada combined.

_____ **3.** Because of its low temperature and terrific winds, Antarctica is like a desert.

_____ **4.** Bears and seals live in the Arctic, while penguins live in the Antarctic.

★ GED PRACTICE ★

Exercise 5

Directions: Read the passage below and answer the questions that follow.

The success of modern agriculture is due in large part to our successful fight against crop diseases. To aid in the fight against diseases caused by insects, chemists developed special types of insect poisons called pesticides.

When pesticides first came out on the market, they were believed to be both safe and effective. Although a few pesticides are still safe enough to use, many of them are now known to cause both air and water pollution. One example is DDT, a once widely used pesticide that is now known to be so dangerous to animal life that its use has been banned in the United States.

Pesticides can be inhaled directly by animals and people living in areas where spraying takes place. Because of this, the spraying of many types of pesticides near residential areas is now strictly controlled and, in some cases, prohibited. Pesticides can also get into animal and human foods. For example, insect-eating animals, including game animals, absorb pesticides when they eat contaminated bugs. Contaminated game animals can pose a serious threat to human health. In·addition, when cows eat grass that has been sprayed with pesticide, both contaminated milk and beef result. Still another problem occurs when pesticides are sprayed over crop fields. These pesticides soak into the ground and can be washed by rain into groundwater and local streams. Then the pesticides are eaten by fish and other aquatic animals.

1. According to the passage, which of the following is true about DDT?

   (1) DDT are the initials of the three people who invented a particular pesticide.
   (2) DDT is the most dangerous pesticide ever used in the United States.
   (3) DDT is still used in many European countries.
   (4) DDT is a pesticide that is now banned in the United States.
   (5) DDT has been found in samples of tuna and other ocean-dwelling fish.

2. According to the passage, what is one way that pesticides get into groundwater?

   (1) Birds carry pesticides to rivers when they go to drink.
   (2) Contaminated fish may bring pesticides to the rivers in which they swim.
   (3) Rain may wash pesticides in the soil into groundwater.
   (4) Wind may carry sprayed pesticides over residential areas and into the reservoirs of groundwater.
   (5) Sprayed insects contaminate groundwater reservoirs.

ANSWERS AND EXPLANATIONS START ON PAGE 287.

Restating Information In Graphics

When you restate information found in graphics, you use words to express information that is presented in pictures or in numbers. Being able to restate information correctly is a skill needed for understanding all types of graphics. On the next few pages we'll show how this skill is used for understanding diagrams.

Skill Builder
Reading Diagrams

For our purposes, a diagram (often called an *illustration*) is a picture or drawing that illustrates one or more ideas. Diagrams are designed in many ways.

- Labeled diagrams contain word labels that name certain objects or that point out things that are taking place.

- Unlabeled diagrams may contain no writing at all.

- Any diagram, whether labeled or not, may have a caption. A caption is a phrase or short paragraph that helps explain what the diagram is about.

Look at the diagram below. This diagram contains both labels and a caption. Using your own words, what point do you think the author is trying to make about translucent materials?

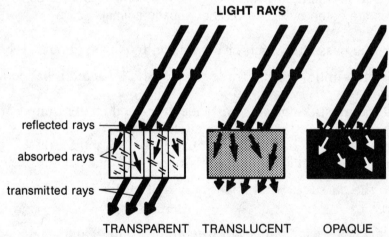

Different types of materials transmit different amounts of light.

Your answer should be that translucent materials transmit only part of the light that strikes them. (As used here, to transmit means "to allow light to pass through.") Looking closely at the diagram, you can also see that the author makes the point that translucent materials reflect part of the light that strikes them. (When light reflects, it bounces off the object that it strikes.) An example of a translucent object is a piece of colored glass.

Exercise 6

Directions: Looking at the diagram on page 24, what point do you think the author is trying to make about transparent and opaque materials? Also, see if you can think of an example of each type of material.

1. transparent: _____

example: _____

2. opaque: _____

example: _____

★ **GED PRACTICE** ★

Exercise 7

Directions: Questions 1–3 are based on the diagram below.

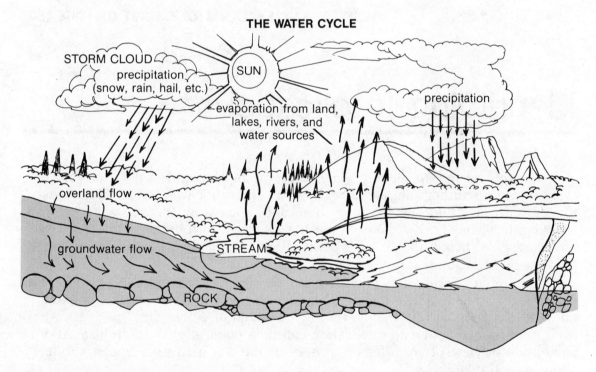

THE WATER CYCLE

1. According to the diagram, which of the following would be the best restatement of the label *precipitation*?

    (1) the mixture of gases that surrounds the Earth
    (2) all sources from which moisture evaporates into the sky
    (3) the seeping of water into the rock layers of the land
    (4) all forms of moisture that fall to the Earth
    (5) the flow of water over the surface of the land

2. What label on this diagram means the same thing as the expression "moisture that rises into the atmosphere from the land and from all water sources"?

   (1) stream
   (2) overland flow
   (3) groundwater flow
   (4) precipitation
   (5) evaporation

3. The artist's key point is that a water cycle is

   (1) the removal of fresh water from land by the actions of both runoff and the growth of vegetation
   (2) the evaporation of water from the land and rivers due to the sun's heat
   (3) the continual back-and-forth movement of water between the Earth's surface and the atmosphere
   (4) the formation of storm clouds over a stream and land at the same time
   (5) the changing of the fresh water found in clouds to the salt water found in the oceans

ANSWERS AND EXPLANATIONS START ON PAGE 287.

Identifying Implications

To *imply* means "to suggest." Therefore, an implication is a point of view or an idea that an author suggests. For example, an author who writes "Scientists may have invented nuclear weapons, but I sure don't want them to work on arms control!" implies that he does not have a lot of faith in the political ability of scientists. Although the author's point of view is not stated directly, you can tell how he feels about the subject.

Although an author may present many details in a passage, it is often left for you to infer additional information. When you *infer*, you are really just making an educated guess at information that is not stated directly.

As mentioned above, an implication can be a point of view or an idea. An implied point of view, often called an *attitude*, is the way an author appears to feel about something.

For an example of an implied idea, read the following paragraph.

Many homes and businesses have installed solar heating units on their roofs. A solar heating unit captures the sun's energy by letting sunlight heat water that circulates through darkly colored pipes. The hot water is then used as a source of heat for the building below.

An implied idea that you can infer from this paragraph is that the cost of heat obtained from a solar heating unit is less than the cost of a comparable amount of electricity. Although cost is not mentioned, you can infer that a solar heating unit is used as a money-saving device because there's no other reason to go to the trouble of installing one.

Exercise 8

Directions: Read the following passage and see if you can identify its implications by answering the questions that follow.

> One of the greatest inventions of the twentieth century is the robot. With its tiny electronic brain humming along, it can be programmed to do just about anything. Since we installed several robots, business has really picked up and we've saved a lot of payroll money.
>
> A robot is a great investment. Robots don't take rest breaks, and they don't get sick. They don't require a lunch room, nor do they need a smoking area. You don't need to provide them with either medical insurance or retirement benefits. What's more, each robot can do the work of several regular employees, and you can run robots twenty-four hours a day, seven days a week.

1. How would you describe the author's attitude toward robots?

_____

2. What does the author imply about the yearly cost of operating a robot compared to the yearly salary of a regular employee?

_____

3. What can you infer about the quality of work done by a robot as compared to the quality of similar work done by a regular employee?

_____

4. From the way the passage is written, do you infer that the author is most likely an assembly-line worker or an owner?

_____

★ **GED PRACTICE** ★

Exercise 9

Directions: Read the passage below and answer the questions that follow.

> Many books have been written—most of them based on questionable research—about the value of exercise as a means of improving one's overall health. Right now, hundreds of health nuts are making a fortune selling exercise books that proclaim exercise to be the answer for everything from weight control to heart disease. Well, hold on just a second, I'm not so sure.
>
> New research is showing that exercise might even be bad for your health,

especially if you're past middle age. According to this research, mild exercise can actually damage muscle tissue. By having mice of different ages run on a treadmill, researchers were able to show that older mice actually were harmed by moderate exercise.

One possible explanation for their findings is that natural muscle breakdown in older mice is simply increased by the effects of exercise. According to the researchers, these findings suggest that there may be an age beyond which a mouse is no longer able to exercise in a beneficial way. This work certainly suggests that it makes a lot of sense for middle-aged or older people to place themselves under a doctor's supervision if they feel they must take up an exercise program.

1. In the first paragraph, the author implies that

   (1) too many exercise books are being sold in bookstores
   (2) weight control and heart disease can't both be related to exercise
   (3) publishing companies charge too much money for the exercise books they publish
   (4) most exercise books are written to make money rather than to provide good medical information
   (5) it would be better if only doctors wrote exercise books

2. Overall, the author implies that the research done on mice

   (1) explains why older mice move more slowly than younger mice
   (2) may apply directly to human beings
   (3) could be the topic of another exercise book
   (4) proves that mice have a lot in common with human beings
   (5) explains why older people find it easy to stick with an exercise program

3. From the author's attitude, you can most reasonably infer that the author is

   (1) a writer who has been unable to get a book on exercise published
   (2) an animal lover who believes that mice are just as valuable as human beings
   (3) a person who is easily convinced that exercise is probably dangerous to one's health
   (4) a person who is not in favor of medical research performed on mice
   (5) a doctor who believes that many older people could improve their health by beginning an exercise program

ANSWERS AND EXPLANATIONS START ON PAGE 288.

Identifying Implications In Graphics

When you identify an implication in a graphic, you're making a good guess at information that's not specifically given. In your study of science, you'll find that this skill is particularly useful when you work with line graphs.

Skill Builder
Reading Line Graphs

A line graph shows information as points (often called *data points*) that lie on a straight or curved line. This line of data points runs across the graph from left to right. A line graph contains both a labeled vertical axis (running up and down along the side of the graph) and a labeled horizontal axis (running across the bottom of the graph). Each data point on the line shows the relationship between two items of information, one taken from each axis. A line graph is especially useful in showing a trend.

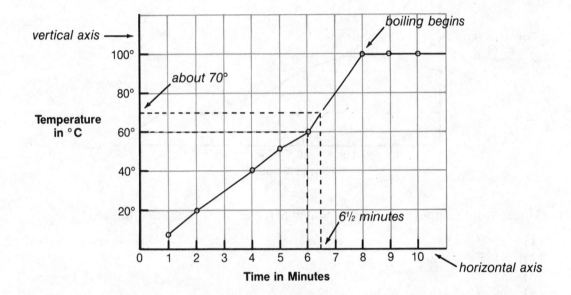

The line graph above shows several temperature readings taken from a pan of water that was placed on a stove for 10 minutes. Each circle represents one data point—the water temperature after a certain time has passed.

As an example, the temperature of the water after 6 minutes is 60°C. (Dotted lines have been drawn as a guide for your eyes.) To read this data point, first find the 6 minutes point on the horizontal axis. Next, move straight up from this point to the indicated data point. Now, from this data point move directly across to the vertical axis. The point you read on the vertical axis is about 60°C.

You can also find the temperature of the water after 6½ minutes even though there is no recorded data point at 6½ minutes. As the second pair of dotted lines show, you treat this point just as you would treat an actual data point. First you find the 6½ minutes point on the horizontal axis. Next, move straight up to a point on the data line—even though this point is not indicated by a circle. Then, read directly across to the temperature scale on the vertical axis. The temperature after 6½ minutes is about 70°C.

Now try identifying a point on the line.

About what temperature is the water when 7 minutes have passed?

Your answer should be about 80°C.

★ **GED PRACTICE** ★

Exercise 10

Directions: Questions 1–3 refer to the line graph below.

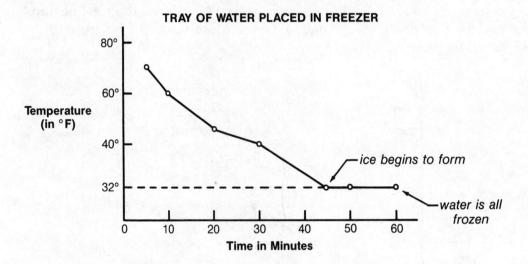

TRAY OF WATER PLACED IN FREEZER

1. About what temperature is the water after 20 minutes have passed?

    (1) 48°F
    (2) 41°F
    (3) 35°F
    (4) 24°F
    (5) 15°F

2. About how long does it take the tray of water to reach a temperature of 35°F?

    (1) 10 minutes
    (2) 20 minutes
    (3) 28 minutes
    (4) 40 minutes
    (5) 55 minutes

3. After the tray had been in the freezer for 50 minutes, its contents would most probably be

    (1) all water at a temperature slightly above 32°F
    (2) all water at a temperature slightly below 32°F
    (3) partly water and partly ice, all at a temperature of 32°F
    (4) all ice at a temperature of 32°F
    (5) all ice at a temperature slightly above 32°F

ANSWERS AND EXPLANATIONS START ON PAGE 288.

2 APPLYING SCIENCE CONCEPTS

Much of what you learn in life is not learned purely for the sake of knowing something, but for the purpose of applying that knowledge. For example, you read a first aid manual in order to help an injured or ill family member or friend. You read about the importance of bandaging a serious wound to stop it from bleeding, and you learn how to clear a person's airway to make sure he or she doesn't suffocate. The quick application of this knowledge can save a life.

On the GED Test, you'll be asked to *apply* knowledge to situations discussed in passages. This application of reading skills is a measure of two abilities:

- the ability to apply given ideas in a new context
- the ability to apply remembered ideas in a new context

Applying Given Ideas in a New Context

Many principles in science apply in a lot of different contexts (situations). One principle you might know about is often called *stimulus-response*. According to this principle, an organism will respond in some way when acted on by a stimulus (something that can be felt, seen, heard, smelled, etc.). For example, if you hit your thumb with a hammer, you pull your thumb back and probably yell! Here, the act of hitting your thumb is the stimulus, and pulling your thumb back and yelling is the response.

Identify the stimulus and response in each of the next two examples:

a. A child throws a cracker into the pond, and several ducks quickly swim over to get the cracker.

Stimulus: _____

Response: _____

b. While driving, Julia hit the brakes after seeing a dog dart in front of her car.

Stimulus: _____

Response: _____

In example a, the stimulus is the cracker hitting the water, and the response is the ducks swimming over. In example b, the stimulus is the dog darting in front of the car, and the response is Julia hitting the brakes. Notice that the stimulus always occurs before the response, even if the response is described first in the sentence.

Exercise 1

Directions: Read the paragraphs below and do the exercise that follows.

Inherited traits are characteristics that are passed on from parents to children. For example, hair color is an inherited trait. Dark-haired parents are likely to have a dark-haired child.

Traits that are a result of changes you make yourself cannot be passed on. For example, if a dark-haired mother dyes her hair blond, *she* will have blond hair, but this characteristic cannot be passed on to any children she might have.

Check the following traits that most probably were inherited by children.

_____ **1.** Elena has pierced ears, just like her mother.

_____ **2.** Jeremy has blue eyes, the same color as both his mother's and father's.

_____ **3.** Joe and his parents go jogging every day, so Joe has developed strong leg muscles.

_____ **4.** Julius stands six feet nine inches tall, two inches taller than his father.

_____ **5.** When he turned thirty, Arnold noticed he was beginning to lose his hair, just as his father had at that age.

Exercise 2

Directions: Read the paragraph below and answer the questions that follow.

In a science class, you have learned that one general principle of science is that objects expand when they are heated and contract when they are cooled. A rock, exposed to the weather, will expand in high temperatures and contract in low temperatures. In fact, it is this expansion and contraction that causes many large rocks to crack and break apart.

Let's see how the expansion/contraction principle might apply in new contexts. Check each action below that is an application of the expansion/contraction principle.

_____ **1.** To help keep it from cracking, a sidewalk is made in sections, with a small space between sections.

_____ **2.** Richard noticed that the metal screen door on his house shuts more easily on a cold day than on a hot day.

_____ **3.** By wearing a white shirt on a hot summer day, Jason kept cooler than he would have been had he worn a dark shirt.

_____ **4.** To open a "stuck" jar of jam, Emmy ran hot water over the metal lid.

_____ **5.** In order to save energy, Yoko replaced her 100-watt light bulbs with special 50-watt bulbs that gave off the same amount of light but didn't get as hot.

★ **GED PRACTICE** ★

Exercise 3

Directions: Read the passage below and answer the question that follows.

The study of the development of different species of animals is filled with fascinating questions. One of the most interesting concerns the discovery of vestigial organs. A vestigial organ in an animal is an organ that seems to have no purpose.

An example of a vestigial organ is the presence of leg bones inside a snake. These small bones are absolutely useless to snakes that exist at the present time. One possible explanation of vestigial organs is that present-day animals evolved from ancestors who needed these organs. According to this idea, snakes inherited the genes that produce leg bones from some ancestral relative among ancient reptiles that did have legs.

Which of the following is the best example of a vestigial organ?

(1) a frog's spleen, an organ that helps destroy germs
(2) the hoof of a horse, an organ to which a metal horseshoe is often attached
(3) the tailbone of a human, a bone having no known use
(4) the shell of a turtle, a heavy object the turtle must carry
(5) eyes of a bat, an animal that flies mainly at night

ANSWERS AND EXPLANATIONS START ON PAGE 288.

Classification Questions

One special use of application questions is with a passage that defines *classes* of things. The passage is followed by several questions that ask you to apply these definitions in new contexts.

When animals and plants live together in the same environment, like a forest or a lake, special nutritional relationships develop among many of the different organisms. These relationships can be classified as follows:

(1) **Predator-prey relationship**—one organism kills and eats a second organism.

(2) **Saprophytic relationship**—an organism takes nutrients from the remains of dead organisms it finds.

(3) **Parasitic relationship**—one organism takes nutrients from the living body of another organism and, in doing so, may harm, but not kill, the other organism.

(4) **Mutualistic relationship**—organisms live together in a way that nutritionally benefits all of the organisms.

(5) **Commensal relationship**—one organism nutritionally benefits from a second organism, while the second organism neither benefits nor is harmed.

Compare the following relationship with the definitions above:

In a freshwater lake, bass live by eating minnows and small crustaceans.

What is the nutritional relationship of bass to minnows and small crustaceans? _____

You are correct if you answered *predator–prey*. One organism (the bass) kills and eats the other organisms (the minnows and small crustaceans).

Here is another example:

> Many tiny lice can live on the body of a bird by slowly eating its feathers. Although lice damage the feathers, they do not kill the bird. However, the bird does not benefit in any way from this relationship.

What is the relationship of the lice to the bird? _____

To answer this question, notice that the bird is harmed but not killed by the lice. You can rule out (1) predator-prey, (2) saprophytic, and (5) commensal as possible answers. Also, since the bird does not benefit from the relationship, (4) mutualistic is not a possible answer either. You are left with (3) parasitic as the correct answer. The lice do take nutrients from part of the body of a living bird and do harm—but not kill—the bird.

★ GED PRACTICE ★

Exercise 4

Directions: For each question below, choose the type of nutritional relationship that is described. Refer back to the definitions on page 34, if necessary.

1. As uninvited guests, small beetles often live in the nest of an ant colony, helping themselves to food supplies built up by the ants. During a prosperous season, when the portion taken by the beetles is not missed, the relationship of beetles to ants is best classified as

    (1) predator-prey
    (2) saprophytic
    (3) parasitic
    (4) mutualistic
    (5) commensal

2. A fungus causes the disease chestnut blight in the native American chestnut tree. This fungus takes nutrients from the tree and damages plant tissue on any part of the tree on which it grows. Fortunately, chestnut trees usually do not die from this disease. The relationship of the chestnut-blight fungus to the chestnut tree is best classified as

    (1) predator-prey
    (2) saprophytic
    (3) parasitic
    (4) mutualistic
    (5) commensal

3. Decay bacteria play an important role in bringing nitrogen, needed for plant growth, back into the soil. These bacteria take nutrients from plant and animal remains, break down the proteins, and release ammonia, a nitrogen compound, into the soil. The relationship of decay bacteria to dead plants and animals is called

   (1) predator-prey
   (2) saprophytic
   (3) parasitic
   (4) mutualistic
   (5) commensal

4. While a herd of gazelle graze close by, a solitary lioness lies quietly in the grass. With a powerful but graceful lunge, the lioness brings down a gazelle that strays too far from the herd. The gazelle provides needed meat for the lioness and its cubs. The relationship of lioness to gazelle is known as

   (1) predator-prey
   (2) saprophytic
   (3) parasitic
   (4) mutualistic
   (5) commensal

5. Some algae live in such close association with a fungus that the two plants together are given the name *lichen*. In a lichen, the fungus captures moisture for the algae and provides a protective skinlike covering. The algae produce the food necessary to support the life of both plants. The relationship of fungus to algae in a lichen is best classified as

   (1) predator-prey
   (2) saprophytic
   (3) parasitic
   (4) mutualistic
   (5) commensal

ANSWERS AND EXPLANATIONS START ON PAGE 288.

Applying Remembered Ideas in a New Context

Some of the questions on the GED Science Test will draw on knowledge you might have from experience or reading rather than from information in passages presented on the test. Below is an example of this type of question. Read it carefully and choose the most reasonable answer.

An animal's color may be related to its need for

(a) absorption of sunlight
(b) protection from predators
(c) easy identification

You are correct if you chose (b) as your answer. A general principle of science is that animals adapt to their environment in a way that gives them the best chance of survival. If an animal's coloring matches its environment, it is less likely to be seen by a predator.

Both in this book and on the GED Test, you may sometimes find that you are just not familiar with the principle or example under discussion. That's perfectly natural. For now, remember these two things: first, you will learn a lot of background information in science as you read this book; and second, very few questions of the kind shown above will actually be on your test, probably one or two at most.

Our purpose in presenting this section is so that you won't be surprised by any question on the GED Science Test. If you do see a question you're unable to answer, make the most reasonable guess you can and then move on to the next question.

Exercise 5

Directions: Each of the three questions below requires that you apply a remembered idea in one way or another. Circle the best answer choice for each question.

1. In the autumn of each year, ducks and geese gather in huge flocks and begin a long journey to a warmer climate before winter begins. This annual journey is for the purpose of

    (1) escaping from natural predators
    (2) leaving before bird hunters begin the fall hunt
    (3) finding food or going to a mating area

2. Erosion is the wearing away of land formations by the actions of nature. Which of the following is *not* one of the causes of erosion of the Rocky Mountains?

    (1) the action of rain water
    (2) the action of wind
    (3) the action of the tides

3. Space flight is perhaps the most exciting and dangerous adventure under-taken by science in the last half of the twentieth century. The main danger of space flight is

   (1) an explosion of the rocket fuel
   (2) being lost in space
   (3) becoming seriously ill while in space

★ **GED PRACTICE** ★

Exercise 6

Directions: Each question below is based on your knowledge of issues in science. Circle the best answer for each question.

1. In a recent magazine advertisement, a national corporation made these statements:

   A. Nuclear power is safe, clean, and efficient.
   B. Nuclear power is now America's second most important power source.
   C. Fuel for nuclear power plants is almost unlimited.

   What serious disadvantage of nuclear power plants does this "pro-nuclear" advertisement fail to point out?

   (1) A nuclear power plant requires a large plot of valuable land for its development.
   (2) Nuclear power plants produce a deadly form of radioactive waste that can't be disposed of safely.
   (3) Nuclear power plants use steam-driven turbines to turn electric generators.
   (4) The energy produced by a nuclear power plant comes from the splitting of atoms.
   (5) Certain religious groups oppose the use of electricity, whatever the type of power plant that's used to produce it.

2. Which of the following is *not* an effort to reduce the amount of air pollution to which the general public is exposed?

   (1) developing efficient engines that use unleaded fuel
   (2) inventing emission control devices that limit exhaust pollutants from automobiles
   (3) restricting the number of hours allowed each day for using wood stoves in certain areas of the country
   (4) reducing the amount of money spent on the problem of acid rain in order to cut down on government spending
   (5) limiting the spraying of pesticides near residential areas

ANSWERS AND EXPLANATIONS START ON PAGE 288.

Applying Ideas From Graphics

You can also apply ideas taken from a graphic. For example, look at the two drawings that make up the diagram below.

These drawings, and others like them, appear in the safety instructions of many types of consumer electrical products. See if you can figure out what safety message the artist wants you to apply to your handling of all electrical products.

For drawing A: _____

_____

For drawing B: _____

_____

Your answers should be something like the following. Drawing A warns you of the danger of dropping or spilling anything into any opening in the body of an electrical product. Not only could you ruin the product; you could also get an electric shock or start a fire. Drawing B shows that only an expert should work on the inner components of an electrical product. An inexperienced person risks his or her own safety trying to solve a problem that requires taking the product apart.

Exercise 7

Directions: Read the following paragraph and its accompanying diagram.

Because of the Earth's rotation, the Earth has been divided into twenty-four different time zones. As shown in the diagram below, there are four different time zones in the continental United States. Each time zone differs by one hour from the time zone on each side of it.

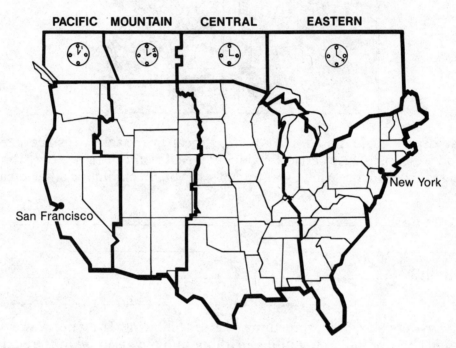

1. Imagine that you're traveling from your home in San Francisco to visit a friend in New York City. If, while in San Francisco, you want to call your friend at 1:00 P.M. New York time, what time should you place the call from San Francisco? _____

2. As you fly from San Francisco to New York, should you set your watch forward or backward in order to show the correct New York time when you arrive? _____

3. While you're in New York, will you feel very tired at 10:00 P.M. each night, or will you feel wide awake? (Assume 10:00 P.M. is your normal bedtime in San Francisco.) _____

★ GED PRACTICE ★

Exercise 8

Directions: Questions 1–3 refer to the diagram shown below.

HUMAN TEETH AND THEIR USES

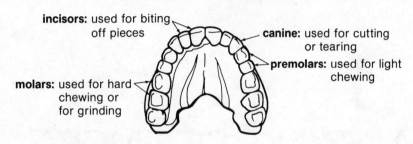

incisors: used for biting off pieces

canine: used for cutting or tearing

premolars: used for light chewing

molars: used for hard chewing or for grinding

1. Which teeth would you use the most in chewing a cut piece of steak before swallowing?

   (1) incisors
   (2) canine
   (3) molars
   (4) both incisors and canine
   (5) both incisors and premolars

2. Which teeth would you be most apt to use to bite off a piece of chicken from a drumstick?

   (1) incisors
   (2) canine
   (3) premolars
   (4) molars
   (5) both premolars and molars

3. Which teeth are you most likely to use for the purpose of cutting a string into two pieces?

   (1) incisors
   (2) canine
   (3) premolars
   (4) molars
   (5) both premolars and molars

ANSWERS AND EXPLANATIONS START ON PAGE 289.

3 ANALYZING SCIENCE MATERIALS

When you analyze something, you look at all of its parts in order to get a better understanding of the whole. On the GED Science Test, you will be tested on your ability to analyze a passage or illustration in four ways:

- distinguishing facts from hypotheses and opinions
- recognizing unstated assumptions
- identifying cause-and-effect relationships
- distinguishing a conclusion from supporting statements

Distinguishing Facts From Hypotheses and Opinions

To begin this section, become familiar with the following definitions:

- A scientific *fact* is a statement, based on evidence, that scientists can agree on. For example, it is a scientific fact, based on geological evidence, that dinosaurs became extinct about 70 million years ago.

- A *hypothesis*, on the other hand, is a reasonable explanation of a scientific fact. Some scientists hypothesize that the dinosaurs became extinct because of the sudden occurrence of an ice age.

- An *opinion* is a personal belief that is often based on a person's own feelings of the way things should be. As an example, a person may have the opinion that the study of dinosaurs is a waste of time and taxpayers' money!

Try classifying each of the following as fact, hypothesis, or opinion. Write *f*, *h*, or *o* on the line before each statement.

_____ **a.** Although any person can lose his or her hair, baldness is much more common in men than in women.

_____ **b.** Because of superior intelligence, human beings are the most important animals that have ever lived.

_____ **c.** The reason that human beings and other primates show genetic and physical similarities may be that each evolved from a common ancestor millions of years ago.

Statement a is a fact. You don't need to be a scientist to observe that there are more bald men than bald women. Statement b is an opinion, based on feelings about the importance of human beings. Science can never provide evidence to prove or disprove value judgments. Statement c is a hypothesis that gives a possible explanation for an observed fact: that human beings and other primates have similar characteristics. No one can prove for sure that human beings and primates do in fact have a common ancestor. In fact, many people strongly believe that no common ancestor exists.

Exercise 1

Directions: Write *f*, *h*, or *o* on the line preceding each statement below to classify the statement as a fact, hypothesis, or opinion.

_____ **1.** Because many people are frightened by snakes, there should never be an effort to save any species of snake.

_____ **2.** Moonlight is actually light from the sun that is reflected off the moon's surface.

_____ **3.** The reason that moon rocks are similar to Earth rocks may be that the moon and Earth were once part of the same cloud of matter in space.

_____ **4.** During winter months, tree roots store food that is used by the plant as it grows new leaves and stems in the spring.

_____ **5.** Regardless of what chemists claim, vitamins produced in a laboratory can't possibly be as healthful as vitamins naturally found in foods.

_____ **6.** The reason that one person is often so strongly attracted to a second person may be smell rather than good looks or personality.

_____ **7.** Air pollution is a negative by-product of the Industrial Revolution.

Exercise 2

Directions: A passage may contain facts, hypotheses, and opinions. As you read the passage below, try your skill at identifying each. Underline each fact and label it _fact._ Do the same for hypotheses and opinions. Then, on the lines below, write one fact, one hypothesis, and one opinion found in the passage.

Can a computer be made to think? This is the question being asked by artificial intelligence researchers around the country. Although even home computers can do thousands of routine calculations each second, it is not known whether a computer can ever be designed that will actually think for itself. In support of the idea, some scientists suggest that a computer is already similar to the human brain. Based on their observations, these scientists believe that the human mind stores and sorts information in the same way a computer does. What's more, they point out, a thinking computer would be a great benefit to our society. One use, for example, would be to provide companionship to lonely people!

1. Fact: _____

_____

2. Hypothesis: _____

_____

3. Opinion: _____

_____

Exercise 3

Directions: Read the passage below and answer the questions that follow it.

Before the year 2000, biologists and chemists, working together, may get rid of most of the diseases that are caused by viruses and bacteria. They may be able to achieve this through successful research in the development of vaccines.

A vaccine is used to prevent a disease, not to cure it. A vaccine is a dose of a germ that is enough to trigger your immune system into action, but not enough to make you sick. For example, a flu vaccine consists of a small dose of flu virus. Once this vaccine is taken, your body responds by making antibodies, a form of protein that acts as a virus fighter. These antibodies prevent more of the same flu virus from entering and attacking cells in your body.

Vaccines that have been very successful are the DPT vaccine that has all but eliminated the three long-feared childhood diseases (diphtheria, tetanus, and pertussis—commonly known as whooping cough) and vaccines for pneumonia, influenza, polio, measles, mumps, german measles, and smallpox. The effectiveness of vaccines is most obvious when parents fail to have their children immunized at proper times. When this happens, the number of children stricken with polio and and other diseases once again rises.

Although vaccines are usually safe, there is an element of risk. A small number of people who take a vaccine actually get the disease itself. For example, it is estimated that one child in 310,000 who takes the DPT vaccine will become ill and suffer brain damage. Yet, without the DPT vaccine, it is claimed that the incidence of death due to whooping cough would be nineteen times higher than it is now and the incidence of brain damage would be four times as high. Because of the potential danger of vaccines, medical research in studies of vaccine safety is continuing. Parents are advised to check with their own doctor or with a local health clinic to see which vaccines are appropriate for their children.

1. Which of the following is a fact that the author could prove by citing scientific evidence?

   (1) Most of the diseases caused by viruses and bacteria will someday be curable by vaccines.
   (2) By the year 2000, scientists will discover a vaccine that will prevent all forms of cancer.
   (3) The beneficial effect of a vaccine occurs because of the production of a person's own antibodies.
   (4) A vaccine is made up of antibodies designed to fight a particular kind of virus or bacteria.
   (5) A flu virus prevents a person who has the flu from being able to infect other people.

2. Remembering that a hypothesis is an explanation of an observed fact, which of the following is a hypothesis?

   (1) A vaccine is a dose of a germ that triggers your immune system into action.
   (2) Someday vaccines will be invented that can cure diseases as well as prevent them.
   (3) On the average, one child in every 310,000 that takes the DPT vaccine will be made ill by it.
   (4) Without vaccines, civilization could not survive another 1,000 years.
   (5) The decrease in childhood diseases during this century has most likely resulted from the use of vaccines.

3. Which of the following is an opinion that can neither be proved nor disproved with scientific evidence?

   (1) Vaccines have been very successful in preventing many diseases caused by viruses and bacteria.
   (2) Because of the risk, all vaccinations should be halted until perfectly safe vaccines can be produced.
   (3) Many cancers are believed to be caused by viruses, and work is being done on possible types of cancer vaccines.
   (4) The success of vaccines has been due to the work of chemists involved in medical research.
   (5) By failing to get their children vaccinated as directed by their doctor, parents risk the health of their children.

ANSWERS AND EXPLANATIONS START ON PAGE 289.

Facts, Hypotheses, and Opinions in Graphics

Questions about facts, hypotheses, and opinions may also be asked about information presented in graphics. Following the Skill Builder, we'll discuss how these types of questions may apply to information on bar graphs.

 ## Skill Builder
Reading Bar Graphs

A *bar graph* gets its name from the bars it uses to present information. The bars may run horizontally (from left to right) or vertically (up and down). In each type of bar graph, a bar represents a value that is determined by two things: (1) the length (or height) of the bar and (2) the bar's position along an axis.

As an example, look at the horizontal bar graph below. By the graph's title at the top, you can see that this graph tells how many calories are used in one hour of each of several activities.

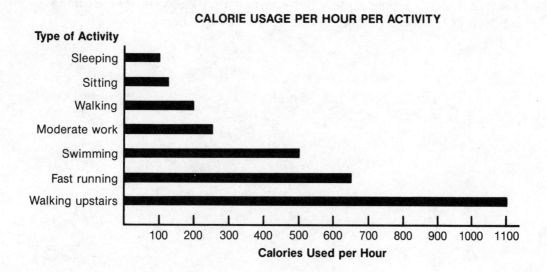

CALORIE USAGE PER HOUR PER ACTIVITY

The label to the left of each bar tells what activity the bar represents. The length of the bar indicates the number of calories used per hour—a value that is read on the horizontal axis directly below the end of the bar. For example, find the end of the bar labeled *walking* and look straight down. You'll see that walking uses about 200 calories per hour.

Now label the following as fact, opinion, or hypothesis.

_____ **a.** Moderate work uses fewer calories than fast running.

_____ **b.** Exercises that use more calories are more fun than exercises that use fewer calories.

_____ **c.** Some people feel better when they exercise because exercise uses up calories that might otherwise be used for an unhealthy activity such as too much worrying.

Statement a is a fact based on information presented on the graph. Moderate work uses only 250 calories per hour, while fast running uses 650 calories per hour. Statement b is an opinion. The bar graph can't give any information about the comparative fun of these two activities. Whether or not something is fun is an opinion. Statement c is a hypothesis because it is a possible explanation of an observed fact, that some people do feel better when they exercise. The explanation may be correct for some people and not correct for others.

★ **GED PRACTICE** ★

Exercise 4

Directions: Questions 1–3 refer to the vertical bar graph below. In this graph, two bars are drawn side by side for each category along the horizontal axis. Each bar gives data for one of the two age groups of people represented.

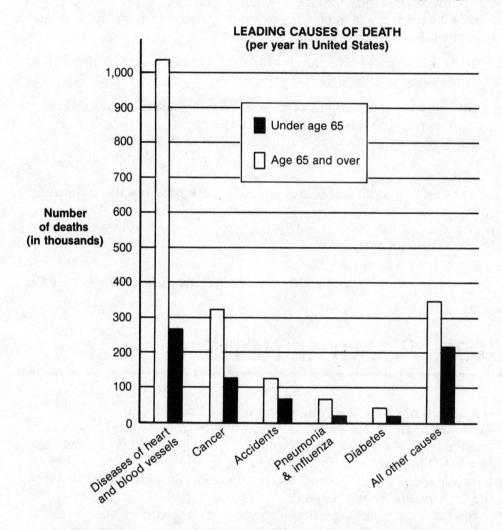

LEADING CAUSES OF DEATH
(per year in United States)

1. Which of the following is a fact that is supported by information given by the graph?

   (1) For people under age 65, accidents are the leading cause of death.
   (2) Cancer is the second leading cause of death in people age 65 and older.
   (3) Diabetes is responsible for more deaths in all age groups than are pneumonia and influenza.
   (4) Most people suffering from cancer are hospitalized unnecessarily.
   (5) More money is spent on heart disease research than on any other area of medical study.

2. Which of the following is an opinion?

(1) Cancer is the most feared of all diseases.
(2) The average hospital stay for cancer is longer than the average hospital stay for heart disease.
(3) The cost of heart transplant operations is now being covered by some insurance companies.
(4) Many terminally ill patients are encouraged to spend their remaining time at home with family members when possible.
(5) In schools where there is accident prevention instruction, accidental student deaths have been reduced.

3. Remembering that a hypothesis is a possible explanation of an observed fact, which of the following is a hypothesis?

(1) The cure rate for certain types of cancer has increased by more than 50 percent during the last twenty-five years.
(2) Recent evidence suggests that heart disease is on the decrease.
(3) Drunk drivers are responsible for more than half of all highway accident deaths.
(4) The American diet, high in fat and sugar, is very possibly the main reason why so many Americans die from heart problems.
(5) By the year 2000, heart disease will no longer be the leading cause of death in the United States.

ANSWERS AND EXPLANATIONS START ON PAGE 289.

Unstated Assumptions

When you make an *assumption*, you act as if something is true without checking to see if you're right. For example, when a light goes out in a room, you immediately change the light bulb even though the problem could be elsewhere. A wire in the wall switch may have popped loose, or the light socket itself may be broken. But, because the problem is most often a burned out light bulb, we all assume that the bulb needs to be changed.

When you read a science passage, it is important to be aware of the author's unstated assumptions. An unstated assumption is something the writer just seems to take for granted. It may even be an idea the writer just didn't think of. Other times it may be a point of view that the writer wants you to take. This is a technique used by salespeople, by politicians, and by others who want you to believe and act in a certain way.

See if you can spot the unstated assumption in the statement below.

When the world's supply of oil runs out, automobile use will decrease drastically.

What unstated assumption is the author making? The writer is assuming that scientists will not be able to find an energy source for automobiles other than the gasoline we now use.

Exercise 5

Directions: In the space following each passage below, answer the question by identifying the unstated assumption indicated by the writer.

1. When life is discovered on another planet, its form will be much different from any of the life forms on Earth.

    What is the writer assuming about other planets? _____

    _____

2. An astronaut stated, "Manned space travel is absolutely necessary if we are to learn about the planets outside of our own solar system."

    What assumption is the astronaut making about information obtained from

    unmanned space travel? _____

    _____

3. To make ice in her freezer as quickly as possible, Rhoda first ran the tap water until it was as cold as she could get it. She then placed a tray full of this cold tap water into the freezer.

    What assumption is Rhoda making about the fastest way to make ice? _____

    _____

4. When most people take aspirin for a headache, or take other medicinal drugs for specific purposes, what assumption are they making about these drugs?

    _____

    _____

5. Doctors recommend that pregnant women do not take any medicinal drugs of any kind unless specifically advised by a doctor. This includes common drugs like aspirin, cold medicine, allergy medicine, and so on.

    Upon what unstated assumption do doctors base this recommendation? _____

    _____

6. Astrology, though not a real science, did help advance the early study of astronomy. Astrologers predict the future by looking at the position of the stars and planets.

    What is an unstated assumption made by astrologers? _____

    _____

Exercise 6

Directions: Read the passage below and do the exercise that follows.

While taking an afternoon hike up a mountain trail, Jerry and Fred had a strange encounter with bees. On the way up the mountain, several bees were always buzzing around Jerry but not around Fred. To see what would happen, Jerry and Fred switched shirts for the walk back down. Jerry gave his orange shirt to Fred, and Jerry wore Fred's brown shirt. Interestingly, on the way down the mountain, several bees now buzzed around Fred but not around Jerry. Jerry concluded that bees are attracted to the color orange but not to the color brown.

Place a check before each statement below that is an unstated assumption that Jerry has made in reaching his conclusion.

_____ **1.** Bees can distinguish one color from another.

_____ **2.** The bees buzzed around Jerry on the way up the mountain and around Fred on the way down.

_____ **3.** Jerry and Fred switched shirts at the top of the mountain.

_____ **4.** It was the color of the shirt and not something else such as shape or smell that attracted the bees.

_____ **5.** Bees have a very good sense of smell.

★ **GED PRACTICE** ★

Exercise 7

Directions: Read the passage below and answer the questions that follow.

When nuclear power was first developed, it was hailed as the energy source of the future. People saw only the positive side of its use: an inexpensive, almost inexhaustible source of energy. Little was said about the radioactive waste that nuclear power plants produce.

Today, the nuclear waste issue is one of the most serious issues of our times. Scientists still know of no way to safely dispose of radioactive waste. If this waste gets into the air or into our drinking water, it could cause cancer, genetic mutations, and death. Therefore, nuclear waste must be stored for the thousands of years that it remains harmful to life. Storage sites must be watched carefully to guard against contamination of the atmosphere and of the groundwater and to guard against the possibility of terrorism. Many communities have resisted the building of storage sites in their area, so it is becoming difficult to find places to store nuclear waste. A growing number of scientists and other citizens are demanding that no more nuclear power plants be built.

1. What unstated assumption is being made by those who are demanding an end to nuclear power plants?

    (1) Nuclear power companies would stand to lose a lot of money if nuclear power plants were to be closed.
    (2) Elected public officials will act to shut down nuclear power plants if enough citizens are concerned.
    (3) Nuclear power provides a small part of the electrical energy being used in the United States.
    (4) Radioactive waste is also produced in the development of nuclear weapons.
    (5) There is already a large amount of radioactive waste in temporary storage sites in the United States.

2. An unstated assumption made by those who favor further development of nuclear power is that

    (1) the demand for electrical energy will decrease in the future due to more efficient consumer products
    (2) nuclear power companies are more concerned about radioactive waste than is the general public
    (3) scientists will someday invent safe methods of disposal of radioactive waste
    (4) nuclear power plants do not produce radioactive waste
    (5) scientists who don't work in the nuclear industry are only trying to scare the public

ANSWERS AND EXPLANATIONS START ON PAGE 289.

Unstated Assumptions in Graphics

You may also find unstated assumptions in graphics. For example, look at the following illustration and caption.

Will you help?

In this graphic, several unstated assumptions are made by the artist. Perhaps the most important assumption is that the reader will recognize this as a polluted lake. The pollution threatens the health of anyone (or anything) living near the lake.

Now see if you can determine two more unstated assumptions by answering the following questions.

a. What assumption does the artist make about how this picture will affect people who see it?

b. What assumption does the artist make about the reader's willingness to help work to create a clean environment?

Answers may vary, but two unstated assumptions made by the artist are a) that the reader will be upset by seeing the environment polluted in this way and b) that the reader will want to help in some way, possibly by demanding government action or by sending money to some environmental organization.

★ **GED PRACTICE** ★

Exercise 8

Directions: These questions refer to the illustration below, which was part of an advertisement from the makers of Goodgrow Fertilizer to show "scientific proof" that Goodgrow is better than Sunshine Fertilizer. Choose the best answer to each question.

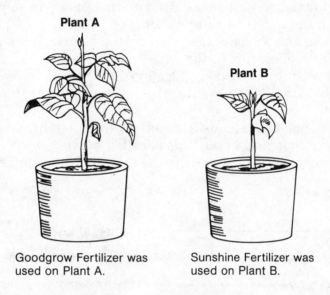

Plant A

Plant B

Goodgrow Fertilizer was used on Plant A.

Sunshine Fertilizer was used on Plant B.

1. Which of the following is an assumption that the makers of Goodgrow Fertilizer want you to make about the two plants?

   (1) Plant A was grown in a different location than Plant B.
   (2) Plant A costs more than Plant B.
   (3) Plant A and Plant B are the same type of plant.
   (4) Plant A is older than Plant B.
   (5) Plant A is taller than Plant B.

2. Which of the following is *not* an assumption that the makers of Goodgrow Fertilizer want you to make about the care the plants received?

   (1) Both plants were given equal amounts of fertilizer.
   (2) Both plants received equal amounts of sunshine.
   (3) Both plants are growing in the same type of soil.
   (4) Both plants were given the same fertilizer.
   (5) Both plants were given equal amounts of water.

ANSWERS AND EXPLANATIONS START ON PAGE 290.

Identifying Cause-and-Effect Relationships

On the evening news we hear that an earthquake in southern California caused extensive damage to nearby cities and towns. During the next few weeks, we hear that frightened residents now demand that earthquake-proof buildings be built to replace those destroyed by the quake.

The earthquake and the later demands by the citizens are a good example of a cause-and-effect relationship. In this type of relationship, you can identify an event (the effect) with the condition (the cause) that made the event occur. In the example above, the *cause* is the earthquake and the *effect* is the action taken by the citizens.

In many cases, one cause leads to an effect that then itself becomes the cause of a second effect, and so on. This is called a *chain of causes and effects*. Below is listed a chain of causes and effects that might be started by an earthquake.

Cause	**Effect**
Earthquake ⟶	Damaged buildings
Damaged buildings ⟶	Action taken by citizens
Action taken by citizens ⟶	New building codes
New building codes ⟶	Safer buildings

On the line provided, write an effect that might result from the construction of safer buildings.

Cause	**Effect**
Safer buildings ⟶	_____

Several answers are possible. Here are two of them: (1) citizens feel safer and (2) the new buildings don't get destroyed in the next earthquake.

In any chain of events, a cause always occurs before the effect. It is important to remember this because a passage may mention the effect first. Look at this sentence:

Jimmy had several fillings before he was six years old because he ate too much candy and did not brush his teeth daily.

See if you can identify the two causes that lead to a single effect.

Causes   **Effect**

As you probably wrote, the two causes are Jimmy's eating too much candy and his failure to brush his teeth. The effect is that he needed work done on his teeth.

Exercise 9

Directions: Read the passage below and do the exercise that follows.

During times of unexpected stress or fright, the human body reacts in a most protective, amazing way. First, the adrenal glands give off into your bloodstream two hormones, adrenaline and noradrenaline. These adrenal hormones can give you extra strength and endurance. When you get a "rush of adrenaline," you might experience some of these changes:

- Your heart beats faster.

- The pupils of your eyes dilate (become wider).

- The liver releases stored sugar, so there is an increased energy supply to the muscles.

- Digestive processes slow down.

- The blood vessels near the surface of your skin constrict (become more narrow), slowing the bleeding of any surface wounds and causing a greater flow of blood to the muscles, brain, and heart.

- The bronchial tubes in your lungs dilate, increasing the rate at which you're able to absorb oxygen.

Because your adrenal glands have this effect, they are often called the glands of "fight or flight." This refers to the fact that a surprised, scared animal will usually flee if given the chance, but will fight if it has no choice. The adrenal hormones prepare the animal for either course of action.

Match each effect listed in the column on the right with its cause listed on the left. Write the correct letter in the space before each number.

Cause	Effect
_____ 1. unexpected stress or fright	**a.** increased muscle energy
_____ 2. adrenal hormones in blood	**b.** increased absorption of oxygen
_____ 3. dilation of bronchial tubes	**c.** the adrenal glands give off two adrenal hormones
_____ 4. release of stored sugar by liver	**d.** increased blood flow to the heart
_____ 5. constriction of surface blood vessels	**e.** increased heart rate

Exercise 10

Directions: Read the following passage and answer the questions after it.

One of the unique features of Earth, "the blue planet," is the presence of liquid water on its surface. The temperature at the Earth's surface makes this possible. If the Earth were much hotter, the oceans would evaporate and water would be found only as a gas in the atmosphere. If the Earth were much colder, the oceans would freeze and remain as an ice blanket, covering most of the Earth's surface. As far as scientists can tell, all other planets in our solar system are either too hot or too cold to allow for the existence of this precious, life-giving substance.

According to the passage, what effect would follow each of these occurrences?

1.   A great increase in the Earth's average temperature

_____

2.   A great decrease in the Earth's average temperature

_____

★ **GED PRACTICE** ★

Exercise 11

Directions: Read the passage below and answer the questions that follow it.

The Mesozoic era, called the Age of the Reptiles, began about 225 million years ago. During this era, the giant reptiles called *dinosaurs*—from the Greek words meaning "terrible lizard"—roamed the earth. For over 150 million years, these wondrous and feared creatures dominated all other life forms. Then, about 70 million years ago, the dinosaurs suddenly disappeared. In fact, the only reptiles that survived this period were the ones we today know as snakes, lizards, turtles, and crocodiles.

The reason for the dinosaurs' extinction remains one of the strangest mysteries in science. According to one popular theory, the Earth collided with a large asteroid or comet from space. This collision kicked a lot of dirt up into the atmosphere. With only a little sunlight able to get through the darkened atmosphere, the temperature of the Earth's surface rapidly decreased. Before long, possibly only a few months, the whole Earth froze, and an ice age began. All tropical forests quickly died, as did all of the animals such as the dinosaurs that depended on the lush vegetation for their survival.

With the disappearance of the dinosaur, another animal form became dominant. This next era, called the Age of the Mammals, is the one we're still in and hope to be in for a long time to come!

1. One effect of an ice age, mentioned in the passage, would be

    (1) the beginning of the Mesozoic era
    (2) a drop in temperature at the Earth's surface
    (3) a collision between the Earth and a comet
    (4) the emergence of mammals
    (5) the death of tropical forests

2. According to the passage, a cause of the end of the Mesozoic era could have been

    (1) the disappearance of dinosaurs from the Earth
    (2) the sudden occurrence of an ice age
    (3) the survival of snakes, lizards, and turtles
    (4) the beginning of the Age of the Mammals
    (5) the rise of human beings as a dominant life form

3. According to the theory presented in the passage, what exactly was the cause of the dinosaurs' death?

    (1) the collision of the Earth with an object from space
    (2) the emergence of mammals as a new life form
    (3) the extremely low temperature of the air
    (4) the disappearance of their food supply
    (5) the lack of sunlight by which to see

ANSWERS AND EXPLANATIONS START ON PAGE 290.

Identifying Cause-and-Effect Relationships in Graphics

A cause-and-effect relationship might be indicated in a graphic as illustrated below. These pictures show two orientations of an outdoor plant at two different times of the day and the position of the sun in the sky at each of these times.

The illustration above shows a cause-and-effect property of plants known as *phototropism.* Phototropism is the movement and growth of plants toward a source of light. As shown here, the movement of the sun (the cause) is followed by the movement of the plant (the effect).

10:00 A.M.   4:00 P.M.

Exercise 12

Directions: Cause-and-effect questions often require you to follow carefully and understand several interrelated steps. The diagram below shows how four main types of rock are related by demonstrating what kinds of causes can change one rock type into another. After looking at this diagram, do the exercise that follows.

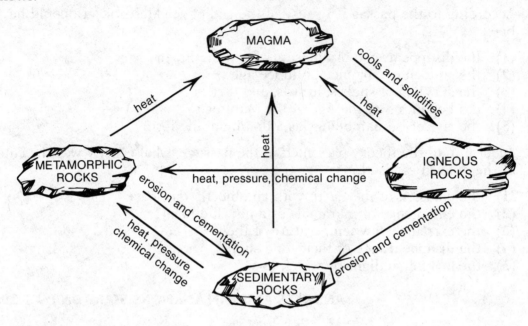

Use the information shown in this diagram to fill in the causes left blank in the list below.

Cause(s)	Effect
1. _____	Igneous rock is changed directly to metamorphic rock
2. _____	Metamorphic rock is changed directly to magma
3. _____	Igneous rock is changed directly to sedimentary rock

★ **GED PRACTICE** ★

Exercise 13

Directions: Questions 1 and 2 refer to the diagram below. Choose the best answer to each of the questions.

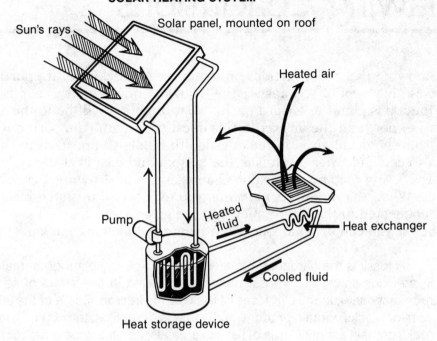

SOLAR HEATING SYSTEM

Sun's rays

Solar panel, mounted on roof

Heated air

Pump

Heated fluid

Heat exchanger

Cooled fluid

Heat storage device

1. Which of the following statements best briefly describes what takes place in the solar heating system?

   (1) Heat exchangers produce heat that is used both to heat a house and to operate a solar panel.
   (2) A heat storage device is used to heat a solar panel.
   (3) Energy from the sun warms a fluid that then circulates in the heating system or stores the captured heat energy.
   (4) Pumps heat a fluid which circulates through both a solar panel and several heat exchangers.
   (5) The solar panel removes heated air from a house so the system serves as an air conditioner.

2. The purpose of the heat exchanger is to

   (1) warm the house by transferring heat from the fluid to the air around the heat exchanger
   (2) cause the fluid to circulate through the heating system
   (3) capture the sun's energy and heat the circulating fluid
   (4) store heat for later use
   (5) measure the temperature in the house

ANSWERS AND EXPLANATIONS START ON PAGE 290.

Drawing Conclusions

Knowing that the directions on a map, read clockwise, are north, east, south, and west, how would you answer the following question: If a map is oriented so that the top is pointing toward north, what direction will be to the left side?

You know that the answer to this question is *west*. You correctly conclude this from the detail given in the question that tells you north is at the top. You can also conclude that south is at the bottom and east is at the right.

Answering the above question is an example of drawing a conclusion from details. When you ***draw a conclusion***, you express an unstated idea that is logically connected to the information you are given.

See if you can draw a conclusion from the following passage.

> A fossil is the hardened remains or traces of any plant or animal that lived in previous times. Many fossils have been found in the layers of sedimentary rock that make up the cliff faces of the Grand Canyon. Some of the 200-million-year-old rocks contain predominantly fossils of reptiles; the 400-million-year-old rocks contain mainly fossils of fishlike animals; and the even older rocks contain only the fossils of worms.

Check each statement below that is a conclusion that can be drawn from the details given in the passage.

_____ **a.** Ancient fishlike animals fed on worms and were themselves devoured by reptiles.

_____ **b.** Each geological time period is characterized by the types of life forms that predominated during that period.

_____ **c.** Only the remains of small animals are preserved in fossils.

Only statement b is a conclusion you can draw from this passage. Fossil evidence allows you to conclude that different types of animals predominated during widely separated time periods. However, this evidence does not allow you to conclude that either statement a or statement c is true. Statement a is an interesting hypothesis but not a conclusion that can be drawn. The passage doesn't give any information about the diets of different animal forms. Statement c is not true and could not be concluded from the passage. The passage does not describe the sizes of the fossils.

Exercise 14

Directions: Read the following paragraph. Then read the statements that follow. Check the statements that are conclusions that can be drawn from the details given in the paragraph.

Smoking during pregnancy is known to affect fetal development. Babies born to mothers who smoke have lower average birth weights and have a higher probability of being born with a lung illness or a birth defect. Also, more miscarriages and stillbirths occur in babies whose mothers smoked during pregnancy.

_____ **1.** To do everything that she can to ensure a healthy baby, a woman should not smoke during pregnancy.

_____ **2.** A child born to a mother who smokes will also have a dependency on cigarettes.

_____ **3.** Women who smoke during pregnancy are likely to suffer more morning sickness than nonsmokers.

★ **GED PRACTICE** ★

Exercise 15

Directions: Read the following passages and answer the questions that follow.

Electricity and water can be a deadly combination. Making contact with an electric current while standing in water, on wet ground, or on a wet floor can cause serious injury or death. Contact with an electric current occurs when you touch an exposed electric wire. It can also occur when an electric appliance shorts out (has some kind of an electrical breakdown inside). You can be injured when the electric current flows from the point of contact through your body and out to the ground by passing through the wet surface.

1. From the information given in the passage, you can conclude that a good safety rule to follow is

   (1) always wear dry shoes inside your house
   (2) turn off all electrical appliances when it's raining
   (3) don't use an electrical product when you're in contact with a wet floor or any other source of water
   (4) don't take a bath or shower when the television is on
   (5) don't use a hair dryer after you shower or bathe

For any substance to burn in air, oxygen gas must be present. Without oxygen, a flame will simply go out. For example, when Erin's science class placed a burning candle in a jar and then placed a lid on the jar, the candle burned for only thirty-five seconds, and then the flame died out.

2. From this observation it is reasonable to conclude that

(1) an open jar contains less oxygen than a closed jar
(2) if the space above a candle flame is blocked, the candle cannot burn for more than thirty-five seconds
(3) a shorter candle would burn for more than thirty-five seconds before going out
(4) a candle will not stay lit in a jar either open or closed
(5) in thirty-five seconds, a candle flame uses up all the oxygen in the jar

ANSWERS AND EXPLANATIONS START ON PAGE 290.

Drawing a Conclusion from a Graphic

To draw a conclusion from a graphic, you express an idea that follows from the graphic itself. This skill is particularly useful for reading a table.

 ## Skill Builder
Reading Tables

A table is a list of words, numbers, or drawings displayed in rows and columns. A row is read from left to right, across the page. A column is read from top to bottom, down the page. Word labels (or symbols) tell what information is contained in each row and column. The table's title may help you understand the general purpose of the table.

Tables, often called *charts*, are especially useful when you want to compare values of one item with another. Such comparisons can help you draw a conclusion about information in a table.

Below is a nutrition chart for six-ounce servings of several different types of food.

Nutritional Information for Six-Ounce Servings of Foods

	Calories	Protein (grams)	Fat (grams)	Carbohydrates (grams)
Chicken:				
light meat	191	36	4	0
dark meat	203	32	7.3	0
Ham	637	39	52.13	0
Round steak	443	49	26	0
Broccoli	44	5.3	.5	7.6
Corn	58	2	.7	13.4
Tofu (soy bean curd)	61	6.8	3.6	2.1
Apples	70	.3	.7	17.6
Pears	106	1.2	.7	26.7

To read a value from the chart, find the row (or column) of the item you're interested in and then read across (or up and down) and stop at the appropriate point. For example, to find the number of calories in a six-ounce serving of ham, you would go to the row labeled *ham* and look across to the column labeled *calories*. As you can see from the shading, there are 637 calories in a six-ounce serving of ham.

Now try reading the chart in order to answer the following questions.

a. How many grams of protein are in a six-ounce serving of round steak? _____

b. How many grams of carbohydrates are in a six-ounce apple? _____

c. Which type of meat contains 7.3 grams of fat in a six-ounce serving? _____

To answer question a, find the row labeled *Round steak* and then read over to the column labeled *Protein*. The answer is 49.

By following the same method, you can see that the answer to question b is 17.6 To find answer c, look at the column labeled *Fat*. Next, read down the column until you come to the number 7.3. You'll find that 7.3 is in the row labeled *dark meat* (under chicken).

After becoming familiar with information contained in a table, it is possible to draw certain conclusions. For example, by comparing the numbers in the table above, you can conclude that meat contains little or no carbohydrates.

Now try drawing a few conclusions:

d. What can you conclude about the fat content of meat compared to the fat content of fruit? _____

e. Which type of food (meat, vegetables, or fruit) contains the highest percentage of carbohydrates? _____

f. What conclusion can you draw about the calorie content of fat? _____

_____

The answer to question d is that meat has a much higher fat content than does fruit. The answer to question e is fruit. The answer to question f is that fat is very high in calories. You can see this most clearly by comparing the values given for ham and round steak. Although ham has less protein than steak, ham contains more fat and is much higher in calories.

Exercise 16

Directions: For each of the questions below the chart, circle your answer from the choices given in parentheses.

Type of Wind	Wind Speed (miles per hr)	What Happens
no wind	0	Smoke rises straight up.
light breeze	1–12	Leaves and twigs move.
moderate breeze	13–24	Small trees sway.
strong breeze	25–36	Hard to walk against wind.
gale	37–48	Branches break on trees. Store windows break.
strong gale	49–72	Trees are uprooted.
hurricane	above 73	Buildings greatly damaged.

1. What kind of wind would be considered safe for children to play in? (*moderate breeze, gale, strong gale*)

2. For which type of predicted wind would it be wise to cover the windows of your house if you live in a wooded area? (*moderate breeze, strong breeze, gale*)

3. If the weather report says that winds are now at 34 miles per hour but are expected to increase by 20 miles per hour more, what type of wind is being predicted? (*strong breeze, strong gale, hurricane*)

★ **GED PRACTICE** ★

Exercise 17

Directions: Questions 1 and 2 refer to the table below. Choose the best answer for each question.

Information About the Planets in Our Solar System					
Name of Planet	Distance from Sun (in miles)	Diameter (in miles)	Length of Year* (in Earth days)	Length of Day** (in Earth days)	Main Elements of Which Planet Is Composed
Mercury	36,187,500	3,050	88	59	nickel, iron, silicon
Venus	67,625,000	7,560	225	243	nickel, iron, silicon
Earth	93,500,000	7,973	365	(1 day = 24 hr.)	nickel, iron, silicon
Mars	142,120,000	4,237	687	1	iron, silicon
Jupiter	486,437,500	89,500	4,329	(10 hr.)	hydrogen
Saturn	891,875,000	75,000	10,585	(10 hr.)	hydrogen
Uranus	1,793,750,000	32,375	30,660	(16 hr.)	hydrogen, helium
Neptune	2,810,625,000	30,937	60,225	(19 hr.)	hydrogen, helium
Pluto	3,687,500,000	1,875	103,660	9	unknown

*A year is the length of time it takes a planet to make one complete orbit around the sun. This time is also called the period of revolution.
**A day is the length of time it takes a planet to make one complete turn on its own axis. This time is also called the period of rotation.

1. From the information shown in the table, which of the following can you conclude to be true?

    (1) The Earth is one of the three largest planets in the solar system.
    (2) The elements found on Earth are not found on any other planet.
    (3) The Earth is the largest of the five small planets in our solar system.
    (4) The Earth is the closest planet to the sun.
    (5) The Earth is the farthest planet from the sun.

2. Not counting the sun, the largest planets contain most of the matter in the solar system. Which two elements make up most of the matter in the solar system?

    (1) iron and silicon
    (2) iron and hydrogen
    (3) silicon and helium
    (4) nickel and iron
    (5) hydrogen and helium

ANSWERS AND EXPLANATIONS START ON PAGE 290.

4
EVALUATING SCIENCE MATERIALS

What do you think when you hear a tobacco company spokesperson make a statement like "Smoking never hurt anyone"? Would you agree with this person? Before you can answer yes or no, you need more information.

First, you need to know what evidence is available. (*Evidence* is any item of information that either supports or opposes a particular point of view.) For example, you need to know about the medical evidence that links smoking to many respiratory diseases and to lung cancer. You also need to know about any evidence that the tobacco company may have that disagrees with or questions the medical findings. Only then, after you've considered both points of view, will you be ready to give an informed opinion yourself.

When you hear or read something, you know you can't always assume it to be true. Too often people are influenced by more than just the facts. And people often don't know all the facts that are necessary in order to reach a sound conclusion. Because of this, it is important in our own decision making to learn to evaluate (judge) evidence objectively.

Scientists also rely on the objective evaluation of evidence. In fact, they have developed a special research method for collecting, organizing, and evaluating evidence. The *scientific method* is simply a logical way to do experiments and reach correct conclusions.

On the GED Science Test, evaluation questions measure your ability to make judgments about the information that's presented to you. On the pages ahead, you'll learn to do this in three ways. Then you'll see how a scientist uses the same skills to do experiments. This section is divided into four parts:

- judging the value of information
- judging the adequacy of information
- recognizing the influence of values
- the scientific method

Judging the Value of Information

Before making a decision or drawing a conclusion, you must judge the value of all available information. Most often this means distinguishing **relevant information** from **irrelevant information**.

- Relevant information includes any facts that directly affect your decision or conclusion.

- Irrelevant information includes any facts that do not affect your decision or conclusion.

For example, suppose you want to know if you can successfully grow a small garden on a plot of land near your home. From your knowledge of a plant's needs, you know that one item of relevant information is the answer to the following question.
Is the type of soil on the land fertile, garden-type soil?

An item of irrelevant information would be the answer to this question:
Should corn be planted before beans are planted?

Notice that this second question may be of interest, but it is not information that will tell you whether or not a garden is possible.
Now you try it. Place a check before each question below that is relevant to whether you'll be able to grow that garden.

_____ **a.** Is there a source of water for the proposed garden?

_____ **b.** How much snow do you get during winter months?

_____ **c.** Should you start the garden from seeds or seedlings?

_____ **d.** Does the plot receive adequate daily sunshine?

_____ **e.** Which store has the best buy on garden supplies?

Only questions a and d should be checked. Water and sunlight are both needed for crops to grow. Questions b, c, and e are not relevant to the needs of crops. The winter snow will not affect summer crops. And how you choose to plant your crops and where you buy your supplies are not questions that relate to whether a garden is possible.

Exercise 1

Directions: Below are some questions about smoking. Put a check next to each question that asks for relevant information about the health risks associated with smoking.

_____ **1.** What is the cost of a pack of cigarettes?

_____ **2.** Is there evidence that links lung cancer to smoking?

_____ **3.** How many different brands of tobacco are on the market today?

_____ **4.** Is smoking a socially acceptable activity?

_____ **5.** Is it true that a person's chance of having a heart attack doubles if he or she is a smoker?

★ GED PRACTICE ★

Exercise 2

Directions: Read the passages below and answer the questions that follow.

Alcohol is a chemical that interferes with the normal functioning of the human body. Its effects can range from loss of coordination to unconsciousness to death. As the following short story shows, alcohol does not mix well with driving.

After having five beers during the first hour at a party, Larry got mad at the hostess and left. Even though he was an alcoholic who had received medical treatment for drinking problems, Larry felt he could "hold his booze." While on the way home, he was stopped by a police officer who noticed that Larry's car had one headlight burned out and was weaving down the highway. The officer gave Larry a breathalyzer test that showed his blood alcohol level to be at .15 percent, .05 percent greater than .10 percent (the level at which a person is legally considered to be too drunk to drive).

1. Which of the following facts would be most relevant to the officer when he has to decide whether Larry is *legally* too drunk to drive?

   (1) Larry is an alcoholic.
   (2) Larry had consumed five drinks.
   (3) Larry's blood alcohol level was above .10 percent.
   (4) Larry had previously received medical treatment.
   (5) Larry's car was weaving down the highway.

2. Which of the following facts is probably *not* related to Larry's drunk driving?

   (1) Larry was unable to drive his car in a straight line.
   (2) Larry took a breathalyzer test.
   (3) Larry's blood alcohol level was above .10 percent.
   (4) Larry's car had a burned out headlight.
   (5) Larry was stopped by a police officer.

Although light and sound are both forms of wave energy, the speed of light is much greater than the speed of sound. In fact, light travels at about 186,000 miles per second, while sound travels at only about 1,100 feet per second. One place you'll directly see the difference between the speeds of light and sound is when you watch a lightning storm.

Lightning is caused by separated electrical charges rushing together in the atmosphere. At the instant the charges come together, both a flash of light and a loud sound are created. Although the flash of lightning reaches your eyes almost at once, the thunder may not reach your ears until several seconds later.

You can use the relative speeds of light and sound to find out how far away the lightning is. One useful rule of thumb is the following: when you see a flash of lightning, start counting slowly, spacing your counts one second apart. For each five seconds you count before you hear the thunder, you can figure that the lightning is about one mile away. (In five seconds, sound travels a distance of about 5,500 feet which is just a little farther than one mile—5,280 feet.) For example, if you see a flash and don't hear thunder until you've counted slowly to ten, you know that the lightning flash occurred about two miles from you.

3. Assume you know that both light and sound are created at the instant that lightning occurs but that you do not know either the speed of light or the speed of sound. From which fact below can you deduce that light travels faster than sound?

   (1) As you move farther away from a lightning storm, the sound of thunder becomes fainter.
   (2) You always see a lightning flash before you hear the thunder that is created with it.
   (3) The speed of sound is about 1,100 feet per second.
   (4) Light and sound are both forms of wave energy.
   (5) One mile is a distance of exactly 5,280 feet.

4. Which item of information below is not related to the "rule of thumb" mentioned in the passage?

   (1) the speed of sound
   (2) the speed of light
   (3) the fact that light and sound are created at the same instant at the point of a lightning flash
   (4) the cause of lightning
   (5) the rate at which you count after seeing the flash

ANSWERS AND EXPLANATIONS START ON PAGE 291.

Judging the Value of Information in Graphics

Being able to identify relevant information is especially useful when you're looking at a graphic. To avoid confusion, remember to look for just the information you need. In the example below, the locations and directions of other wind patterns are not relevant to the question you're answering.

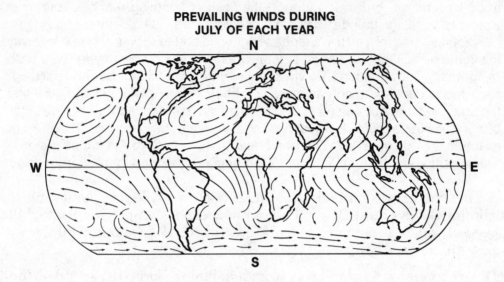

**PREVAILING WINDS DURING
JULY OF EACH YEAR**

Now try answering this question: In July, in what direction do the prevailing winds blow over the eastern United States? _____

The answer is *from south to north.* To find this answer you need to look only at the eastern part of the United States. Then see in which direction the arrows are drawn.

Exercise 3

Directions: The following questions refer to the diagram above.

1. In what direction do the prevailing July winds blow over the western part of the United States? _____

2. In what direction do the prevailing July winds blow off the southern tip of South America? _____

3. In which of the following studies would the diagram above be of *least* relevance?

   (1) ocean water current movement
   (2) the prediction of weather
   (3) the prediction of volcanic eruptions
   (4) ocean navigation

★ GED PRACTICE ★

Exercise 4

Directions: Questions 1–3 refer to information from the illustration below.

BEAK STRUCTURES OF NORTH AMERICAN BIRDS

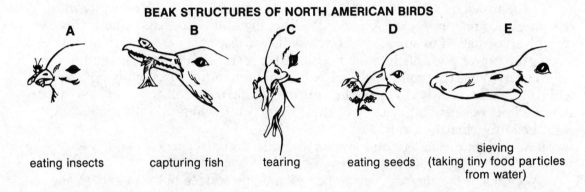

A	B	C	D	E
eating insects	capturing fish	tearing	eating seeds	sieving (taking tiny food particles from water)

1. Which two drawings above would be of most interest to someone studying different beak structures of birds that get their food from rivers and lakes?

   (1) A and C
   (2) B and D
   (3) C and E
   (4) B and E
   (5) D and E

2. Which drawings above show beak structures that are best adapted for eating small land animals?

   (1) A and C
   (2) A, B, and C
   (3) B and D
   (4) C and E
   (5) D and E

3. The drawings would have the *least* relevance to a person interested in

   (1) the eating habits of birds
   (2) the way animals have adapted to their environments
   (3) the beak structure of birds
   (4) bird-watching
   (5) the brain sizes of different birds

ANSWERS AND EXPLANATIONS START ON PAGE 291.

Judging the Adequacy of Information

In the previous section, you learned to distinguish between relevant and irrelevant information. A closely related skill is the ability to determine if there is enough information to support a conclusion. For example, suppose that, during a storm, the power goes off in your house just a second after you plugged in an old toaster. What can you conclude? Not really anything! There may be trouble with the power lines because of the storm, or your own house power may have switched off because of a faulty toaster. Until you have more information, you can't be sure what the trouble is.

Read the next passage and answer the question after it.

A tide is the alternate rising and falling of the surface of the ocean. At any point along a coast, a rising tide occurs at a regular interval and is later followed by a falling tide. A rising tide is called a *flood tide*, and a falling tide is called an *ebb tide*. Oceanographers often keep tide tables to tell you when tides occur.

Which item of information below would you need to know in order to be sure of what type of tide will next occur in Depot Bay?

(a) how long it's been since the last tide
(b) whether the previous tide was an ebb tide or a flood tide
(c) the highest water level of the last flood tide

According to the passage, an ebb tide follows a flood tide, and vice versa. Thus, answer (b) is the information you need. If, for example, the previous tide was an ebb tide, then the next tide will be a flood tide. Answers (a) and (c) refer to the tide but do not help you determine what type of tide the next one will be.

Exercise 5

Directions: Check your skill at identifying missing information in the next two passages. Read each passage and question and then circle your answer choice.

1. Competition for food determines where animals can live in a forest. When two different animals eat the same foods, each animal may have to find its own region of the forest where it has sole access to that particular food supply.

   Which item of information below would you need to know in order to decide whether or not owls and hawks can live in the same part of the forest?

   (1) whether owls and hawks use the same hunting methods
   (2) whether owls and hawks eat the same daily amount of food
   (3) whether owls and hawks eat the same sources of food

2. The exhaust gas from a diesel engine is darker in color than the exhaust gas from a gasoline engine. Because of the danger of air pollution, it would be safer for the general population if diesel engines were no longer produced.

    Which item of information below would you want to know before you would agree with this author's opinion?

    (1) whether diesel exhaust smells worse than gasoline exhaust
    (2) whether diesel exhaust produces more dangerous air pollution than gasoline exhaust
    (3) whether diesel fuel costs more or less than gasoline

★ GED PRACTICE ★

Exercise 6

Directions: Read the following passages and answer the questions that come after them.

> Brenda and Sharon had the following conversation.
>
> SHARON: "I wonder why there are seasons. For instance, why does winter occur at the same time each year and summer six months later?"
>
> BRENDA: "I'm not sure exactly. But I think it may have something to do with the movement of the Earth around the sun."
>
> SHARON: "How could the Earth's movement have anything to do with the weather?"
>
> BRENDA: "Well, I know that the Earth's orbit around the sun is not a perfect circle. And, because it isn't, the Earth is a little closer to the sun during part of the year and a little farther away six months later. I think that summer occurs when the Earth is closest to the sun and that winter occurs when the Earth is farthest from the sun."

1. Which of the following additional facts would tend to show that Brenda's hypothesis is incorrect?

    (1) Though moonlight can be very bright, it doesn't feel hot, as sunlight does, when you stand directly in it.
    (2) Out of the billions of stars in the universe, the sun is the closest star to the Earth.
    (3) The moon reflects sunlight and helps illuminate the Earth.
    (4) Light is a form of energy that is changed into heat energy when it strikes the Earth.
    (5) Countries that lie south of the equator experience winter during the same months that countries north of the equator experience summer.

Agriculture, perhaps more than other study in the twentieth century, has shown how biologists and chemists can work together to provide for the needs of the Earth's people. Due to the success of modern agricultural techniques, developed countries such as the United States are now capable of producing more food each year than all their own citizens could possibly eat. In fact, the United States sells much of the food it produces to other countries. What a wonderful feeling to know you live in a country where every citizen has more than enough food for each meal!

2. Which of the following items of information would you want to know before you could agree with the author's final statement?

   (1) whether the United States imports as much food as it exports
   (2) whether the economic system in the United States ensures that poor people have plenty of food to eat
   (3) whether the cost of food is about the same in each state of the United States
   (4) whether the United States uses more food at home than it exports
   (5) whether the United States is at a condition of full employment

The density (weight per unit volume) of one liquid can often be compared with the density of a second liquid by combining the liquids in the same container. When two liquids are combined, either one liquid will float on the other, or the liquids will mix freely. When one liquid floats on the other, you know that the liquid on top has the lesser density. As an example, oil floats on water, so you can conclude that oil is less dense than water.

Liquids that freely mix together are said to be *miscible*. When two liquids are miscible, simply combining them won't give you any information about which liquid has the lesser (or greater) density. For example, water and alcohol are miscible in all proportions. Mixing them tells you nothing about whether alcohol is more dense than water or vice versa.

3. Which of the following facts would enable you to conclude that the density of water is greater than the density of gasoline?

   (1) Gasoline and alcohol are miscible.
   (2) Gasoline and oil are miscible.
   (3) Water that condenses in a car's gas tank can prevent the car from starting.
   (4) Gasoline will float when combined with water.
   (5) Water will not put out a gasoline fire.

4. Which of the following items of information would you need to know in order to determine whether alcohol will float on oil?

   A. whether or not oil and alcohol are miscible
   B. whether the density of alcohol is less than the density of water
   C. whether the density of alcohol is less than the density of oil

   (1) A only   (4) A and B only
   (2) B only   (5) A and C only
   (3) C only

ANSWERS AND EXPLANATIONS START ON PAGE 291.

Judging the Adequacy of Information from Graphics

The question of the adequacy of information also occurs with all types of graphics. Most often, you'll be asked to decide whether a graphic contains enough information to support a certain conclusion. For example, look at the following chart.

Average Weights for Men and Women		
	Weight in Pounds	
Height	**Women**	**Men**
5'4"	124–138	135–145
5'5"	127–141	137–148
5'6"	130–144	139–151
5'7"	133–147	142–154
5'8"	136–150	145–157
5'9"	139–153	148–160

See if you can decide which of the following statements is a conclusion that is supported by the chart.

a. At birth, baby girls tend to be shorter than baby boys.
b. Between age two and age five, girls and boys are about equal in weight.
c. Adult men tend to be heavier than adult women.

Although all three statements are true, only c is supported by information given in the chart. The chart says nothing about the comparative sizes of babies or of children. Although you may also know that a and b are true, your own knowledge is not what's being tested on this question! To get the correct answer, you must consider only the information that appears on the graphic itself.

Exercise 7

Directions: Look at the chart below. Then place a check next to each of the statements listed that is supported by information from the chart.

Properties of Metals and Nonmetals

Properties	Metals	Nonmetals
Common Phase (at room temperature)	Solids, except mercury (a liquid) Examples: copper, iron, gold, aluminum	Solids, liquids, or gases Examples: glass, wood, plastic, oxygen
Luster	Bright and shiny	Dull-looking
Color	Silver-gray, except for gold and copper	Various colors
Electrical Conductivity	Very good conductors	Very poor conductors
Heat Conductivity	Very good conductors	Very poor conductors

_____ **1.** Iron, a metal, is a better conductor of heat than is glass, a nonmetal.

_____ **2.** Gold is not considered a metal because it does not have the normal silver-gray metallic color.

_____ **3.** Of the two metals, copper is a better conductor of electricity than aluminum.

_____ **4.** Mercury is an example of a liquid metal.

_____ **5.** Many gases are considered to be metals.

★ **GED PRACTICE** ★

Exercise 8

Directions: Each of the questions below is related to a graphic. Find the appropriate graphic and circle the best answer to each question.

Questions 1 and 2 refer to the drawings below.

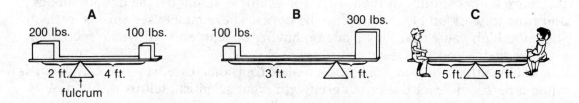

1. Assume that levers A and B are balanced. You can conclude that for a lever to be balanced,

    (1) equal weights must be placed on each side
    (2) weights must be placed at equal distances from the fulcrum
    (3) the sum of the two weights must not be greater than 200 pounds
    (4) the product of each weight times its distance from the fulcrum must be the same on both sides of the lever
    (5) the larger weight must be placed twice as far from the fulcrum as is the smaller weight

2. Assume that the teeter-totter in drawing C is moving. What item of information would you need to know in order to determine whether the teeter-totter will balance when the children stop it?

    (1) the sum of the weights of the children
    (2) the height of each child
    (3) the average weight of the children
    (4) the weight of the teeter-totter
    (5) the weight of each child

ANSWERS AND EXPLANATIONS START ON PAGE 291.

Recognizing Values

A *value* is a personal belief about the way to live one's own life. It can be a religious belief, or it can be the way a person believes he or she should act when around other people.

People often express their values by writing letters to newspapers, by voting for certain political candidates, or by donating money or time to organizations that have values similar to their own. For example, many people donate money and time to work on cleaning up public parks. These people see this as a way to show the high value that they place on having a clean and enjoyable recreation area for themselves and their neighbors.

Values affect the way each of us makes decisions. One way this can occur is when a personal belief does not agree with what scientists tell us is a fact. A good example is the question of evolution. Though scientific evidence strongly supports the basic principles of evolution, many religious groups oppose these ideas on the grounds that evolution does not agree with religious teachings. In this case, a person may be forced to decide between two competing values: the value a person places on certain religious teachings versus the value the person places on certain scientific evidence.

Here's an example for you to try. The paragraph below describes a situation. On the line beneath the paragraph, write the two competing values you think are in conflict in this situation.

Reggie is nineteen and has a job at a factory. The men he works with all chew tobacco. To feel "like the other men," Reggie also started to chew tobacco about three weeks ago. Last night, for the first time, Reggie heard about medical evidence that strongly indicates that chewing tobacco can cause cancer of the mouth. Because Reggie is concerned about his health, he finds himself having to make an uncomfortable choice.

What two values are in conflict in Reggie's situation?

_____

Reggie is in a very common situation. He is faced with choosing between (1) the value he places on wanting to feel accepted by the group he works with and (2) the value he places on his health.

Exercise 9

Directions: In each situation described below, a person must choose between two competing values. On the line beneath each paragraph, express in your own words the values you believe are in conflict.

1. According to Betty's religious beliefs, she is not allowed to have a medical operation of any type. Recently, though, Betty found out that she needs an operation on her fallopian tubes if she ever wants to give birth to a child, a lifelong dream of hers.

_____

2. Jay, a physicist, has just found out that the company he works for has accepted a government contract to do work in nuclear weapons research. Jay is strongly opposed to the use of nuclear weapons, and he refuses to take part in the project.

_____

3. Wilma, a housewife, drives an older car. She has been told that she can either use regular gas or unleaded gas. Regular gas is about 10 cents less per gallon, but it creates a dangerous form of air pollution because it contains lead. Unleaded gas will not harm her older engine and is safer for the environment, but it costs more.

_____

★ GED PRACTICE ★

Exercise 10

Directions: Read the following passage and answer the questions below.

On October 26, 1984, surgeons at Loma Linda Hospital in southern California removed the failing heart of a two-week-old baby girl and replaced it with the heart of a baboon. Baby Fae, as the girl was known to the press, was the first infant ever to receive a heart from a nonhuman species. Following surgery, Baby Fae astounded the world by how well her body seemed to accept the baboon's heart. Yet, a short twenty days later, Baby Fae died from heart and kidney failure, following her body's eventual rejection of the new heart.

Baby Fae's short life and sad death focused the world's attention on the possibility of cross-species heart transplants. The use of a baboon heart as a replacement for a failing human heart has brought mixed feelings from the general public. Many doctors and others have come out in strong support of this procedure. They feel that, for medicine to progress, doctors must be allowed to try radical new procedures. According to this view, the surgery performed on Baby Fae, though very difficult for relatives and friends, was part of the price that must be paid for medical knowledge.

On the other hand, many animals' rights groups protested the Loma Linda operation, describing it as tinkering with human and animal life. In fact, several groups demonstrated outside the Loma Linda hospital after news of the operation was announced. The members of these groups believe that destroying animals for the sake of medical research is morally wrong. They point out that respect for life must be given to all animals, as well as human beings, because we all share the Earth together.

1. Which of the following best represents a value shown by those who favor the baboon heart transplant procedure?

   (1) Medical experimentation is the most important thing to consider, regardless of the deaths of a few infants.
   (2) It is better to transplant a baboon heart than another human heart because a baboon is not another person.
   (3) The life of a baboon has much less value than the life of an infant human being.
   (4) The life of a baboon has an equal value to the life of an infant human being.
   (5) Baboon heart transplants should be tried only on those infants whose parents have adequate medical insurance.

2. Which of the following bests represents a value of an animals' rights group that opposes the use of baboons and other animals for medical experimentation where the animal suffers and may die?

   (1) The rights to life and freedom from suffering extend equally to human beings and animals.
   (2) Baboons and other animals should be given all the legal rights that human beings have.
   (3) The life of a healthy baboon is more important to society than the life of a very sick child.
   (4) Because of its difference in shape, a baboon heart is not a suitable replacement for a human heart.
   (5) Replacing a human heart with a baboon heart will create a child without a human soul.

3. Many people feel that while it is all right to raise animals such as cows for slaughter, it is not all right to take the lives of baboons and other animals that show a high level of intelligence. What value is being shown in this position?

   (1) Food production for human consumption is more important than any rights an animal might otherwise have.
   (2) Humans should value animals of high intelligence more than they value animals of lower intelligence.
   (3) Any animal that is not raised as a source of human food should not be used for medical experimentation.
   (4) The only justification for killing an animal is for use as a source of food.
   (5) Animals that are physically similar to human beings ought to be treated differently than animals that aren't.

ANSWERS AND EXPLANATIONS START ON PAGE 291.

Recognizing Values in Graphics

On the previous few pages, you saw that personal values may influence how a person makes decisions. On the next few pages we will discuss how values may also be reflected in graphics. An artist or author may use graphics as a means of expressing his or her values in the hope that the reader will be influenced to support the presented point of view.

The use of graphics to express values is common in both social studies and science. In science, artists may focus on controversial scientific research such as genetic engineering or on the use of science in a way that provokes social controversy, such as the development of expensive military weapons systems.

The two types of graphics in which artists most often express values are diagrams and cartoons. As an example, look at the following cartoon. The subject of the drawing is genetic engineering, the study of how scientists can alter genes in a plant or animal cell in order to produce organisms with new characteristics.

"Dangerous? No, our work is simply with plants!"

As you look at this cartoon, answer these two questions:

a. How do you think the artist feels about genetic engineering?

_____

b. What feeling do you think the artist would like you to have about genetic

engineering? _____

As you can see, the artist is very concerned about the potential dangers of genetic engineering. Answers may vary, but one answer to a is that the author believes that scientists might create a dangerous, uncontrollable organism. Though the person-eating plant is meant to be an amusing exaggeration, the cartoon is an effective way for the artist to make a point. Answers to question b may also vary. However, you can be sure that the artist would like you to become aware of the potential dangers of this research.

Exercise 11

Directions: Refer again to the drawing of the person-eating plant and answer the next three questions, choosing the best answer from among the choices given.

1. What positive aspect of genetic engineering is the author failing to point out?

   (1) Genetic engineering research is being carried out by many large pharmaceutical companies interested in making money.
   (2) Genetic engineering may lead to new types of food crops, medicinal drugs, and other things beneficial to society.
   (3) Genetic engineering is a new science, and it's too early to tell how successful or dangerous its results will be.

2. Basing your answer on what you've learned about the artist's values as expressed by the cartoon, which of the following words would best describe the artist's attitude toward scientific research in general?

   (1) excited
   (2) indifferent
   (3) cautious

3. Which of the following organizations is most likely to express values similar to the artist's?

   (1) an environmental protection group
   (2) a group of politicians
   (3) a private company involved in genetic engineering

★ **GED PRACTICE** ★

Exercise 12

Directions: Questions 1–3 refer to the illustration below.

YOUR TAX DOLLARS AT WORK

In Space   and   at Home

1. Which of the following best expresses the point of view that the artist is try-
    ing to present in the drawing above?

    (1) All scientific research for military purposes should be canceled.
    (2) Spending tax dollars on military weapons in space is the cause of pov-
    erty and other social problems.
    (3) Much of the tax money spent for space-based military weapons would
    be better spent if it were used to help eliminate poverty and other social
    problems.
    (4) Money spent for military spacecraft will help lead to a solution for
    poverty.
    (5) Poor people should get jobs so that they can help provide tax money for
    space-based weapons.

2. Which of the following words best describes the artist's attitude toward gov-
    ernment spending priorities?

    (1) happy
    (2) indifferent
    (3) excited
    (4) uninformed
    (5) concerned

3. Which of the following best expresses a point of view that opposes the artist's point of view?

   (1) Spending tax money for space-based weapons is more important to the United States at this time than spending the same money to help fight poverty—also an important problem.
   (2) Poverty among some citizens is a desired feature of a growing economy.
   (3) Poor countries should not tell a rich country like the United States how to spend its own tax money.
   (4) Money spent for weapons research should come from private companies, not from tax dollars.
   (5) The placing of military weapons in space should be put under strict control of the United Nations.

ANSWERS AND EXPLANATIONS START ON PAGE 292.

The Scientific Method

Most of the scientific knowledge we have today has come from careful observation and experimentation. In each experiment that is performed, a scientist carefully forms a hypothesis, evaluates evidence, and reaches conclusions. As mentioned before, the steps followed by scientists in the ongoing search for knowledge are part of a logical process called the *scientific method*.

As we identify each of the five steps of the scientific method, we'll show how each might actually be used in a real experiment.

1. **The first step of the scientific method is to identify the problem to be investigated.**
   Example: Suppose a biologist notices that the tomato plants in her lab are growing at a faster rate than usual. She wants to find out why this is happening.

2. **The second step is to collect information.**
   Example: The biologist asks the lab assistants if anything unusual has happened to the tomato plants lately. She also checks the records. She discovers that the plants had been accidentally treated with a certain synthetic hormone. She looks in books and journals to get more information about this hormone.

3. **The third step is to make a hypothesis.**
   Example: The biologist's hypothesis is that the synthetic hormone causes tomato plants to grow at a faster rate.

4. **The fourth step is to test the hypothesis by trying an experiment and recording the results.**
   Example: The biologist tests her hypothesis by doing the following experiment. She grows tomato plants in two planters. One group of plants, called

the *experimental group*, will be treated with the synthetic hormone. The second group of plants, called the *control group*, will not be treated with the hormone. Both the experimental group and the control group will be given equal amounts of water and sunshine.

The purpose of the control group is to let the biologist know what would happen to the plants if they stayed in their natural state and did not receive hormones. Only by comparing the growth rates of the plants in the experimental group with that of the plants in the control group can the biologist find evidence of an increased growth rate (if the increased growth occurs).

On a weekly basis, the biologist measures and records the height of each plant in both the control and experimental groups. An example of one week's data is illustrated below.

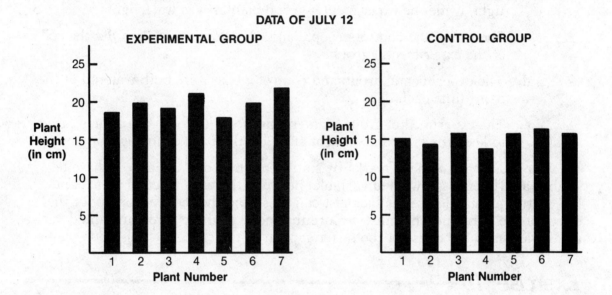

DATA OF JULY 12

5. **The fifth step is to draw conclusions.**
Example: After two months, the plants in the experimental group are taller, on the average, than the plants in the control group. From the data obtained, the biologist concludes that the synthetic hormone does in fact increase the rate at which tomato plants grow.

If there had been no difference in size between the experimental group plants and the control group plants, the biologist would probably conclude that the synthetic hormone did not cause the increased growth rate. Then she would have to throw out her hypothesis and form a new hypothesis about why the plants had started growing more quickly. She would have to repeat the whole process, running a new experiment to test her hypothesis and drawing conclusions based on the new experimental results.

The biologist will want to run this experiment a second time to make sure that the same results can be obtained. When she does the experiment again, she will use new seeds and new soil. This helps ensure that the only difference between the two groups of plants is the use of the synthetic hormone.

Before reaching a conclusion, the biologist must make sure there are no **unwanted variables**. An unwanted variable is any unplanned difference that exists between the experimental group and the control group. An unwanted variable can affect the outcome of an experiment and can cause the reported results to be meaningless. In the experiment described above, an unwanted variable would be any difference other than the use of synthetic hormone on the experimental plants.

Place a check beside each statement below that identifies an unwanted variable in the experiment described above.

_____ **a.** Both the experimental group and the control group received equal amounts of sunshine.

_____ **b.** The planter in which the control group was planted was not watertight, while the experimental-group planter was watertight.

_____ **c.** The soil of the control group contained more rocks than did the soil of the experimental group.

_____ **d.** The experimental group and control group were both watered at the same time each day.

_____ **e.** The experimental-group planter was closer to the space heater (used to keep the laboratory warm at night) than the control-group planter.

You should place check marks by statements b, c, and e. Each of these describes a difference (unwanted variable) between the experimental plants and the control plants. Before the biologist can be sure of her conclusion about the effect of the hormone, she must be sure that none of these three unwanted variables was really the cause of the faster growth in the experimental-group plants.

Exercise 13

Directions: Answer each of the following questions.

1. Following are phrases that summarize each of the five steps of the scientific method. Write these phrases in the correct order: draw conclusions, collect information, perform experiments, identify a problem, form a hypothesis

   a. _____   **c.** _____   **e.** _____

   b. _____   **d.** _____

2. In the plant hormone experiment, why did the biologist grow a control group of plants as well as the experimental group of plants?

   _____

3. Why is it better that the biologist grew several plants in each planter rather than just one plant in each? _____

★ **GED PRACTICE** ★

Exercise 14 ─────────────────

Directions: Questions 1–3 refer to the information below.

Jason, a psychologist, wants to determine if mice suffer from any form of anxiety or tension when they are forced to live in crowded conditions.

1. Which of the following experimental conditions will be best suited to provide evidence on which Jason can base a conclusion?

   (1) Place a group of six mice in each of two identical small cages, each so small that the mice have only a few inches of distance between one another at all times.
   (2) Place a group of six mice in each of two identical large cages, each large enough so that the mice can have several feet of distance between one another if they so choose.
   (3) Place a single group of twelve mice in one small cage.
   (4) Place a single group of twelve mice in one large cage.
   (5) Place one group of six mice in a small cage and a second group of six mice in a large cage.

2. Suppose that Jason does his experiment in the following way. He places a group of six mice in a small cage and a second group of six mice in a large cage. Now let's suppose that the crowded mice *do* show more signs of anxiety than the uncrowded mice. How can Jason best double-check his hypothesis that it is the crowding together that is causing these mice to experience this anxiety?

   (1) Do the experiment a second time, only this time place two mice in each cage.
   (2) Contact his friends to see if they think his hypothesis is reasonable.
   (3) Do the experiment a second time, only this time use two new groups of mice.
   (4) Do the experiment a second time, only this time do it with hamsters.
   (5) Do the experiment a second time, only this time place mice in the large cage and hamsters in the small cage.

3. Jason believes that the findings from his mice studies might also apply to human beings. Of the following types of research, the most relevant evidence to support Jason's belief would come from studies dealing with

   (1) the anxiety and depression levels of people living in crowded conditions in an inner-city neighborhood
   (2) the rate of teenage pregnancies in cities that have a population of one million or more
   (3) the anxiety levels of farmers struggling to exist during low-income years
   (4) the anxiety levels of people living in a small midwestern town
   (5) the rate of crime occurring in large cities where there is a high rate of drug use

Exercise 15

Directions: In many experiments, the use of a control group does not apply. An example is the experiment below. Read the description of the experiment and answer the questions that follow.

Wanda knows that the force of gravity pulls all objects toward the surface of the Earth. She now wants to determine whether heavier objects fall at a faster rate than lighter objects. To find out, Wanda decided to try experiments in which she would use a three-pound brick, a one-pound rock, and a paper clip that weighs a fraction of an ounce. In each of three experiments, Wanda dropped two objects side by side from a height of three feet and observed them as they fell. When she completed the experiments, Wanda recorded the results shown in the table below.

Experiment	Objects dropped	Observed results
#1	3-lb. brick and 1-lb. rock	Both brick and rock reached the ground at the same time. Both fell at the same rate.
#2	3-lb. brick and paper clip	Both brick and paper clip reached the ground at the same time. Both fell at the same rate.
#3	1-lb. rock and paper clip	Both rock and paper clip reached the ground at the same time. Both fell at the same rate.

1. From the results of her experiment, Wanda can conclude that for fairly short distances,

   (1) all heavy objects fall more quickly than light objects
   (2) metal objects fall more quickly than bricks
   (3) some heavy and light objects fall at the same rate
   (4) heavy objects fall more slowly than light objects
   (5) objects made of different substances fall at different rates

2. Suppose that Wanda now does the same experiment with a paper clip and a leaf. This time, even though the objects are about the same weight, they do not fall at the same rate: the paper clip falls much more quickly and reaches the ground much sooner.

   Which of the following can Wanda most reasonably conclude *from this observation*?

   (1) The rate at which a light object falls depends on its weight.
   (2) Very light objects fall at different rates, and these rates depend on the time of day the objects are dropped.
   (3) Man-made objects fall more quickly than objects from nature.
   (4) The rate at which a light object falls depends on how large the surface of the object is.
   (5) The rate at which a heavy object falls depends on how large the surface of the object is.

3. Noticing that a paper clip falls much more quickly than a leaf, Wanda forms a new hypothesis to explain this new discovery:

   > Very light objects fall at different rates because of the effect of air resistance. Air resistance slows an object with a large surface much more than it slows an object with a small surface. Over short distances, heavy objects with small surfaces are not noticeably affected by air resistance.

   To test her hypothesis about very light objects, Wanda should do an experiment in which she drops

   (1) a pin and a needle
   (2) a piece of notebook paper and a book
   (3) a paper plate and a china plate
   (4) a green leaf and a brown leaf
   (5) a piece of notebook paper and a small plastic spoon

4. After doing all four experiments, Wanda had another hypothesis. She wondered whether all objects would fall at the same rate if there were no air resistance. Which of the following would be the most ideal place to test Wanda's hypothesis?

   (1) in the pressurized passenger cabin of an airplane flying at 35,000 feet
   (2) standing underwater on the bottom of a swimming pool
   (3) in the "weightless" condition of an orbiting space shuttle
   (4) on the surface of the moon, a body that has gravity but no air
   (5) in a very still room where the windows are closed and there is no air movement

ANSWERS AND EXPLANATIONS START ON PAGE 292.

5
PLANT AND ANIMAL BIOLOGY

Imagine for a moment what it's like to sleep in a meadow. Until you fall a-sleep, you listen to the chirping of crickets, the croaking of frogs, and the occasional buzzing of a bothersome mosquito. Unless you're used to these sounds, you're probably surprised at how much of a racket these little animals can make!

But you soon grow used to the noise, and the next thing you know you're awakening to the first rays of sunlight. Your sleeping bag and the grass around you are moist with morning dew—but at least the crickets and frogs are quiet! The only sounds you hear now are those of insects busily starting their day. Small bees hover above the flowers, looking for blossoms from which to take the sweet nectar they need for making honey. A butterfly alights on a dandelion a few feet away. Beyond the butterfly, spring buttercups slowly open their golden petals toward the morning light. And just beyond the buttercups, a robin pulls a worm from the grass and flies off to feed its young. Sitting up and starting to feel hungry yourself, you are amazed at the variety of life and activity around you.

Sleeping in a meadow is quite an educational experience. It gives you a glimpse into the world of plants and animals—some big, some small, but all living out their lives in their own ways while sharing the Earth together.

Biology is the study of all these living things, from plants and animals too small to be seen by the human eye to huge redwood trees, elephants, and whales. The interests of biologists are almost as numerous as the one and one-half million types of *organisms* (living things) known to be on the Earth. Much of this interest focuses on the study of plant and animal structures and on life cycles.

Of recent interest is the field of ecology. *Ecology* is the study of the relationship of organisms to their environment. An *environment* is all the living and nonliving things that affect an organism's life in some way.

The study of biology really began thousands of years ago, when people first attempted to understand living things. In fact, the word *biology* comes from two Greek words: *bios*, which means "life," and *logos*, which means "study of." Even though the study of life has been going on during all this time, one important principle—called *biogenesis*—is only about 150 years old.

According to this principle, life can come only from life. Each organism must come from the reproduction of other organisms. This idea seems obvious to us today. But, before the mid-1800s, it was widely believed that insects and worms could form from rotting soil! People also believed that frogs formed in clouds and fell to Earth during rainstorms!

Today, biologists know quite a lot about the types of organisms that inhabit the Earth. Many of these have been identified and studied, and they are broadly classified into two groups: plants and animals. The study of plants is called *botany*, and the study of animals is called *zoology*. This chapter will focus on many of the characteristics of life that are of interest in both botany and zoology, characteristics that are common to all living things.

Exercise 1: Overview of Plant and Animal Biology

Directions: Match each item on the left with the phrase that best describes it on the right. Write the letter of the phrase on the line before the correct number.

_____ **1.** botany

_____ **2.** ecology

_____ **3.** biology

_____ **4.** environment

_____ **5.** zoology

a. the study of all living things

b. the study of animals

c. the study of the relationship of organisms to their surroundings

d. the study of plants

e. all the things that affect the life of an organism

★ **GED PRACTICE** ★

Exercise 2: Plant and Animal Biology

Directions: Choose the best answer for each question below.

1. Which of the following best summarizes the first two paragraphs of the overview on page 92?

   (1) A meadow is a cold damp place at night, and you'll want to take plenty of warm clothes if you camp there.
   (2) By sleeping overnight in a meadow, you can hear firsthand how much noise small animals can make.
   (3) A meadow is filled with a variety of life forms, each going about an activity that is part of its life cycle.
   (4) Some animals eat plants, while some animals eat other animals.
   (5) Many baby animals, such as small robins, depend on their mothers to provide them with food.

2. Which of the following statements is an opinion, not a fact?

   (1) Frogs eat insects, a fact that makes them more important to humans than worms are.

   (2) Certain types of animals hunt for food mainly at night, while other animals hunt mainly during the day.

   (3) The study of an organism includes the way in which it interacts with other organisms.

   (4) Many flowers respond to the sun's coming over the horizon by opening their petals.

   (5) Both plants and animals exhibit behavior that helps ensure their survival.

Questions 3–5 are based on the following passage.

In a famous experiment performed in the seventeenth century, Francesco Redi wanted to disprove the common belief that meat, when left to rot, would turn into maggots. (Maggots are the newly hatched, crawling stage of flies that later mature to become adult flies.) Redi believed that an organism such as a maggot could result only from the reproduction of parent organisms of the same type. To prove this, Redi performed the experiment shown below. He placed a piece of meat to rot in each of two jars. The control jar was covered with a piece of cloth. Although air could pass through the cloth, the flies couldn't. The experimental jar was left open.

EXPERIMENT BEGINS

control jar   experimental jar

As the experiment begins, no maggots are on the meat in either jar. Flies can lay eggs only in the experimental jar.

SEVERAL WEEKS LATER

control jar   experimental jar

Several weeks later, maggots cover the meat in the experimental jar. No maggots have appeared on meat in the control jar.

3. For what purpose did Redi place the cloth over the control jar?

   (1) to keep dirt off the meat in the control jar

   (2) to keep the smell of rotting meat from leaving the control jar

   (3) to keep fresh air from circulating around the rotting meat in the control jar

   (4) to give the flies two places to lay their eggs, on the rotting meat and on the cloth

   (5) to prevent flies from laying eggs on the meat in the control jar

4. The diagram on page 94 shows the results of Redi's experiment. What is the most reasonable conclusion that can be drawn from these results?

   (1) Rotting meat will turn into maggots only when the meat is left open to fresh air.
   (2) Maggots will turn into flies only when they get their nutrients from rotting meat.
   (3) The effect of the cloth is to slow down the rotting process by about a week.
   (4) Maggots appear on rotten meat only after hatching from eggs that flies have laid on the meat.
   (5) Flies are able to reproduce only when there is a source of rotten meat on which to lay their eggs.

5. Which of the following factors should Redi have been most careful about when he began his experiment?

   (1) that both jars were exactly the same size
   (2) that both pieces of meat were free of insect eggs or larvae
   (3) that the temperature of each jar would be kept constant
   (4) that both pieces of meat were exactly the same size
   (5) that no flies would ever be allowed to enter the room in which the experiment was to be performed

ANSWERS AND EXPLANATIONS START ON PAGE 292.

Characteristics of Living Things

Key Words

cell—the basic unit of all living things
food—a substance that helps an organism grow and provides it with energy
response—a reaction, usually expressed as a change in an organism's activity
stimulus—anything that causes an organism to react

Seeing a squirrel or dog is a commonplace experience that's easily taken for granted. Too often we forget just how unique and remarkable life is. Perhaps it is a good idea from time to time to remember that, of all the planets in the solar system (and possibly of all the planets in the universe), Earth is the only one that contains life. This means that Earth is a very special place. Earth has just the right combination of chemical elements and climatic conditions needed to produce and sustain an incredible variety of living things.

What Does It Mean to Be a Living Thing?

To answer this question, first notice that living things are certainly different from nonliving things. For example, you don't have much in common with a chair or a glass. However, you're also very different from a tree or a bird, and they—like you—are living things. In defining living things, scientists have found it more useful to look at how living things are similar to one another than to look at how they are different. Below are some characteristics common to all organisms, both plants and animals.

All living things go through a life cycle that can be divided into five stages: beginning, growth, maturity, decline, and death. During the beginning stage, an organism takes shape. For animals, the beginning is the time preceding birth. Growth is the period when an organism grows to its mature size and develops the ability to reproduce. During maturity, an organism uses energy mainly for the maintenance of life. During decline, an organism is not as able to keep itself in top shape, and it may become less active.

In order to go through this life cycle, living things need energy. Everyone is familiar with the feeling of hunger. This feeling is just your body's way of telling you that it needs a source of energy. You and all other organisms use energy to carry on daily activities. Green plants get energy from glucose, a food sugar that they produce by combining sunlight energy, carbon dioxide gas, and water. Animals cannot produce their own food directly, so they use the food energy produced by plants. Animals either eat the plants themselves or eat other animals that eat plants.

All living things can reproduce, or make more of their own kind. Each individual animal or plant will eventually complete the life cycle and die. Reproduction makes it possible for each type of organism to continue to exist.

All living things respond to things that happen around them. An organism will react to a stimulus, or change, in its environment. A stimulus may be something seen, heard, felt, smelled, or tasted. Living things always respond to a stimulus in a way that helps them in their constant struggle to survive. For example, when a deer hears a mountain lion growl, it bolts. The big cat's growl is the stimulus. The deer's reaction—running away—is called a response.

Finally, all living things are made up of basic units called cells. Cells carry out important life activities during each stage of an organism's life. There are tiny organisms made up of only one cell, and there are organisms, such as ourselves, that are made up of trillions of cells.

Exercise 3: The Life Cycle

Directions: In each blank, write the stage of development and growth (beginning, growth, maturity, decline, death) during which each of the following usually occurs in the life cycle of a human being.

_____ **1.** growth of permanent teeth

_____ **2.** great-grandchildren

_____ **3.** existence as a fetus

_____ **4.** decay and decomposition of the body

_____ **5.** years of work and raising a family

★ **GED PRACTICE** ★

Exercise 4: Living Things

Directions: Choose the best answer to each question below.

1. What name is given to the basic unit of all living things?

    (1) energy
    (2) environment
    (3) organ
    (4) response
    (5) cell

2. What is most likely to be true of a mouse that responds more slowly to a cat's hissing than most other mice?

    (1) It will have a slower than average growth rate.
    (2) It will have a shorter than average life span.
    (3) It will use less than an average amount of energy for its daily activities.
    (4) It will be rejected by other mice.
    (5) It will have a longer than average life span.

3. Nonliving things also change when their environment changes. For example, a puddle of water will freeze solid when the water temperature drops below 32°F. Which of the following statements tells the most important difference between a puddle freezing and an animal's response to freezing temperature?

    (1) An animal responds more slowly to temperature change.
    (2) An animal does not freeze because it is not made of pure water.
    (3) An animal does not freeze as quickly as a puddle does.
    (4) An animal responds to freezing temperatures in a way that best ensures its own survival.
    (5) An animal freezes solid at a different temperature from that at which a puddle freezes.

ANSWERS AND EXPLANATIONS START ON PAGE 293.

Characteristics of Flowering Plants

Besides being delicious and nutritious, what do oranges, apples, strawberries, tomatoes, avocados, grapes, and hickory nuts all have in common? One thing is that they are all produced by flowering plants. Spring flowers on these plants give way to summer fruit. Now, how about broccoli, cabbage, and cauliflower—what do they have in common? This answer may surprise you: the parts of them that we eat are flowers!

Flowering plants are only one of many types of plants, but they play a special role in our lives. They provide us with fruits, nuts, vegetables, and, of course, flowers. Because of their importance, much is now known about both the structure and the behavior of these plants.

Like all other plants, flowering plants are faced with basic survival needs. They need a source of energy, a source of water and minerals, and an efficient means of reproduction. On the next two pages we'll discuss how flowering plants meet these needs. A picture of a flowering plant is shown below.

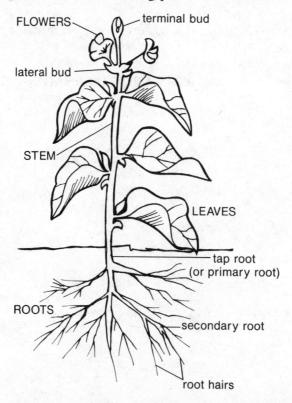

FLOWERS
terminal bud
lateral bud
STEM
LEAVES
tap root (or primary root)
ROOTS
secondary root
root hairs

PARTS OF A FLOWER

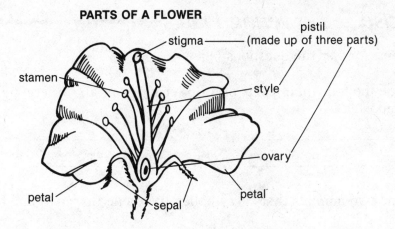

Unlike animals, which move around in search of food, most plants spend their entire life in one spot. A plant can do this because of its roots. Roots both anchor a plant in the ground and absorb water and minerals from the soil. Plants such as grass have a system of small branching roots. Most larger flowering plants have a single large root, called a *tap root* or primary root, and numerous smaller *secondary roots*.

Growing above the ground are the stem and leaves of a plant. The stem holds the leaves up to sunlight and conducts water and minerals from the roots to the leaves. Stems such as those found on small wildflowers may be shorter than an inch. The trunks of trees, which are also stems, may grow to be hundreds of feet tall. One of the most noticeable features of stems is their buds, the part where new growth takes place. On the top of the stem is a terminal bud from which the plant grows taller. Along the sides of the stem are lateral buds that develop into branches, leaves, or flowers.

It is in the leaves that plants carry on photosynthesis, the production of food from sunlight energy, water, and carbon dioxide gas. The larger a plant grows, the more leaves it will usually have. In many plants, leaves and stems form as a single structure. The prickly stem of a desert cactus is an example.

Reproduction of Flowering Plants

Flowers are the parts of plants in which reproduction occurs. Inside the petals, the large brightly colored parts of an open flower, are the stamens and the pistil. Stamens are the male reproductive structures, and pistils are the female reproductive structures.

Flowering plants reproduce by a process called pollination. During this process, pollen—a grain that contains the male sex cell—leaves the stamen and gets deposited on a stigma, the top part of a pistil. From the stigma, the pollen moves through the style, a tube that connects the stigma with the ovary. The female sex cell is contained in the ovary. When male and female cells join in the ovary, they form a fertilized egg that develops into a seed. Usually, a new plant grows from the seed.

Many plants self-pollinate. This means that the plant's pollen fertilizes the same plant's eggs to produce seeds. However, not all plants are able to do this. These other plants must be fertilized by pollen from a second plant. Since plants can't go and search for mates, they must rely on nature to carry pollen to them. Pollen is carried by wind, water, and animals. Bees, butterflies, and hummingbirds are the best-known animal pollinators.

Exercise 5: Flowering Plants

Directions: Answer the questions below.

1. Name the four main parts of a flowering plant and briefly tell why each part is important.

    a. _____   c. _____

    b. _____   d. _____

2. Name two animals that carry pollen from one flower to another.

    a. _____   b. _____

3. Read each statement below. Circle *T* if the statement is true or *F* if the statement is false.

    T F **a.** Photosynthesis is the production of food from the sun's energy.

    T F **b.** A flowering plant contains only female reproductive parts.

    T F **c.** A plant's stem absorbs water and minerals from the soil.

★ **GED PRACTICE** ★

Exercise 6: Plant Responses

Directions: Questions 1–4 are based on the following information.

The responses made by plants to environmental stimuli can be classified in various ways. Below are five types of responses to common stimuli.

(1) **Phototropism**—the bending (or growth) of a plant toward a source of light

(2) **Touch response**—the movement of leaves or other parts of a plant in response to being touched

(3) **Positive geotropism**—the downward growth of a plant root in the direction of gravity

(4) **Negative geotropism**—the upward growth of a plant stem, directly away from the direction of gravity

(5) **Circadian rhythm**—a natural pattern of plant activity that takes place in a twenty-four hour cycle

1. When an insect enters the open leaves of a Venus's-flytrap, the plant's leaves snap shut and trap the insect. The plant's reaction is an example of

    (1) phototropism
    (2) touch response
    (3) positive geotropism
    (4) negative geotropism
    (5) circadian rhythm

2. Morning glories open their petals each morning when the sun comes up and close them each night at dusk. This daily activity is an example of

(1) phototropism
(2) touch response
(3) positive geotropism
(4) negative geotropism
(5) circadian rhythm

3. When she planted flowers in the spring, Marlene accidentally planted her tulip bulbs upside down. Later, when she found out about her mistake, Marlene dug up a bulb and found that the root had simply sprouted from the top and was now growing downward—deeper into the soil, passing along the side of the bulb. This response of the bulb root is known as

(1) phototropism
(2) touch response
(3) positive geotropism
(4) negative geotropism
(5) circadian rhythm

4. On clear days, the large yellow-rayed flowers of Bob's mature sunflower plants slowly follow the sun as it moves. This plant movement is a response best classified as

(1) phototropism
(2) touch response
(3) positive geotropism
(4) negative geotropism
(5) circadian rhythm

ANSWERS AND EXPLANATIONS START ON PAGE 293.

 Writing Activity 1——————————————

Part of what makes each area of the world unique is its plants and trees. When we think of the desert, we imagine cactus plants, and when we think of California, we picture palm trees or giant redwood trees.

Think about the variety of plants in your environment. On a sheet of scrap paper, jot down the names of plants and trees that grow in the area where you live. Then write one paragraph describing those plants.

ANSWERS WILL VARY.

Animal Characteristics

If living things are to survive, they must be adapted to cope with the conditions of the place in which they live. A sea gull, for example, is well suited for life along the coast. A sea gull has long, angled wings that help it glide in coastal air currents as it hunts for food. These wings are also well oiled in order to deflect ocean water as the gull picks its prey from the surf. The gull's webbed feet enable it to walk on the sand and paddle on the water's surface.

As exemplified by the sea gull, traits that help an animal to survive tend to be more complex than those shown by plants. Since an animal has a brain and a variety of sense organs, animal traits involve not only body shape, size, and color, but also patterns of behavior. In addition to the sense of touch, most animals can see, hear, taste, and smell. These senses give animals a wide range of experiences unknown to plants. Also, animals have developed means of movement that plants don't have. Animals can swim, fly, crawl, walk, dig, and burrow. Although no one animal can do all of these, many animals can do more than one.

The complex behavior patterns of most animals are concerned mainly with the constant struggle to survive and reproduce. The types of animals alive on Earth today are those that have been successful in this struggle. Although most animals die young, enough of each type survive until their reproductive years to ensure that their type does not become **extinct** (disappear from the Earth).

The behavior exhibited by different animals varies greatly. Many animals are predators, hunters of other animals. Predators such as sharks and lions are powerfully built, can move rapidly, and have teeth designed to rip a prey (hunted animal) apart. The bodies of these animals are ideally suited for the type of aggressive behavior required of successful hunters. Other animals are not hunters; they are simply the hunted. For these animals, survival depends on one or more types of animal defenses.

Animal Defenses

One type of animal defense is simply the ability to move quickly. Animals such as antelopes and gazelles rely on alertness, speed, and endurance to outrun lions or other predators that hunt them.

An animal's coloring can be a defense. One type of protective coloring is called **camouflage**—the animal's colors enable it to blend into its surroundings and not be seen by predators. For example, green-colored snakes and frogs live in green weeds. And to hide from their enemies, rabbits and weasels have earth-colored fur in the summer and white fur in the winter.

For some animals, it's an advantage to be highly visible. An animal's distinctive coloring may be a defense, warning predators of previous bad experiences with that type of animal. The black and white stripes of a skunk—warning of the horrible smell it emits when approached—may be the most familiar example.

Some animals rely on a strong or menacing outer layer for protection. The armadillo, for example, has a covering of tough, bony plates that predators cannot grasp. Clams and snails have shells that they can pull back into and hide. The North American porcupine has sharp fishhook-like quills that cover its body and, if touched, can come out and cause painful wounds. Similarly, the porcupine fish has sharp spines that stick out of its body like thorns.

For many animals, the best defense is simply to fight back. Some animals fight back by biting, kicking, or ramming. The baboon fights with sharp teeth and powerful jaws. Elk and deer fight by kicking with sharp feet and by ramming a predator with their antlers. Other animals resist their attackers with chemical weapons. Ants and bees use stingers to inject poison, while many snakes and spiders inject poison with fangs.

Finally, some animals play dead when attacked. For example, when an opossum is attacked, it closes its eyes and goes limp. Many predators will not bother with an animal that appears dead.

Exercise 7: Animal Defenses

Directions: Answer each question below.

1. Match each word on the left with the phrase that is the best description on the right. Write the letter of the phrase on the line before the correct number.

    _____ **a.** behavior

    _____ **b.** predator

    _____ **c.** prey

    _____ **d.** adaptation

    _____ **e.** camouflage

    (1) the process of becoming suited for an environment

    (2) the actions or reactions of a living thing

    (3) a hunted animal

    (4) a type of protective coloring

    (5) an animal that hunts other animals

2. For what purpose do animals rely on animal defenses?

    _____

Exercise 8: Social Insects

Directions: Questions 1–3 are based on the following information.

Many animals live with their own kind for the purposes of feeding, reproducing, and migrating and for mutual protection. Fish swim together in schools, elephants roam together in herds, wolves hunt together in packs, and ducks migrate together in flocks. The most complex living arrangement, though, occurs with the social insects: ants, bees, wasps, and termites. Social insects form groups in which the needs of the group are more important than the needs of any particular member. Each individual is specially adapted to perform a function for the group, not for itself. In fact, the group's survival often depends on individuals giving up their own lives!

Social insects are characterized by several kinds of group behavior. They live together, forming a colony or hive; they care for their young; they often feed each other as well as their young; and they usually all stem from the same female parent who is the lone queen of the colony or hive.

Each type of member of a social-insect group differs in both shape and function from other types. For example, a honeybee hive consists of a single queen bee, many worker bees (underdeveloped female bees), and many drones (male bees). The sole job of the queen, the largest honeybee, is to lay the eggs. A worker's job is more varied: she must gather nectar, feed and care for the queen and drones, and keep the hive clean and cool. A drone's only task is to fertilize the queen bee when she is aloft in the "marriage flight." After the drone performs this single task, he dies.

If the hive is attacked, the workers fight back and sting the aggressor. Once a worker has stung the aggressor, the worker dies. Unlike other animal associations, social-insect groups place the survival of the group at a much higher level of importance than the survival of any individual in the group, except for perhaps one—the queen.

1. Which of the following is the best summary of key points made in the passage on social insects?

   (1) Social insects work together, each member of a group playing a role to aid in the survival of the group.
   (2) Social insects form loose, but cooperative, group living associations.
   (3) Social-insect groups place low value on the lives of those members designated as workers.
   (4) Social-insect groups are inefficient because many members do little or no work.
   (5) Members of social-insect groups must often sacrifice their own lives.

2. Which of the following would *best* explain the presence of a lot of dead worker bees on the ground in an area around a beehive?

    (1) The hive was hit by a falling branch.
    (2) The worker bees accidentally gathered poison nectar.
    (3) The worker bees had mated with the drones.
    (4) The hive was disturbed by a bear looking for honey.
    (5) The drones killed the worker bees to make more room in the crowded hive for newly developing bees.

3. In what important way does a social-insect group differ from a human social group?

    (1) Social insects join together to better accomplish a group purpose.
    (2) Social insects share the group's labor in an orderly way.
    (3) Some members of a social-insect group give up their lives as a natural result of performing their role for the group.
    (4) Social insects care for and feed the young who are members of the group.
    (5) Each member of a social-insect group specializes in a certain type of work.

ANSWERS AND EXPLANATIONS START ON PAGE 293.

 Writing Activity 2 ———————————————

Even though animals don't talk to one another in a language like English or Spanish, they do communicate! When a dog bares its teeth and snarls at another dog, it is probably warning the other dog not to come any closer. When a cat purrs, it is expressing contentment.

Some instances of animals communicating aren't quite so easy to observe. Whales, for example, communicate through a sophisticated language of cries and calls that echo for miles under water. Researchers suspect that frogs communicate by thumping their throats on the ground and that even rats vocalize in order to communicate.

Have you ever watched animals communicate with each other? Have you ever seen animals communicating with people? In one or two paragraphs, describe what you have observed.

SAMPLE ANSWERS START ON PAGE 293.

Growth of Living Things

Cells: The Building Blocks of Life

Key Words

cell membrane—a membrane that holds a cell together as a single unit
chromosomes—carriers of hereditary information
nucleus—the control center of a cell
protoplasm—the complex chemical compounds that are the substance of life

---

Though the exact date of its invention is unknown, the development of the microscope was a great leap forward in the work of biologists in the seventeenth century. For the first time, they could see beyond the limits of the naked human eye. The British scientist Robert Hooke, after looking at slices of cork with the new instrument, was amazed at the tiny boxlike cavities out of which the cork was made. Because these cavities reminded him of cells (rooms) in a monastery, he gave the name *cells* to these tiny units of cork.

Today biologists know that cells are the basic units from which all living things are made. A cell is the smallest living unit that carries on the activities of the life of an organism. A cell is made up of protoplasm, complex chemical compounds that are the substance of life. Illustrated below are sample plant and animal cells.

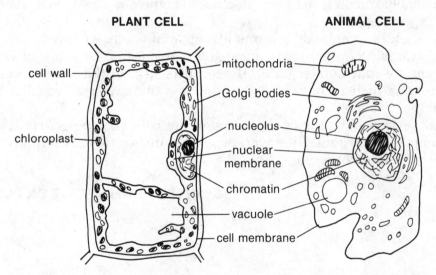

Though cells of plants and animals differ in some ways, they do have several common characteristics.

Each cell has a cell membrane. This membrane separates the cell from other cells and holds it together as a unit. The cell membrane is not solid, but is permeable, allowing needed substances to pass in and out of the cell. Food molecules, needed to provide energy, pass into the cell, while waste products produced within the cell pass out of it.

Each cell contains a single large oval or round body called the nucleus. The nucleus controls the activities of the cell. A smaller round body within the nucleus, called the *nucleolus*, is responsible for the making of protein used in new cell growth. Also within the nucleus are strands of chromatin. When a cell divides, the chromatin forms chromosomes—rod-shaped structures that carry hereditary information.

Each cell contains cytoplasm. Cytoplasm is the name given to all the protoplasm that is outside the nucleus. Mitochondria are the centers of respiration in a cell. These objects release the energy that provides for all of a cell's activities. Golgi bodies are involved in preparing important types of protein substances for movement out of the cell. Vacuoles are fluid-filled cavities that temporarily hold both food materials and waste products.

As the illustration shows, a plant cell has two special structures not found in an animal cell. These are the cell wall and chloroplasts. A cell wall surrounds the cell membrane of most plant cells. This wall both supports and protects the cell. In many plants, the cell wall is tough but flexible. Cell walls are what make vegetables like celery crunchy to bite and chew. In plants such as trees, cell walls are thick and rigid, which enables them to provide the tree with great strength.

Chloroplasts contain chlorophyll, the green pigment that is used to capture sunlight energy. The plant uses this energy from the sun to produce glucose, a food sugar that the plant itself uses as its source of energy. As mentioned on page 99, this process is called *photosynthesis*.

Exercise 9: Cell Structure

Directions: Match each item on the left with the phrase that best describes it on the right. Write the letter of the phrase on the line before the correct number.

_____ **1.** cell wall

_____ **2.** cell nucleus

_____ **3.** mitochondria

_____ **4.** vacuole

_____ **5.** cell membrane

a. the body in a cell that controls the cell's activity

b. the surface layer of a cell through which certain substances can pass

c. a cavity within a cell

d. the outer rigid layer of a plant cell

e. bodies that release energy used for all cell activities

★ **GED PRACTICE** ★

Exercise 10: Cell Functions

Directions: Choose the best answer to each of the questions below.

1. Which of the following bodies is found in plant cells but not in animal cells?

    (1) cytoplasm
    (2) nucleolus
    (3) cell membrane
    (4) Golgi bodies
    (5) cell wall

2. A one-celled animal reproduces by simply dividing itself into two equal parts. Which body in the nucleus of the original cell contains hereditary information that will be passed on to the two newly formed cells?

    (1)   the nucleolus
    (2)   the strands of chromatin
    (3)   the Golgi bodies
    (4)   the vacuole
    (5)   the mitochondria

3. Mushrooms, like other fungi, do not carry on photosynthesis. Instead, they obtain their nutrients by absorbing them from other living or dead organisms. Knowing this, which of the following bodies would you *not* expect to find in a mushroom cell?

    (1)   cytoplasm
    (2)   a cell wall
    (3)   chloroplasts
    (4)   a nucleus
    (5)   strands of chromatin

ANSWERS AND EXPLANATIONS START ON PAGE 293.

The Structure of Organisms

Key Words

one-celled—consisting of only one cell
many-celled—consisting of more than one cell
cell specialization—the presence of different kinds of cells in an organism, where each cell has a specific function
tissue—a group of cells that are alike in structure and function
organ—a group of different kinds of tissues working together

Which do you think is the largest: a bone cell from a giraffe, a bone cell from a frog, or a stem cell from a rosebush? Because the giraffe is so large, most people would say that the bone cell of a giraffe is huge compared to the other two cells. However, that's not correct. Biologists have discovered that the cells of all organisms are about the same size, averaging a few ten-thousandths of an inch across. A giraffe is larger than a frog or rosebush simply because it is made up of many more cells. This fact is a clue that helps us understand how organisms grow.

One-Celled Organisms

In the late seventeenth century, Antonie van Leeuwenhoek—famous mainly for the improvements he made in microscope design—was looking through one of his instruments at a sample of pond water. Surprised as could be, he used the word *beasties* to describe the tiny creatures he watched scurrying about in the drop of water!

The beasties of van Leeuwenhoek are known today simply as one-celled organisms. The most common examples are blue-green bacteria and amoebas. Tiny as each one is, though, every one-celled organism is a complete living thing. And, although they do not grow larger, these one-celled creatures carry on all of the life activities that characterize the more familiar many-celled organisms.

Many-Celled Organisms

Many-celled organisms such as giraffes, frogs, and rosebushes are similar to one-celled organisms in that each of them begins life as a single cell. However, a many-celled organism doesn't stay a single cell. And, as the organism grows, other important differences become apparent.

One difference is that specialized kinds of cells develop. As an example, a frog begins life as a single fertilized egg cell. Then, as more cells form and the frog grows, new types of cells are produced that take on special roles in the frog. These new cells include muscle cells, nerve cells, fat cells, bone cells, and brain cells, to name just a few. Groups of the same type of cell usually develop together and are called tissue. A group of muscle cells in a frog's leg is one example of a tissue. The skin of a tomato is another.

A many-celled organism also shows a high degree of organization not found in a simple one-celled organism. Not only do tissue cells work together, but groups of different types of tissue cells often work together, forming a structure called an organ. A frog's leg is an organ that is made up of muscle tissue, bone tissue, nerve tissue, fat tissue, and skin tissue. Other examples of a frog's organs are its eyes, heart, lungs, and stomach.

Several organs working together are called an *organ system*. The digestive system of a frog is an organ system that provides the frog with a way of getting energy from food sources. The digestive system includes the mouth, stomach, small and large intestines, and other organs. Other systems common to most animals are the respiratory system (used for breathing), the circulatory system (used for moving blood), the nervous system (used for transmitting messages to and from the brain), the reproductive system (used for reproduction), and the excretory system (used for the elimination of waste). Vertebrates (animals with backbones) also have a skeletal system that serves as a support structure.

Exercise 11: The Structure of Organisms ───────

Directions: Circle *T* for each statement below that is true and *F* for each statement that is false.

T F **1.** Cells grow in size in proportion to the size of an organism.

T F **2.** One-celled organisms carry on all of the basic life activities of many-celled organisms.

T F **3.** Groups of organs work together in a structure called a tissue.

T F **4.** Both plants and animals have tissues and organs.

T F **5.** Each kind of cell has its own structure and performs a special function for an organism.

Exercise 12: Cell Specialization

Directions: Choose the best answer for each statement or question below.

1. One similarity of one-celled and many-celled organisms is that

    (1) each is made up of only one cell
    (2) each is made up of more than one cell
    (3) each contains tissue
    (4) each starts life as a single cell
    (5) each develops organ systems

2. Which of the following would a doctor need to know in order to determine the function of a sample of tissue taken from his patient?

    (1) the weight of the tissue sample
    (2) the length and width of the tissue sample
    (3) the number of cells contained in the tissue sample
    (4) the organ the sample was taken from
    (5) the type of cells that make up the tissue

ANSWERS AND EXPLANATIONS START ON PAGE 294.

Writing Activity 3

Just as animals have organs such as eyes, lungs, and hearts, so do humans. Sometimes people become seriously ill when an organ like a kidney or liver fails. Many people carry cards in their wallets that state that, in the event of their accidental death, they would be willing to donate organs to people who would otherwise die or, for example, be blind.

Would you be willing to be an organ donor? Jot down all the reasons you can think of for being an organ donor and all the reasons against it. Then pick *one* side of the issue and write a paragraph stating your opinion.

SAMPLE ANSWERS START ON PAGE 294.

The Mechanism of Heredity

Key Words

chromosomes—rod-shaped structures that carry genes

genes—a hereditary unit contained in a chromosome; each gene controls one hereditary trait

heredity—the passing of certain traits, through genes, from parents to their offspring

species—genetically similar organisms that can mate and produce fertile offspring

trait—a characteristic, or distinguishing feature, of an organism

How do newly produced cells know what they're supposed to do? This question puzzled biologists for a long time. As we'll see, the answer is related to the answer of a second question: why do children tend to look so much like their parents?

Research has now provided answers to both of these questions. Biologists have discovered that an organism grows by a process called *cell division*. During cell division, known as *mitosis*, one cell (called the *parent cell*) divides into two new cells (called *daughter cells*). During mitosis a set of coded instructions is passed on from the parent cell to each of the two daughter cells. Each instruction is actually a complex chemical called a gene. These instructions control the activities of both daughter cells and make sure these cells perform their proper functions.

The genes are carried in chromosomes, rod-shaped structures made of chromatin and found in a cell's nucleus. Hundreds of genes make up each chromosome.

Just before a cell divides, the chromatin forms a second set of identical chromosomes. During cell division, two daughter cells form from the parent cell, and each daughter cell receives one set of the chromosomes. In this way, each new cell has the same set of activity-controlling genes as the parent cell that formed it.

Reproduction and Heredity

Biologists have also discovered that chromosomes play a major role in mating, while genes play an essential part in heredity. Different organisms have different numbers of chromosomes. Organisms that have the same number of chromosomes look alike and are said to be in the same species. In most cases, members of the same species can mate and produce fertile offspring (offspring capable of reproducing). When a male and a female mate, chromosomes from a male sex cell combine with the chromosomes of a female sex cell. Together, they make up the chromosomes of the fertilized egg—the one-celled first stage of the offspring. In this way, every offspring receives an equal number of chromosomes from each parent.

The genes carried in the chromosomes determine the traits of the offspring. Animals, for example, may inherit eye color, hair color, and height. Two inheritable traits in plants are flower color and leaf shape.

When male and female organisms mate, their offspring always receives two genes for each inheritable trait. One gene for each trait comes from each parent. For example, each parent shown below has two eye-color genes, which we've labeled *Br* for brown and *Bl* for blue. The mother has one *Bl* gene and one *Br* gene. The father has two *Bl* genes. A child of this couple will inherit one eye-color gene from each parent. The child may receive any of the four possible combinations of genes as shown.

Eye color, like every other inheritable trait, depends on the presence or absence of a **dominant** gene. For example, a *Br* gene is dominant over a *Bl* gene. Because of this, a person who has either one or two *Br* genes will have brown eyes. A person will have blue eyes only if he or she has two *Bl* genes, like children #3 and #4 in the diagram above. *Bl* genes are said to be **recessive**.

In the example above, the mother has brown eyes and the father has blue eyes. The child's eyes will be brown if he inherits a *Br* gene. Two of the four possible gene combinations result in the child inheriting a *Br* gene and two don't. Therefore, the child is equally likely to be born with brown eyes or blue eyes. This will also be true for any other child this couple may have in the future.

Exercise 13: Chromosomes and Genes ——————

Directions: Complete each sentence by filling in the blanks with the correct word(s).

1. _____ is the passing of traits, through genes, from parents to offspring.

2. Chromosomes are made of the _____ found in a cell's _____.

3. A _____ is an individual instruction that is transmitted from parent to offspring.

4. An offspring receives _____ gene(s) for each inheritable trait.
(number)

5. Each member of a species has the same number of _____.

★ **GED PRACTICE** ★

Exercise 14: The Mechanism of Heredity

Directions: Choose the best answer for each question or statement below.

1. Which of the following statements best summarizes the role played by genes in heredity?

(1) A gene may be either dominant or recessive.
(2) An organism receives identical genes from each of its parents.
(3) The number of an organism's genes determines which two organisms are able to mate.
(4) Genes carry the hereditary messages that determine an organism's traits.
(5) Genes always occur in pairs and determine how many chromosomes an organism has.

2. Which of the following pairs of animals is least likely to be genetically related?

(1) pheasants and turkeys
(2) gorillas and horses
(3) bees and wasps
(4) alligators and crocodiles
(5) robins and sparrows

3. The best experiment to try in order to determine which personality traits are inherited and which are formed by a person's upbringing would be to compare the personalities of

(1) identical twins who were separated at birth and raised in different families
(2) an older sister and younger brother who were raised in the same family
(3) two adopted children who were raised separately in two families that live in the same city
(4) two unrelated children of the same age who were raised in different cultures
(5) two unrelated adults who were raised in different cultures

Questions 4 and 5 refer to the following information.

Each parent organism contains two genes for every inheritable trait. One or both of these genes may be the dominant gene for that particular trait. Remember, though, that during reproduction each parent passes on to its offspring only one gene from each pair of its own genes.

Below we show two parent pea plants, A and B. Plant A (*TT*) has two tall-plant genes, while plant B (*tt*) has two short-plant genes. The first generation offspring are all *Tt*, inheriting one gene from each parent plant. (Notice that all first-generation plants will inherit a *T* from plant A and a *t* from plant B.)

Plants C and D are first-generation offspring that produce second-generation offspring.

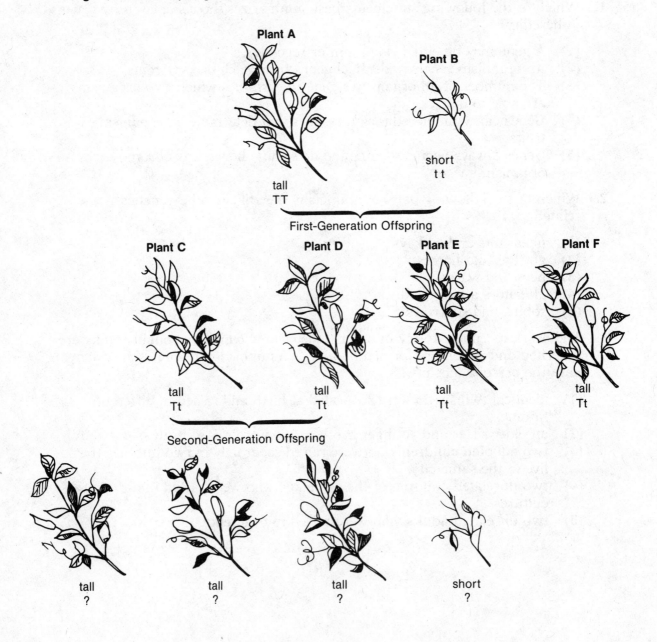

4. From the illustration, you can conclude that

   (1) both plants A and B have a dominant gene for tallness
   (2) neither plant A nor B has a dominant gene for tallness
   (3) each first generation offspring plant has two dominant genes
   (4) the *T* gene is dominant, while the *t* gene is recessive
   (5) the *t* gene is dominant, while the *T* gene is recessive

5. Which of the following correctly labels the gene combinations that are possible in the second generation plants produced by crossing plants C and D?

   (1) *TT, TT, TT, tt*
   (2) *TT, TT, tt, tt*
   (3) *TT, tt, tt, tt*
   (4) *TT, Tt, Tt, tt*
   (5) *Tt, Tt, Tt, Tt*

ANSWERS AND EXPLANATIONS START ON PAGE 294.

Communities of Living Things

Ecosystems

> ### Key Words
>
> *ecosystem*—a community of plants and animals living together with nonliving things
> *food chain*—the order in which organisms depend on other organisms as sources of food
> *habitat*—a place, or home, where organisms live
> *pollution*—the placing in the environment of substances (pollutants) that are dangerous to the health of organisms
> *population*—the number of organisms of the same species living in the same habitat or region
> *resource*—any needed, or useful, thing that is available to organisms in an ecosystem

Many different kinds of animals and plants live in and around a pond. The survival of each of these organisms depends on the others. Many animals eat plants, and plants depend on animals for waste products that provide nutrients. Along the shore, insects eat plants, frogs eat insects, snakes eat frogs, and birds eat snakes. Within the pond, small fish feed on plankton—tiny plant and animal life that floats in great numbers in the water. Bass, other large fish, and perhaps a few ducks eat the smaller fish. Through this interdependence, called a food chain, each organism plays a role in the total life of the pond.

A pond is just one example of a habitat, or home, of a community of living things. Other types of habitats are forests, grasslands, deserts, mountains, rivers, and oceans. A community of organisms, together with its habitat and all the other nonliving things that affect the community, is called an ecosystem. Examples of nonliving resources that are important in an ecosystem are adequate sunshine, clean water, and clean air.

There are many types of relationships among the plants and animals in an ecosystem. One is nutritional and leads to food chains. In every food chain, organisms either produce their own food or obtain food by eating other organisms. Algae and green plants, for example, make food from nutrients they find in water and soil. Mushrooms and other fungi can't make food, so they take nutrients from trees and other plants. Animals don't make their own food either and must obtain it by eating plants and other animals.

A second relationship in a community is based on competition for limited resources. For example, in a pond, both bass and ducks eat small fish. The more successful the ducks are, the less food there will be for the bass. Each of these animals has other sources of food, so this competition is not likely to lead to the death of one of them. However, competition among members of the same species is much more intense. Because each has exactly the same needs and is after the exact same resources, all members of a species often directly compete, with starvation waiting for the poorest competitors. Besides food, animals might also compete for resources such as mating partners and space in which to live.

In a stable ecosystem, the population of each plant or animal stays about constant. The number of each species that die is balanced by the number of their newborn that survive.

Disruptive changes can easily upset the stability of an ecosystem. Destructive acts of nature can occur. A forest fire can destroy all plant and animal life in a forest, along a river, and around the shore of a pond. It can also pollute a pond with ash. A flood or mudslide can wipe out the side of a mountain, flood the banks of a river, and dump tons of sediment into a pond—destroying life along the shore and within the pond as well. Pollution from acts of human beings can also affect an ecosystem. A chemical spill or pesticides sprayed overhead can kill all plant and animal life with which it comes in contact. A housing development along the bank of a river or on the shore of a pond can bring both garbage and noise pollution, in addition to direct physical destruction of these habitats.

Exercise 15: Ecosystems

Directions: Match each item on the left with the best example on the right. Write the letter of the example on the line before the correct number.

_____ 1. resource

_____ 2. population

_____ 3. ecosystem

_____ 4. act of nature

_____ 5. human-caused disaster

a. a volcanic eruption

b. a pond and all the organisms in it

c. clean water

d. a chemical spill into a river

e. the number of frogs living next to Juniper Lake

Exercise 16: Communities of Living Things────

Directions: Choose the best answer for each question or statement below.

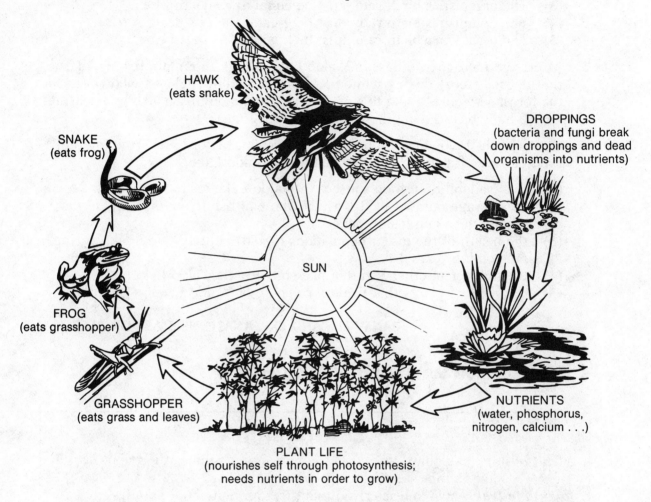

HAWK
(eats snake)

SNAKE
(eats frog)

DROPPINGS
(bacteria and fungi break
down droppings and dead
organisms into nutrients)

SUN

FROG
(eats grasshopper)

GRASSHOPPER
(eats grass and leaves)

NUTRIENTS
(water, phosphorus,
nitrogen, calcium . . .)

PLANT LIFE
(nourishes self through photosynthesis;
needs nutrients in order to grow)

1. Based on the diagram above, what most likely would happen to the animal populations after chemical spraying kills most of the region's mosquitoes and gnats, both of which are sources of food for frogs?

   (1) a decrease in frogs and a decrease in grasshoppers
   (2) a decrease in frogs and an increase in grasshoppers
   (3) an increase in both frogs and snakes
   (4) a decrease in snakes and an increase in hawks
   (5) an increase in both snakes and hawks

2. In order for the population of an organism in a habitat to increase, which of the following must be true?

   (1) The organism's reproduction time must be short compared to the reproduction time of other organisms in the habitat.
   (2) The organism must have no natural predators.
   (3) The organism's birth rate must be equal to its death rate.
   (4) The organism's birth rate must be greater than its death rate.
   (5) The organism's birth rate must be less than its death rate.

3. At present there are no bass in Waldo Lake, a high-mountain fishing lake that doesn't freeze during winter. Richard, a wildlife biologist who works for the forest service, is going to start a bass population in the lake by releasing 10,000 baby bass during the warm month of June.

Which of the following will be the *least* relevant factor in determining the eventual size of a stable bass population in Waldo Lake?

   (1) the availability of food sources in Waldo Lake for bass
   (2) the average number of fishermen who will fish for bass in Waldo Lake during the coming summers
   (3) the health of the insect populations in and around Waldo Lake during the coming years
   (4) the number of other fish that presently live in Waldo Lake
   (5) the types of plants that live on the shore of Waldo Lake

ANSWERS AND EXPLANATIONS START ON PAGE 294.

Charles Darwin's Discoveries

Key Words

evolution—the idea that a species may change over time, both in appearance and in inherited behavior patterns

favorable trait—any characteristic that gives an individual an advantage in the struggle for survival

genetic variation—a difference in appearance or behavior that can be inherited by offspring

natural selection—the idea that individuals with favorable traits are the most likely members of a species to survive and reproduce

---

In 1832, a twenty-four-year-old naturalist named Charles Darwin sailed from England aboard Her Majesty's Ship *Beagle*. During the next three years, Darwin explored the rain forests of South America and hiked throughout the Galapagos Islands located off that continent's western shore. These explorations revealed things to Darwin that forever changed his ideas about the nature of life on Earth.

On the Galapagos Islands, Darwin saw creatures that existed nowhere else in the world. He saw tortoises that seemed to be the same as the small land tortoises of South America. However, the island tortoises were huge, large enough to ride! He saw small birds called *finches* that seemed to be like the finches found on the continent, only they weren't quite the same. The island finches had different beak shapes and eating habits from the South American variety.

Thinking about how similar the island animals were to the continent animals, Darwin concluded that each island species had originally come from the continent, perhaps thousands of years ago or more. At that distant time, each island species must have been exactly like its mainland relatives.

To account for the differences that he saw, Darwin concluded that each species, once on the islands, had become isolated from the mainland. Then, because the island environment had fewer life forms and much harsher conditions than the mainland, the island species slowly changed through many generations. There were changes in both appearance and behavior. The island species that he saw now were visibly different from their South American relatives, but they were much better suited (or fit) for the island environment. Darwin used the word *evolution* to refer to this process of gradual change.

Darwin's Theory of Evolution

Darwin's theory can be summarized as follows:

- **First, there are genetic variations among the members of every species.** Many of these variations, called favorable traits, may actually aid in an individual's struggle for survival. For example, a hawk that has long claws will be able to kill prey more easily than a competing hawk that has short claws.

- **Second, an ecosystem can support only a certain number of organisms of any one species.** Competition for food, water, and a place to live limit the population growth of each species. There are also threats to life such as predators and disease.

- **Third, members of a species that are most likely to survive during a time of changing environmental conditions are those with favorable traits.** For example, during a time of limited prey, the hawks with long claws are much more likely to capture prey than are the hawks with short claws. By surviving, long-claw hawks will likely reproduce and pass on this favorable trait to their offspring. But short-claw hawks are not so lucky. It is likely that many of these hawks will starve to death and not produce offspring. Because of this, the unfavorable trait of short claws will slowly be eliminated in this species of hawk.

The idea that individuals with favorable traits are the most likely members of a species to survive, reproduce, and pass on those traits is known as the principle of natural selection. Natural selection, a key principle in Darwin's theory, ensures that only favorable traits are likely to be passed on to future generations. Darwin realized that natural selection, operating over thousands of years or more, would lead to just the type of world that he saw: one in which organisms were superbly adapted to the environmental conditions around them.

Exercise 17: Darwin's Theory

Directions: Choose the best answer for each question or statement below.

1. Which of the following best summarizes Darwin's theory of evolution?

   (1) Organisms purposely change in order to adapt to changing environmental conditions.
   (2) Organisms change over time, and those that are the most fit have the best chance of surviving and passing on their own characteristics.
   (3) Although many life forms are now extinct, living organisms have not changed since the beginning of life on Earth.
   (4) Genetic traits are passed from one generation of an organism to the next generation.
   (5) All organisms have an equal opportunity to learn to adapt to changing environmental conditions.

2. From the list below, choose the trait that would be most useful for birds on a small island that is hit periodically by severe storms that kill most of the island's land animals.

   (1) longer claws, useful for carrying twigs
   (2) a high-pitched vocal cry, useful for attracting mates
   (3) darker-colored tail feathers, useful for camouflage
   (4) a wider beak, capable of capturing insects and tiny fish swimming in water
   (5) sharper claws, useful for killing small rodents

3. The most important factor in determining what shape of beak would be the most favorable trait for a bird is

   (1) the types of food sources in the bird's habitat
   (2) the bird's average life expectancy
   (3) the type of predator that hunts the bird
   (4) the bird's nesting habits
   (5) the times during the day or night that the bird hunts

4. Which of the following observations best supports Darwin's theory of evolution?

   (1) Offspring of organisms tend to look and behave in ways that are very similar to their parents.
   (2) Dinosaurs were once the dominant life form on Earth, but now they are extinct.
   (3) If polar bears were not a protected species, they would soon become extinct because of hunters.
   (4) Certain genetic diseases such as sickle-cell anemia can be inherited.
   (5) Fossils show that many of today's organisms are similar to, but not identical to, organisms that are now extinct.

Questions 5 and 6 refer to the following passage.

Before Darwin's ideas were published, Jean Lamarck, a French biologist, proposed a different idea of how organisms obtained favorable traits. According to Lamarck, an individual organism could acquire certain favorable traits by its own efforts. Lamarck believed that these traits would then be inherited by all of the organism's future offspring.

Lamarck's most famous example was the giraffe. He claimed that giraffes once had short legs and short necks. But then, as they strained to reach leaves higher up on trees, giraffes stretched their necks and legs, a little bit at a time. In this way the bodies of giraffes changed shape. When each "stretched" giraffe reproduced, its offspring were born with the favorable traits of long necks and long legs!

Since the time of Darwin, biologists have concluded that Lamarck was incorrect. Although organisms can adapt their own bodies to the conditions of their environment, they cannot automatically pass these acquired traits on to offspring.

5. Which of the following is the best example of an inherited trait that Lamarck would have said was acquired by a previous generation?

   (1) the strength of a bullfrog's hindlegs
   (2) the thickness of a sheep's wool
   (3) the uselessness of a penguin's wings for flying
   (4) the amount of hair on a gorilla's body
   (5) the whiteness of a polar bear's fur

6. According to Lamarck's theory, which of the following factors most influenced a change in shape in giraffes?

   (1) a genetic variation that proved to be favorable
   (2) an abundance of vegetation close to the ground
   (3) the great depth of rivers during frequent floods
   (4) a scarcity of vegetation close to the ground
   (5) the need to be larger than its predators

ANSWERS AND EXPLANATIONS START ON PAGE 294.

 Writing Activity 4

Botanists estimate that approximately one-fourth of all species of organisms on Earth face extinction during the next ten to thirty years. The endangered species include unique plants and animals that could possibly provide new forms of energy or even a cure for cancer. These species may die out because their habitat—the rain forests of Latin America, Africa, and Australia—is being destroyed. Major causes of this destruction are rapid population growth, the need for land on which to raise crops, and the world's demand for timber.

Is it important to protect these plants and animals, or would our money and time be better spent on other projects? Pick *one* side of the issue and write a paragraph explaining your viewpoint.

SAMPLE ANSWERS START ON PAGE 295.

6 HUMAN BIOLOGY

Animals, as a rule, stay in the environment for which they're best adapted for survival. You may find lots of penguins living near the South Pole, but you'd be surprised to see even one in the Sahara Desert! Likewise, while you expect to see camels in the Sahara Desert, you wouldn't expect one to live near the South Pole. Penguins and camels, like almost all other animals on Earth, show no desire or ability to venture away from their home environment. Even animals that migrate spend their lives in only two homes for which they're specially adapted.

The one exception to the rule is human beings. Humans by nature—naked and without thick skin or a coat of fur—are adapted only to life on land where the temperature is mild. Compared to most other animals, we don't seem very fit for survival even there! We aren't very strong, we can't run very fast, we can't fly, and we can't fight very well. But here we are! By inventing clothes, forms of shelter, weapons for hunting, and other survival aids, we have done things that no other animal, no matter how well adapted, has ever done. We have made homes on all the continents and islands of the Earth. We have lowered ourselves to the bottom of the ocean, and we have flown to the top of the atmosphere and to the moon. Perhaps most important, we have produced a culture where the least fit have as much opportunity to survive and prosper as do the most fit. These are remarkable achievements.

What makes human beings unique? Most certainly it is the power of the human mind. Although many of our survival needs are the same as those of other animals, our means of meeting those needs are much more complex. We can anticipate and plan for the future, we learn from experience (both our own and the experiences of others), and we have free choice. Other animals have none of these abilities. While an ant can build only an anthill, we can build a skyscraper, a school, a church, or a sports stadium. While other animals spend their time in a constant search for food, we can pursue goals that help lead to fulfilling work and recreational lives. Although it's fun to think about our special talents, the study of human biology is also about the similarities that are found in all life forms. We know we differ from other animals, but in what ways are we the same?

One important discovery is that human beings may be biologically related to many different species. Similarities in body structure suggest that humans and other animals have similar genetic codes for the formation of many different organs. The arm bones of a human, for example, are very similar to the leg bones of a dog as well as to the forelimb bones of a bird.

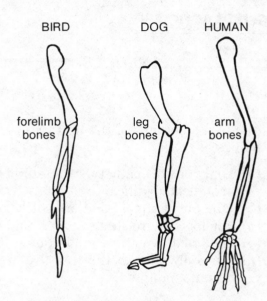

Similar bone structure indicates that many different species of animals may be biologically related.

Biologists have also discovered that the chemical makeup of a human is much like that of other animals. For example, the proteins in the human body differ in structure by less than 1 percent from the proteins in the body of a chimpanzee. Because of these structural and chemical similarities, biologists now think that human beings may share many more characteristics of other life forms. They hope to use this information to help understand the biological origin of human life as well as the origin of other forms of life.

Biologists classify all animals according to body structure and function. Different species that look very much alike tend to be placed in the same classification group. For example, cattle and sheep are classified in a group that does not include chickens or salmon. Human beings are classified in a large group called **mammals** and are given the biological name *Homo sapiens*. We are also placed in a small subgroup called primates. **Primates** are mammals that can walk erect on two legs. This subgroup includes human beings, apes, and monkeys.

We'll begin our study of human biology by discussing the most unusual organ of the human body, the brain.

Exercise 1: Overview of Human Biology

Directions: Answer each of the questions below.

1. Complete each sentence by filling in the blanks with the correct word(s).

   a. Biologists classify animals according to their _____.

   b. _____ is the biological name given to the animal species better known as human beings.

2. Name two types of evidence that suggest that human beings are biologically related to other animals.

a. _____

b. _____

★ **GED PRACTICE** ★

Exercise 2: Evolution ━━━━━━━━━━

Directions: Choose the best answer to each question below.

1. The best summary of the first two paragraphs of the overview is that human beings are

    (1) only one of many types of animals that are able to change their environment significantly
    (2) the only animals that are solely adapted to life on land
    (3) biologically related to other animals
    (4) adapted by nature to life on all the land masses of the Earth
    (5) the only animals that can live in environments for which their bodies are not adapted

2. According to the reading selection, human beings are classified in a group called *primates.* Which of the following animals is also a primate?

    (1) goat
    (2) gorilla
    (3) dolphin
    (4) sparrow
    (5) horse

Questions 3 and 4 are based on the following passage.

    The publication in the last half of the nineteenth century of Charles Darwin's ideas on evolution and natural selection started a bitter controversy among biologists, religious leaders, and the general public. This controversy centered around Darwin's conclusions that both plant and animal species change over time and that new species may develop in the process. A particular point of contention was Darwin's suggestion that human beings, like other animals, evolve as a result of natural selection.

    The idea of human evolution remains today as one of the most discussed and debated ideas in biology. Many people now believe that human beings did, in fact, evolve from a simpler life form, most probably an apelike primate that lived millions of years ago. According to this idea, the evolution of these prehuman primates resulted in the formation of several new species. One of these species is *Homo sapiens*, or human beings. If this conclusion is correct, human beings are related to other modern primates much more closely than scientists before Darwin's time could ever have imagined.

3. Charles Darwin noticed certain similarities between the physical features of chimpanzees and those of orangutans. Based on his beliefs, which of the following conclusions could he most likely have drawn?

   (1) Chimpanzees are not biologically related to orangutans in any way.
   (2) Either the chimpanzee or the orangutan, but not both, evolved from an apelike primate that lived millions of years ago.
   (3) Chimpanzees evolved from orangutans that lived millions of years ago.
   (4) Chimpanzees and orangutans both evolved from the same apelike primate that lived millions of years ago.
   (5) Neither chimpanzees nor orangutans evolved at all during the last few million years.

4. Which of the following discoveries would be the best evidence that human beings and modern apes may have evolved from a common ancestor?

   (1) With proper training, an ape can learn to communicate in simple sign language with human beings.
   (2) Apes can be raised from babies to adulthood by human beings.
   (3) Ancient skulls have been discovered that show both humanlike and apelike features.
   (4) Apes can walk upright on their two back legs in a way that's similar to how human beings walk.
   (5) Apes in the wild form family groups similar to the family groups formed by human beings.

ANSWERS AND EXPLANATIONS START ON PAGE 295.

 Writing Activity 1

In order to test new products or develop cures for diseases, scientists often experiment on such animals as rats, monkeys, dogs, and cats. For example, in order to find out if a new eye cosmetic is safe for humans, researchers might place the product in a monkey's eye even though the animal might be injured or blinded.

Do you believe that such experiments are fair and necessary? Make a list of reasons that support your point of view. When you are finished, reread the list carefully and cross out any reasons or examples that do *not* support your point of view.

SAMPLE ANSWERS START ON PAGE 295.

The Human Brain

Key Words

brain hemisphere—one of the two halves of the human brain
emotion—a strong feeling such as joy or sadness
intelligence—the ability to acquire and apply knowledge
intuition—problem-solving insight that is based on inner feelings
logic—careful reasoning used to solve problems
neuron—a nerve cell

The human brain is often described as the most marvelous, yet mysterious, organ in the human body. You use yours in everything that you do. Because of your brain, you have special qualities that make you unique among all other living organisms. From it comes the personality that is the "you" whom other people know!

As you read this page, your brain receives electrical signals from your eyes. Somehow—nobody knows how—you change these signals into the thoughts of your conscious mind. You then remember some of these thoughts and simply forget others. Yet, as familiar as these processes are to you, scientists do not yet know what the conscious mind is or how it is actually related to the brain. This mystery—often called the *mind-brain problem*—will undoubtedly remain one of the most challenging and exciting areas of brain research well into the twenty-first century. In this section we'll mention a few of the most important discoveries about the mind and brain.

Seen from above, the human brain looks much like a large gray walnut. Its typical weight is about three pounds. Although we usually think of the brain as a single unit, it is actually divided into two halves. Each half, called a hemisphere, is joined to the other half by bundles of nerve fibers. Biologists believe that these nerve fibers enable the two halves of the brain to communicate with each other.

If brain tissue is examined under a microscope, it is seen to consist of nerve cells called neurons. Although the exact number is unknown, each human brain is believed to contain more than ten billion neurons! These neurons form an interconnected network of cells through which electrical and chemical messages pass. Because these messages occur at all hours of day and night, scientists believe that they must be directly related to mental activities that take place both while we're awake and while we're asleep and dreaming.

TOP VIEW OF HUMAN BRAIN

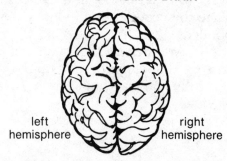

left hemisphere   right hemisphere

The two halves of the human brain are connected in the center by bundles of nerve fibers.

Because it has so many neurons, the human brain has the capacity to store more information than is in all the libraries in the world. However, we don't use our brain power just to memorize information. We can use books and computers to do that! Instead, we use our brain power to carry out the more complex activities of intelligent living beings. The brain thinks, feels, stores memories, and interprets. It also responds to sight, sound, touch, and other body sensations and controls body movement and body growth.

Localization of Brain Functions

Each of our body sensations and movements is controlled by one of the brain hemispheres. The left hemisphere controls the right side of the body, and the right hemisphere controls the left side of the body. If one hemisphere is damaged, the opposite side of the body may be partly or completely paralyzed. This often occurs with accident and stroke victims.

Besides controlling sensations and movements, the brain provides us with intelligence and emotions. Intelligence is the ability to acquire and apply knowledge; emotions are our inner feelings. Each hemisphere appears to play a special role in the many ways in which knowledge and feelings are acquired and remembered. The left hemisphere appears to be more important for reasoning skills such as mathematics and science and language skills. The right hemisphere is more important for spatial-relations skills, artistic skills, and imagination. This division of skills has led many researchers to comment that the two halves of the brain are much like the two ways we deal with problem solving: the left half gives us logic, while the right half gives us intuition.

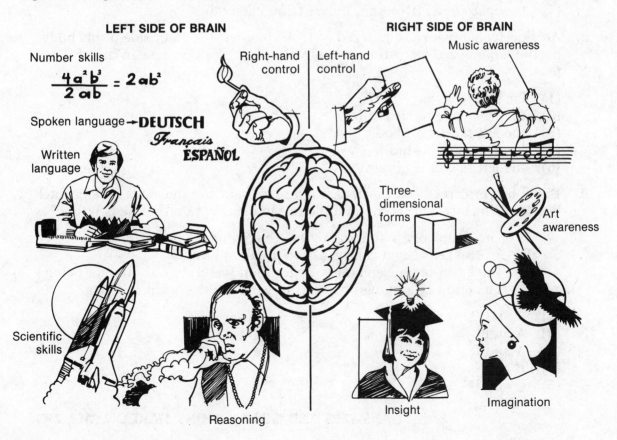

LEFT SIDE OF BRAIN

RIGHT SIDE OF BRAIN

Number skills

$$\frac{4a^2b^3}{2ab} = 2ab^2$$

Spoken language → DEUTSCH Français ESPAÑOL

Written language

Right-hand control

Left-hand control

Music awareness

Scientific skills

Three-dimensional forms

Art awareness

Reasoning

Insight

Imagination

Exercise 3: The Human Brain━━━━━━━

Directions: Complete each sentence below by filling in the blanks with the correct word(s).

1. The human brain is divided into _____ hemispheres.
    (number)

2. The _____ hemisphere of the brain controls the right side of the body, while the _____ hemisphere controls the left side of the body.

3. The cells that make up the human brain are called _____.

★ **GED PRACTICE** ★

Exercise 4: Brain Functions━━━━━━━

Directions: Choose the best answer for each question or statement below.

1. For what purpose do bundles of nerve fibers join the two brain hemispheres?

    (1) to enable dreaming to occur while we sleep
    (2) to hold the two brain halves close together
    (3) to enable the two brain halves to exchange information
    (4) to enable blood to flow from one side to the other
    (5) to separate the two brain halves from each other

2. An elderly man who has suffered a stroke that left the right side of his body partially paralyzed has most probably experienced a decrease in blood flow to

    (1) his heart
    (2) the right side of his brain
    (3) the left side of his body
    (4) both sides of his brain
    (5) the left side of his brain

3. David has incorrectly assumed that a larger brain size indicates greater intelligence. Which two ideas can Maddie use to demonstrate that he is wrong?

    A. The brains of all human adults are about the same size.
    B. A teenager's brain is larger than a baby's brain.
    C. The brain of an elephant is larger than the brain of a human being.
    D. The brain of a human being is larger than the brain of a dog.

    (1) A and B
    (2) A and C
    (3) A and D
    (4) B and C
    (5) C and D

ANSWERS AND EXPLANATIONS START ON PAGE 295.

Writing Activity 2

Some researchers say that people are either right-brained or left-brained. A right-brained person is more artistic, imaginative, and intuitive—the right half of the brain dominates the personality. In contrast, a left-brained person is more logical and is good at dealing with numbers and language.

Do you believe this theory? Have you observed that you or your friends are particularly right-brained or left-brained? Write a paragraph stating your opinion. Be sure to give examples to support your point of view. It may be helpful to describe the personalities of people you know.

ANSWERS WILL VARY.

Taking Care of Your Body

A Long and Healthy Life

> ### Key Words
>
> *aging*—changes that take place in an organism as it grows older
> *life expectancy*—the average life span of an animal or plant
> *stress*—inner tension caused by emotionally upsetting feelings

Have you ever wished for a magic pill or magic formula that would let you live happily forever? If you have, don't feel alone! It's a very common, natural wish that has a long history. Spanish explorers of the sixteenth century even tried to find a fountain of youth in what is now the state of Florida. The water of this legendary fountain, which no one has yet found, was believed to restore youth and good health to those who drank it.

Biologists today don't expect that anyone will find a magical fountain of youth. Growing older is a natural part of the life cycle that can't be reversed. As human beings grow older, organs such as the heart and lungs may stop functioning properly. Sight and hearing may become impaired. And the human body becomes more likely to come down with serious illnesses from which it cannot recover.

Considered together, changes that bring about the decline of an organism are called aging. Because of aging, many biologists believe that there may be a maximum age limit to which even the healthiest organisms can live. For human beings, this maximum age limit is about 110 years. Body cells seem to have an internal clock that determines the maximum life span of each species.

Perhaps the most important thing you can learn from your study of human biology is that you have a lot of control over how the aging process occurs in your own life. Having a long and healthy life and living beyond average life expectancy are not necessarily matters of luck. They can be planned for. In fact, within our control are many physical and mental factors that have much to do with aging. For example, although half the deaths each year in the United States are caused by heart and blood vessel disease, these diseases are almost unknown in many countries of the world. Why is this so? The answer is related to our lifestyle!

Recent research indicates that each of us can do many things to help prevent heart and blood vessel disease. For example, we can avoid eating a lot of fatty meat (mainly fatty beef and pork). Eating too much of these types of animal fats can lead to the clogging and hardening of blood vessels. We can cut back on smoking and hopefully quit entirely. We can limit the amount of alcohol we drink and the amount of sugar we eat. We can exercise regularly and strengthen the heart and other organs. And we can remember to take time out each day for ourselves, time just to relax. Exercise, recreation, and relaxation all reduce stress—inner tension that is hard on all body organs.

There is also a lot we can do to decrease our risk of getting cancer, the second leading cause of death. By not smoking, we also greatly reduce the chances of getting lung cancer. Recent evidence suggests that by eating a diet high in fiber we can reduce the chances of getting cancer of the digestive system. Good sources of fiber are fresh fruits and vegetables and foods made from whole grains.

Evidence also suggests that by keeping our weight down we can reduce our chances of getting many diseases, including heart disease and diabetes. Although eating is enjoyable to the mind, overeating is slow torture to the body.

One final thing we can do is to try to keep aware of advances made in health education. Information is often available free of charge from county health clinics or schools.

Exercise 5: A Long and Healthy Life———————

Directions: Circle *T* for each statement below that is true and *F* for each statement that is false.

T F **1.** Many biologists believe that each species has a natural maximum life span.

T F **2.** There is much you can do to help prevent many diseases.

T F **3.** Mental attitude is not a factor that is related to good health.

T F **4.** Doctors believe that smoking increases a person's chances of getting both lung cancer and heart disease.

Exercise 6: Aging and Life Span

Directions: Choose the best answer to each question below.

1. The leading cause of death of people in the United States is

    (1) heart disease
    (2) cancer
    (3) accidents
    (4) childhood diseases
    (5) alcoholism

2. People in the United States have a higher incidence of heart disease than people in many poorer countries. This problem is *most likely* related to the fact that people in the United States

    (1) pay more for medical insurance
    (2) use more labor-saving devices and thus get less exercise
    (3) have a higher life expectancy
    (4) have more unavoidable sources of stress
    (5) eat more whole grains

Questions 3 and 4 are based on the following information.

In 1900, U.S. citizens could expect to live an average of forty-seven years. Today, the average life expectancy in the United States has risen significantly—to about seventy-five years. There are several reasons for this increase. First, fewer children are dying. Laws now prohibit child labor, which caused many deaths and injuries at the turn of the century. Better nutrition and new vaccinations against disease help ensure children's health. Second, adult Americans are healthier. Workplace safety laws and advances in medicine and technology have protected more and more adults. And finally, increased education throughout the twentieth century has brought about a new public awareness of health and safety.

3. Which of the following is *not* one of the reasons given for the increase in average life expectancy in the United States during the twentieth century?

    (1) increased average income
    (2) better nutrition
    (3) improved working conditions
    (4) development of vaccines
    (5) increased education

4. Which of the following items of information would be *least* important to a researcher studying ways to increase life expectancy in the United States?

   (1) the quantities and types of food eaten by people in the United States
   (2) the smoking and drinking habits of people in the United States
   (3) the leading causes of death of people in the United States
   (4) the amount of money the average American household spends on food each year
   (5) the percent of people receiving adequate medical care

Questions 5 and 6 refer to the following passage.

In order to observe the relation between aging and the amount of food an organism consumes, a researcher did the following experiment. He placed four mice in each of two cages and fed each group of mice the same type of food. He kept the food trays in cage 1 full at all times. The mice in cage 1 could eat any time and any amount they wanted. He placed only small portions of food in cage 2. The mice in cage 2 were purposely underfed. The results of his experiment were as follows:

- The mice in cage 1 seemed to lack energy and were sick a lot. They all died before reaching the average life expectancy of a mouse.

- The mice in cage 2 were energetic and healthy. They all lived long beyond the average life expectancy of a mouse.

5. The most reasonable conclusion that you can draw from the results reported in the passage above is that

   (1) the death of the mice in cage 1 was related to the type of food they ate
   (2) the mice in cage 2 would probably have lived beyond their life expectancy even if they hadn't been underfed
   (3) underfeeding slows the aging process in mice
   (4) overfeeding slows the aging process in mice
   (5) neither overfeeding nor underfeeding affects the aging process in mice

6. Which of the following would be the *least* important item of information that the researcher would want to have before drawing a conclusion about his experimental results?

   (1) the exact causes of death of the mice in cage 1
   (2) the time of day that the mice in cage 2 were fed
   (3) the average daily amount of food consumed by each group of mice
   (4) the daily amount consumed by a normal mouse
   (5) the life expectancy of a mouse fed an average amount

ANSWERS AND EXPLANATIONS START ON PAGE 296.

Writing Activity 3

Even though aging is a natural part of the life cycle, many people worry about growing older. Some fear that they will face discrimination in a society that values youth. Other people worry that they'll be lonely or become sick.

How do you feel about growing older? Make a list of concerns that you have about aging and then think of some of the benefits of being a senior citizen.

SAMPLE ANSWERS BEGIN ON PAGE 296.

Nutrition

Key Words

food—a substance that helps an organism grow and provides it with energy
calories—a measure of the energy provided by food
nutrients—food substances that the body needs for growth and repair
nutrition—the study of the health value of food

How does a piece of chocolate cake and a milk shake sound to you for lunch? If you're hungry, it may sound pretty good—unless, of course, you're on a diet! Then you may not want the weight gain this food will give you.

While a piece of cake and a milk shake provide lots of calories, they do not provide the nutrients your body needs. Calories are a measure of food energy. We all need calories for daily activities and during sleep, but many people eat more calories than they need. These excess calories are stored as unwanted body fat. Nutrients, on the other hand, are food substances that the body can use for tissue growth and repair, as well as for energy. Without nutrients, the human body ceases to function properly, and sickness and death can result. A well-balanced diet is made up of foods that provide an adequate, but not excessive, number of calories while supplying all the nutrients needed for good health.

Nutrition is the study of the health value of food. Nutritionists have discovered that the most important nutrients found in food are carbohydrates, fats, protein, and vitamins and minerals. Many types of food are major sources of one type of nutrient but also contain smaller amounts of the other nutrients.

- Carbohydrates are our main sources of food energy. Bread, rice, potatoes, fruits, and grain cereals are some healthful sources of carbohydrates. These sources also contain important vitamins, minerals, and protein. Less healthful sources include sugar and sugar-sweetened desserts such as cakes, cookies, doughnuts, and ice cream. Healthful sources are low in calories, while less healthful sources are high in calories and contribute to unwanted weight gain. What's more, evidence now indicates that sugar and sugary products contribute to heart disease and diabetes as well as to tooth decay.

- Fats are another energy source. Some fats should be eaten only occasionally and in limited amounts. These fats are found in beef, pork, chicken, and many dairy products. As indicated on page 130, these fats are known to contribute to heart and blood vessel disease. For cooking, oil from vegetable sources should be used instead of oil made from animal fat. One exception is fish oil. Recent research has shown that fish oil, though an animal source, does not seem to carry the risk for heart disease as the other animal fats do.

- Protein is vital to body growth and to the repair of body tissues. The most healthful sources of animal protein are lean beef, chicken, fish, and dairy products. Good sources of protein from vegetables include grain products, potatoes, and beans.

- Vitamins and minerals are chemicals that are used by the body in small amounts. Though they contain no calories, vitamins and minerals are important for proper body growth, for body activity, and for the prevention of certain diseases. The most common sources of vitamins and minerals are fruits and vegetables. Many people also supplement their diets with vitamin and mineral pills.

- Water, which makes up more than two-thirds of your body weight, is also an important part of your diet. Water is used in the digestion of food, in the production of blood, and in the elimination of body waste. Water also helps regulate body temperature.

As a general rule, in a well-balanced diet, 55 to 60 percent of the calories come from carbohydrates, no more than 30 percent come from fats, and 10 to 15 percent come from proteins. The exact number of calories your body requires on a daily basis depends on your age, your body size, and your activity level. If you increase your activity level, you need more calories and nutrients. Information about diet and nutrition is available in bookstores, schools, and county health clinics.

Exercise 7: Nutrition

Directions: Match each word on the left with the best descriptive phrase on the right. Write the letter of the phrase on the line before the correct number.

_____ 1. calorie

_____ 2. water

_____ 3. carbohydrate

_____ 4. protein

_____ 5. vitamins

a. needed for cell growth and repair

b. a measure of food energy

c. needed by the body in small amounts

d. an energy-providing nutrient

e. helps regulate body temperature

Exercise 8: Diet and Exercise

Directions: Choose the best answer to each question below.

1. What does the human body do with the excess food calories present in such foods as chocolate cake and milk shakes?

    (1) It stores them as muscle tissue.
    (2) It stores them as nerve tissue.
    (3) It passes them through the digestive system.
    (4) It digests them only when the body needs it.
    (5) It stores them as fat tissue.

2. Of the following, the person who probably needs the least number of calories during an average day is

    (1) a pregnant housewife
    (2) a professional football player
    (3) an accountant
    (4) a construction worker
    (5) a waitress

3. Which of the following describes the relationship between food intake and exercise?

    (1) The more a person exercises, the less need he has for nutrients.
    (2) The more a person exercises, the fewer calories he can eat each day without gaining weight.
    (3) The amount of exercise a person gets each day has nothing to do with weight gain or weight loss.
    (4) The more a person exercises, the more calories he can eat each day without gaining weight.
    (5) The less a person exercises, the more need he has for nutrients.

4. To advise a patient about how to lose weight slowly in a healthful way, a doctor would need to know all of the following *except*

    (1) the person's present weight
    (2) the present state of the person's health
    (3) the average weight of other patients who are the same age and sex
    (4) the amount of exercise the person presently gets
    (5) the amount and types of food the person presently eats

Questions 5 and 6 are based on the following information.

Nutritionists categorize food in four food groups. The food groups, recommended servings, and nutrients provided by each group are shown in the chart on page 136.

The Basic Food Groups

	Meat	Dairy	Fruits and Vegetables	Grain Products Cereal, Bread

How many servings per day?	2
	3 for
	  teenagers
		2–3 for
		  children
		  under 9
		3–4 for
		  children 9
		  through teens
		3 for
		  pregnant
		  women
		4 for nursing
		  mothers
		2 for adults
			4 (include 1 dark green or deep yellow vegetable for vitamin A and 1 citrus fruit or juice for vitamin C)	3 to 4 servings per day (at least one cereal)

What do you get from this group?	Protein Fats Minerals B vitamins	Calcium Phosphorus Protein Vitamin A Riboflavin	Vitamins A and C Minerals Fiber	Starch Fiber Protein Vitamins Minerals

5. According to the chart above, the most important sources of fiber are the

   (1) meat and fruits-and-vegetables groups
   (2) fruits-and-vegetables and grain products groups
   (3) dairy and fruits-and-vegetables groups
   (4) dairy and grain products groups
   (5) meat and grain products groups

6. According to the chart, which of the following people should drink the most milk on a daily basis?

   (1) a child, age seven
   (2) a young adult, age twenty-one
   (3) a pregnant woman, age twenty-three
   (4) a nursing mother, age twenty-one
   (5) a retired man, age seventy-six

ANSWERS AND EXPLANATIONS START ON PAGE 296.

Systems of the Human Body

Body Structure and Movement

Key Words

skeleton—a body's internal structure of bones and cartilage

bone—dense tissue that gives the body form, support, and protection

muscle—body tissue that can shorten and cause movement of body parts or fluid

nerve—body tissue that is used to carry electrical messages back and forth between the brain and spinal cord and all other parts of the body

THE HUMAN SKELETON

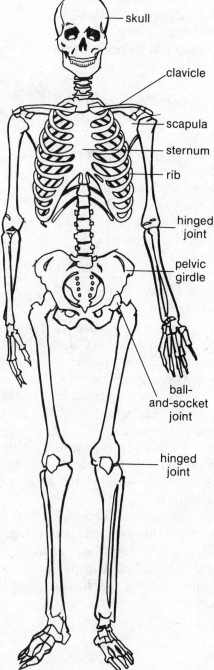

skull

clavicle

scapula

sternum

rib

hinged joint

pelvic girdle

ball-and-socket joint

hinged joint

Like the frame of a house, your skeleton gives form to your body. It also provides protection for internal organs. A typical human skeleton, shown at right, is made up of about 200 bones and numerous joints.

The shape of the skeleton allows for great freedom of movement while at the same time providing strength and protection. The skull surrounds and protects the brain, while the bones of the upper spine (backbone) support the skull and allow you to turn your head without turning your body. The ribs form an enclosed upper-body cavity that protects the most important internal organs. The numerous bones in the hands allow for many types of highly skilled thumb and finger movements, from tying shoes, to assembling machines, to playing musical instruments. The numerous bones of the feet help provide for balance and ease of movement while a person is in a standing posture.

Joints are formed where two bones come together. To prevent the bones from grinding against each other, the surfaces of contact are covered with cartilage, a tough but flexible tissue. Cartilage is also the tissue that makes up the tough part of both your nose and ears.

There are three main types of joints. Ball-and-socket joints, such as those found in the shoulders and hips, allow for wide circular motion. Hinged joints, such as those in the elbows and knees, allow for back-and-forth motion. Finally, joints such as those found in wrists and ankles allow limited motion in many directions.

Movement in the human body is made possible by muscles. A muscle is a special type of tissue that has the ability to contract (to shorten or pull together). Muscles are connected to bone by tendons—strong, fibrous connective tissue. Because a muscle can only contract, every joint is controlled by opposing muscles. This enables back-and-forth movement to occur. As shown at right, you contract your biceps muscle to bend your arm, but you contract your triceps muscle to straighten it.

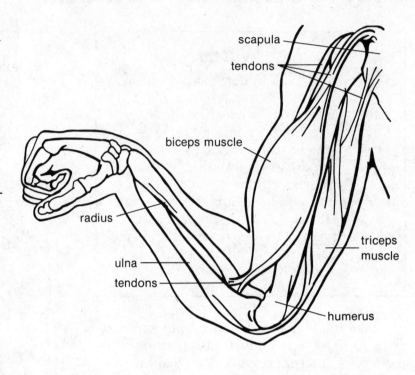

Muscles are usually spoken of as being either voluntary or involuntary. Voluntary muscles are those that you can consciously control. Muscles that you use to control bone movement are all voluntary muscles. When you raise your hand, you consciously use the voluntary muscles of the arm and shoulder.

Involuntary muscles are those over which you normally have no conscious control. The muscles of the lungs, stomach, intestines, heart, and blood vessels are examples.

Both voluntary and involuntary muscles produce heat as they contract and relax. This is the reason you feel so warm when you exercise. It's also the reason that people often jump up and down to keep warm while waiting in line on a cold day!

To control the working of all its muscles, and to sense stimuli both inside and outside of itself, the human body contains a network of nerves that thread throughout the body. These nerves are like tiny wires that carry electrical signals called nerve impulses. Each nerve connects with the spinal cord, a large central nerve within the spine that serves as the communication link with the brain.

When you decide to move your arm, your brain sends a nerve impulse down the spinal cord and out the correct nerve. The impulse reaches the muscles involved and causes them to contract and raise your arm.

If you cut your finger, a nerve impulse is sent from the point of the cut to the brain by way of the spinal cord. It is only when this impulse reaches your brain that you feel pain. Pain and all other sensations actually occur within your brain, although the stimulus that produces each sensation may occur anywhere on your body. As you can imagine, nerve impulses are very complex and race back and forth in a fraction of a second between your brain and points on your body.

THE HUMAN NERVOUS SYSTEM

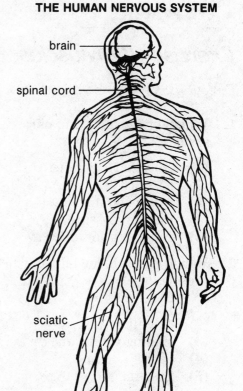

brain

spinal cord

sciatic nerve

Exercise 9: Body Structure and Movement

Directions: Circle *T* for each statement below that is true and *F* for each statement that is false.

T F **1.** Nerve impulses travel both to and from the brain.

T F **2.** Only involuntary muscles are controlled by the nervous system.

T F **3.** A joint is a break in a bone.

T F **4.** Voluntary muscles can be controlled by conscious decision making.

T F **5.** The bones that give protection to the internal organs within the chest are called femur bones.

Exercise 10: Muscles and the Nervous System ————

Directions: Choose the best answer to each question.

1. Which of the following phrases best sums up the function of the nervous system?

   (1) communication network
   (2) support structure
   (3) waste elimination
   (4) food processing
   (5) transport and delivery

2. Which of the following activities is the best example of a use of involuntary muscles?

   (1) jumping rope
   (2) driving a car
   (3) signing your name
   (4) lifting weights
   (5) breathing

3. Damage to the spinal cord can interfere with any nerve impulses that must flow past the injured point on their way to and from the brain. A person who falls and seriously injures his or her lower back might experience temporary loss of feeling

   (1) in the arms
   (2) on the right side of the body
   (3) on the left side of the body
   (4) in the legs
   (5) in the shoulders

4. A young girl quickly pulls her hand away after accidentally touching a hot burner on the stove. During this incident, four things quickly happen, although not necessarily in the following order:

   A. pain felt
   B. muscles contract to pull hand back
   C. nerve impulse sent from hand to brain
   D. nerve impulse sent from brain to hand

The order in which these four things actually happen is:

(1) A, C, B, D
(2) C, A, D, B
(3) B, A, C, D
(4) A, D, C, B
(5) C, D, A, B

5. Together with information given in the reading selection, which of the following facts best supports the hypothesis that the purpose of shivering is to generate heat when the body is cold?

(1) Shivering is an involuntary action.
(2) Shivering occurs mainly in the upper part of the body.
(3) Shivering is movement caused by muscles that rapidly contract and relax.
(4) Shivering interferes with normal speech.
(5) The amount that a person shivers may depend on how long it's been since he or she has last eaten.

ANSWERS AND EXPLANATIONS START ON PAGE 296.

Eating and Breathing

Key Words

digestion—the process by which the body breaks down food into nutrients that cells can use
respiration—the chemical mixing of oxygen gas and food sugar, resulting in the release of energy and carbon dioxide gas

Among life's great pleasures, eating rates pretty high for most people. However, when we talk about eating, we usually think only about tasting, chewing, and swallowing. That's the fun part, but it's only the first step of the process called digestion, the breaking down of food into nutrients that the body's cells can use. As shown on page 142, the human digestive system consists of many more parts than just the mouth.

THE HUMAN DIGESTIVE SYSTEM

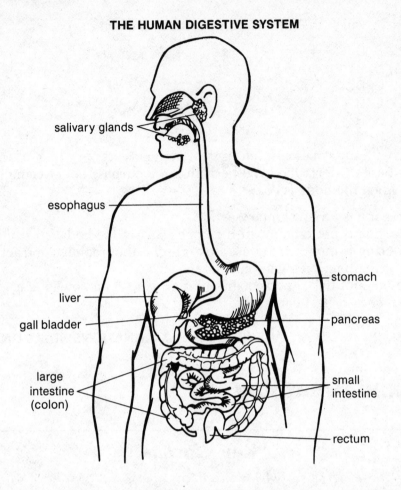

salivary glands

esophagus

liver

gall bladder

large
intestine
(colon)

stomach

pancreas

small
intestine

rectum

After food is chewed and swallowed, it passes down the esophagus and into the stomach, the body's main organ of digestion. In the stomach, the food is churned in digestive juices much like a washing machine churns clothes in soapy water. After being in the stomach for two to five hours, the partially digested food passes into the small intestine.

With the help of digestive juices from the liver and pancreas, the small intestine completes the digestion process. From here the digested nutrients and water pass through the walls of the intestine and into the bloodstream, where they will travel to the body's cells. Waste products continue through the small intestine and move into the large intestine, where they are prepared for passage out of the body.

Closely related to the body's need for food is its need for oxygen. Oxygen is only one of many gases found in air, but it is the gas that cells use for respiration—the process in which food sugar is broken down and energy and carbon dioxide gas are released. This energy powers all of the cell's activities, while the carbon dioxide gas is a waste product.

THE HUMAN RESPIRATORY SYSTEM

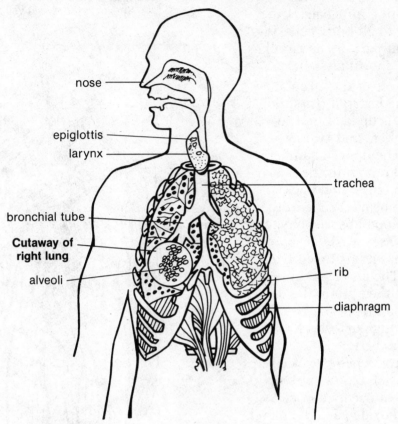

nose

epiglottis

larynx

trachea

bronchial tube

Cutaway of right lung

alveoli

rib

diaphragm

   In order to get oxygen into our blood, we breathe air. As shown above, in-haled air passes through the nose and mouth, down the trachea (windpipe), and into the lungs. The epiglottis, a muscle that works like a trapdoor, allows the air to enter the trachea, but closes the opening to the trachea when food or water is swallowed. Bronchial tubes branch off the trachea and carry the air into each of two lungs. In the lungs, the bronchial tubes branch into even smaller tubes that end in millions of little air sacs. It is in these tiny air sacs that blood vessels ab-sorb the oxygen from the air. At the same time, the blood releases the waste car-bon dioxide gas it has brought from the body cells.

Blood, which serves the body by transporting nutrients, water, and oxygen to all body cells, is an important part of the circulatory system shown at right.

The center of the circulatory system is the heart, a fist-sized muscle that is divided into two upper chambers and two lower chambers. The upper chambers pump blood out from the heart, through the lungs, and back again to the heart. While in the lungs, the blood absorbs oxygen gas and releases waste carbon dioxide gas that it has taken from body cells. The lower chambers of the heart then pump the oxygen-rich blood from the heart and out through arteries to the rest of the body.

When it reaches body cells, the oxygen-rich blood gives up its oxygen and nutrients and picks up carbon dioxide gas. The blood, now rich in carbon dioxide, leaves the cells and returns through veins to the upper chambers of the heart. From there the carbon dioxide-rich blood begins the flow cycle once again.

HUMAN CIRCULATORY SYSTEM
(major arteries and veins)

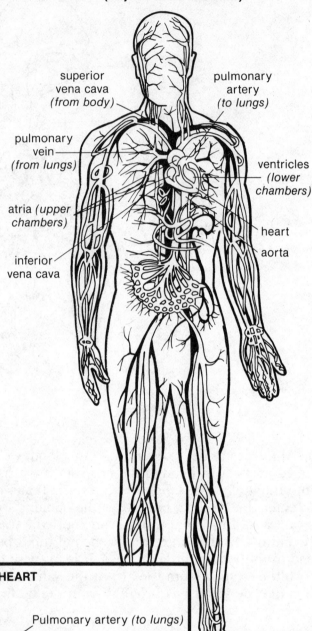

superior vena cava *(from body)*

pulmonary artery *(to lungs)*

pulmonary vein *(from lungs)*

ventricles *(lower chambers)*

atria *(upper chambers)*

heart

aorta

inferior vena cava

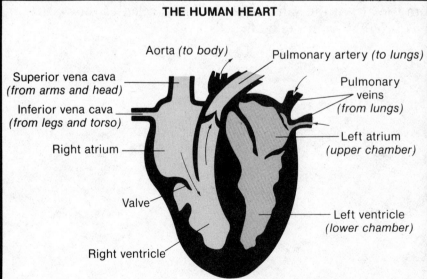

THE HUMAN HEART

Aorta *(to body)*

Pulmonary artery *(to lungs)*

Superior vena cava *(from arms and head)*

Inferior vena cava *(from legs and torso)*

Pulmonary veins *(from lungs)*

Right atrium

Left atrium *(upper chamber)*

Valve

Left ventricle *(lower chamber)*

Right ventricle

Exercise 11: Eating and Breathing

Directions: Match each word on the left with the best definition on the right. Write the letter of the definition on the line before the correct number.

_____ **1.** heart

_____ **2.** lungs

_____ **3.** stomach

_____ **4.** arteries and veins

_____ **5.** small intestine

a. organs in which blood takes oxygen from the air

b. primary organ of digestion

c. organ from which digested food enters bloodstream

d. muscle responsible for pumping blood

e. tubes that carry blood

★ **GED PRACTICE** ★

Exercise 12: The Circulatory and Digestive Systems

Directions: Choose the best answer to each of the questions below.

1. What function is performed by the epiglottis?

  (1) It prevents food from entering the trachea.
  (2) It prevents food from entering the esophagus.
  (3) It prevents air from entering the trachea.
  (4) It prevents air from entering the esophagus.
  (5) It produces the sounds of speech.

2. Which of the following phrases best sums up the function of the circulatory system?

  (1) communication network
  (2) support structure
  (3) waste elimination
  (4) food processing
  (5) transport and delivery

3. What is the most likely reason that being overweight puts an extra burden on the heart of the overweight person?

  (1) A person who is overweight often feels self-conscious.
  (2) The heart of an overweight person must pump a greater amount of blood in order to nourish the extra fat cells.
  (3) An overweight person has an increased risk of developing diabetes.
  (4) The heart of an overweight person tends to tire quickly.
  (5) An overweight person may not consume enough protein.

4. Which of the following comments about an artificial heart is most likely based on human values rather than on scientific evidence?

   (1) An artifical heart is a mechanical pump that takes the place of a seriously damaged human heart.

   (2) Implanted artificial hearts have shown a high failure rate because of unusual blood-clotting problems.

   (3) After its design is perfected, an artificial heart may give a patient a longer life expectancy than a transplanted human heart.

   (4) The decision to implant an artificial heart ought to be left solely up to the patient and his or her doctor, regardless of the risks involved.

   (5) Today's artificial heart may best be used as a temporary life-support measure that keeps a patient alive until a human heart can be obtained for transplant.

ANSWERS AND EXPLANATIONS START ON PAGE 297.

 Writing Activity 4

   White blood cells, part of the circulatory system, help the body fight disease. The HIV virus—the virus that can lead to AIDS—infects certain white blood cells, impairing the body's ability to fight off disease. Victims of AIDS (acquired immune deficiency syndrome) are susceptible to diseases that a normal immune system could fight off easily.

   The HIV virus is transmitted through body fluids. It is most often spread through sexual contact, the use of intravenous needles, and blood transfusions as well as from infected mothers to their babies during childbirth and breast-feeding.

   Because sexual contact has been the most common form of HIV transmission, the medical community and AIDS activists have worked hard to spread the "safe sex" message. Billboards and TV commercials often use blunt language about condoms and sexual practices. Some public schools now give free condoms to high school students. Parents are urged to discuss sex and safety with their children.

   Many Americans, however, are offended by this open discussion of sex. They feel that, regardless of health concerns, sexual practices should not be discussed so openly. Many point out that abstinence is the only *true* form of safe sex, and that the words "safe sex" are misleading.

   Do you agree that we should have open discussion of AIDS and of sexual practices—even with children and teenagers? Write two or three paragraphs describing your opinion.

SAMPLE ANSWERS CAN BE FOUND ON PAGE 297.

Reproduction and Human Genetics

Key Words

egg cell—the female sex cell
sperm cell—the male sex cell
fertilized egg cell—the one-cell first stage of a human being
fetus—the name given to the beginning stage (prebirth stage) of a human being
amniocentesis—the examination of amniotic fluid in order to detect possible genetic problems in a fetus

One important human body system we have not yet discussed is the reproductive system. Unlike other body systems, the reproductive system does more than maintain your functioning as an individual; it also provides you with a means of creating another person, a person very much like yourself. And, unlike the organs of other body systems, reproductive organs are distinctly different in males and females.

Reproduction starts with the union of a male sex cell (a sperm) and a female sex cell (an egg). The combined cell, called a fertilized egg cell, develops quickly into a ball of many cells that implants itself on the inner wall of the female uterus. Here it develops into a fetus, the name given to the beginning (prebirth) stage of a human being. For the nine months that the fetus grows, it receives nourishment from the mother's circulatory system.

Inherited Traits

Reproduction results in a new individual who has many of the features (traits) of each parent. These traits are passed from parents to child by genes, chemical messengers that make up the strands of chromosomes present in each body cell. Sperm and egg cells bring hereditary information from each parent and combine it to produce the unique mixture of traits acquired by the child.

In the nucleus of each of your body cells is a set of forty-six chromosomes. These chromosomes are arranged as twenty-three pairs and contain about 100,000 genes that determine all your traits. For example, whether you have your mother's nose, your father's hands, or your grandfather's hairline are all determined by your genes.

The only human body cells that do not contain forty-six chromosomes are the female egg cell and the male sperm cell. Each of these cells has only one set of twenty-three unpaired chromosomes. However, a fertilized egg cell is also a cell with forty-six chromosomes (twenty-three pairs): twenty-three unpaired chromosomes in the egg are joined by twenty-three from the sperm. In this way, the fertilized egg receives exactly half of its genes from the male parent and half from the female parent.

In most cases, a single fertilized egg develops into a single fetus. Once in a while, though, a fertilized egg will separate into two cells that move away from each other. Each of these cells may develop into a fully formed fetus. The two children that are born are known as *identical twins*. Because they form from the same fertilized egg cell, identical twins are genetically identical. Each has exactly the same set of chromosomes and genes. *Fraternal twins*, on the other hand, develop when two egg cells are fertilized by two sperm cells during the same reproductive cycle. Although fraternal twins develop in the mother-to-be's uterus at the same time, they are no more alike than regular brothers and sisters who may be born years apart.

Prenatal Care

Protecting the health of a developing fetus is the best way to ensure that a healthy baby will be born. This care is called prenatal care. To provide good prenatal care, a mother-to-be needs good nutrition, healthful exercise, and periodic medical checkups.

Because substances in the mother's blood can affect the health of the developing fetus, a mother-to-be should avoid smoking, drinking alcohol, and taking any medicines or drugs of any kind except those prescribed by her doctor. She should also avoid all sources of chemical fumes such as garden sprays, oven cleansers, and other household chemicals. These fumes contain chemicals that could possibly harm the fetus.

Genetic Disorders

Once in a while a gene will change structure and cease to function properly. This changed gene can produce an inheritable trait. Such a defective gene will usually not cause any problem that affects a child's health or abilities. However, some defective genes do lead to harmful traits that result in generation after generation of illnesses or disabilities. Examples of inheritable genetic disorders are sickle-cell anemia, hemophilia, color blindness, and dwarfism.

Many types of genetic disorders can be detected in adults. When two people who have known defective genes decide to have children, they can get genetic counseling. In genetic counseling they can find out what their chances are of having a child with a particular genetic illness or disability.

Today, genetic defects can be detected in a fetus during the early months of pregnancy. Doctors use a procedure called amniocentesis, in which a needle and syringe are used to collect a sample of loose cells from the fetus. These cells are present in amniotic fluid that surrounds the developing fetus. By studying this fluid, doctors are able to identify certain types of defective genes. Although some diseases caused by defective genes can be treated, most of them cannot.

Exercise 13: Reproduction and Human Genetics

Directions: Circle *T* for each statement below that is true and *F* for each statement that is false.

T F **1.** Genetic counseling is an attempt to resolve marriage problems caused by differences in inherited traits.

T F **2.** Color blindness can be inherited.

T F **3.** Except for egg and sperm cells, all cells of a human body contain twenty-three pairs of chromosomes.

T F **4.** Fraternal twins may be born years apart.

T F **5.** The health of a developing fetus depends, in part, on the care the mother-to-be gives to her own body.

★ **GED PRACTICE** ★

Exercise 14: Pregnancy and Prenatal Care——

Directions: Choose the best answer to each question below.

1. Which of the following is *not* true about identical twins?

   (1) Identical twins form from two fertilized eggs.
   (2) Identical twins have the exact same genetic makeup.
   (3) Identical twins form from a single fertilized egg.
   (4) Identical twins are more alike than are fraternal twins.
   (5) Identical twins are always of the same sex.

2. The female egg cell differs from other cells in a woman's body because it has

   (1) twice as many chromosomes as all other cells
   (2) twenty-three more chromosomes than all other cells
   (3) no chromosomes
   (4) twenty-three fewer chromosomes than all other cells
   (5) chromosomes but not genes

3. Which of the following activities should a mother-to-be avoid during the months of pregnancy?

   (1) going to music concerts
   (2) taking daily walks
   (3) cooking meals at home
   (4) taking naps
   (5) painting the baby's room

4. If a woman who is a social drinker discovers she is two months pregnant, what is the *best* way for her to protect the health of the fetus?

   (1) to stop drinking any alcoholic drinks for at least four more months
   (2) to make sure she drinks alcohol only with meals
   (3) to slowly decrease her alcohol consumption over the remainder of the pregnancy
   (4) to stop drinking alcoholic beverages until after the birth of the child
   (5) to continue social drinking as usual

Questions 5-7 refer to the following passage and diagrams.

Sickle-cell anemia is an inheritable blood disease that affects about 50,000 Americans, most of them American blacks. There is no known cure for this disease. Symptoms include slowness in growth, swelling of the feet and hands, aching joints, and pain caused by clogged blood vessels. Many children die of sickle-cell anemia before they reach their teenage years.

Sickle-cell anemia affects red blood cells. A healthy red blood cell has a doughnut shape, but the red blood cell of a person who has sickle-cell anemia is shaped like a sickle; it is elongated and narrow. Sickle cells tend to clump together and clog blood vessels. This results in a lack of oxygen reaching the tissues of the body and causes the symptoms mentioned.

Sickle-cell anemia is known to be caused by a single gene that affects the shape and function of red blood cells. About 9 percent of all American blacks are carriers of a single sickle-cell gene. However, because this gene is recessive, only those who have inherited two sickle-cell genes display symptoms of the disease. Carriers of a single sickle-cell gene do not suffer symptoms of the disease. Because it is a genetic disease, sickle-cell anemia is not contagious.

It is now possible with prenatal testing to determine if a fetus has either one or two sickle-cell genes. The diagrams below illustrate how either the sickle-cell trait (one sickle-cell gene) or the sickle-cell disease (two sickle-cell genes) can be passed on to offspring.

HOW PARENTS PASS ON SICKLE-CELL ANEMIA

NN = normal blood
NS = sickle-cell trait
SS = sickle-cell disease

5. Which of the following phrases does *not* correctly describe sickle-cell anemia?

   (1) a blood disease
   (2) an inheritable disease
   (3) a contagious disease
   (4) a disease caused by defective genes
   (5) symptoms include clogging of blood vessels

6. Diagram A on page 150 shows the gene combinations of a child who could be born to the parents illustrated. The father is a normal blood cell (NN) person, and the mother is a sickle-cell trait (NS) person (a person with a single sickle-cell gene). What are the chances that the child will also be a carrier of the sickle-cell trait?

   (1) 0% (no chance)
   (2) 25% (one chance in four)
   (3) 50% (two chances in four)
   (4) 75% (three chances in four)
   (5) 100% (the child will be a carrier of the sickle-cell trait)

7. Diagram B above shows the gene combinations of a child who could be born to two people who each have the sickle-cell trait (NS). What are the chances that the child will suffer from the disease of sickle-cell anemia?

   (1) 0% (no chance)
   (2) 25% (one chance in four)
   (3) 50% (two chances in four)
   (4) 75% (three chances in four)
   (5) 100% (the child will have it with certainty)

ANSWERS AND EXPLANATIONS START ON PAGE 297.

7

EARTH SCIENCE

"That's one small step for man, one giant leap for mankind." With these famous words, the American astronaut Neil Armstrong stepped off the ladder of the *Eagle* lander and became the first person to stand on the surface of the moon. That day, July 20, 1969, marked the beginning of a new era in human history. For the first time, a human being walked on a body other than the Earth. Yet, as remarkable as this achievement may seem, many scientists believe that the moon voyage was just the first step in the eventual human colonization of other planets! In this view, Earth will someday be thought of as the mother planet of a human family that may reach far beyond the Earth itself.

The study of the structure of the Earth, the forces that change it, and the Earth's location in space is known as *earth science*. Fortunately for us, but unfortunately for space travelers, the Earth is believed to be the most livable of all the known planets. In this chapter, we'll look at some of the features of our evolving home planet. Topics will be chosen from the following related studies that make up the field of earth science.

Astronomy, one of the oldest sciences, is the study of the heavenly bodies in the universe. Astronomers study the structure and life cycles of stars, planets, comets, and other objects in space. From this study, astronomers hope to gain a better understanding of both the creation and the evolution of the Earth. With the development of space vehicles and orbiting space stations, astronomy promises to play an even more important role in the future.

Geology is the study of the composition and structure of the Earth itself. Geologists seek to understand how land and water formations develop and change over time. Many geologists study natural events such as volcanoes and earthquakes that often threaten human safety. Other geologists work for companies whose interests lie in the development of natural resources such as coal and oil and economically important minerals such as gold. Still other geologists work in environmental studies. Their concern is with the geological impact that human life is having on the Earth and its ecosystems (plant and animal life cycles).

Oceanography is the study of the earth's oceans. Oceanographers study the movement of ocean water and its effects on weather. They also study the land formations on the bottom of the oceans. As evidenced by offshore oil rigs, the ocean bottom is proving to be a rich source of natural resources.

Meteorology is the study of the Earth's atmosphere, the covering of air that surrounds our planet. Meteorologists use information about atmospheric conditions to gain an understanding of weather. Each day, using millions of temperature and air pressure readings from around the world, the United States Weather Bureau forecasts the coming weather. Weather forecasts are especially useful as an early warning of approaching storms.

Paleontology is the study of the fossils of prehistoric plants and animals. Through their work, paleontologists are able to tell us much about ancient life forms and about the geological history of our planet. Using scientific dating techniques, they have developed a geological calendar that traces simple life forms back more than two billion years.

We'll begin this chapter by discussing a topic from astronomy: the location of the Earth in space.

Exercise 1: Overview of Earth Science

Directions: In each blank, write the name of the type of scientist (astronomer, geologist, oceanographer, meteorologist, or paleontologist) you would expect to find doing each of the following activities.

_____ 1. working for an oil company that is interested in drilling for oil off the California coast

_____ 2. writing an article on the nature of comets

_____ 3. trying to identify a bone chip thought to be over 1 million years old

_____ 4. taking seismic measurements on Mount St. Helens in order to predict a possible volcanic eruption

_____ 5. working as a weatherman for a local television station

Exercise 2: Studying the Earth━━━━

Directions: Choose the best answer to each question below.

1. Which of the following statements is an accurate summary of several ideas given in the reading selection?

   (1) The Earth is a quiet, unchanging planet.
   (2) Several planets are known to contain some form of life.
   (3) The Earth undergoes constant change, both from natural processes and from the actions of human beings.
   (4) The Earth was created at the same time that all other bodies in the universe were created.
   (5) The study of geology is concerned mainly with finding economically important natural resources.

Questions 2 and 3 refer to the following information.

   While discussing the possibility of life on other planets, a group of astronomers made the following statements.

   A. The winding valleys on the surface of Mars may be ancient riverbeds, carved at a time when water flowed on the Martian surface.

   B. Data sent back in 1976 by the *Viking* lander from the surface of Mars did not indicate that the element carbon was present in the Martian soil.

   C. Further exploration of the Martian surface should be our top priority.

   D. The first astronauts will probably land on the planet Mars before the year 2025.

2. Remembering that a hypothesis is a reasonable explanation of an observed fact, which of the above statements is a hypothesis?

   (1) A only
   (2) B only
   (3) C only
   (4) D only
   (5) B and D only

3. Which of the above statements is most likely a fact?

   (1) A only
   (2) B only
   (3) A and C only
   (4) B and C only
   (5) B and D only

4. Which item of information below would be of most relevance to an environmental geologist working for the federal government?

 (1) the cause of the dinosaurs' extinction
 (2) the daily national weather forecast
 (3) the yearly movement of an Alaskan glacier
 (4) the life cycle of a star
 (5) the location of toxic waste dumps

ANSWERS AND EXPLANATIONS START ON PAGE 298.

The Earth in Space

Key Words

galaxy—a group of a large number of stars
gravity—a force of attraction that exists between any two objects in the universe
orbit—the path followed by one body as it moves around a second body (Used as a verb, to *orbit* means to "travel in an orbit.")
planet—any body that moves in an orbit around a star
solar system—the sun and all the objects that are in orbits around the sun

Thousands of years ago, the Greeks observed the night sky with a feeling of religious wonder. As they watched from night to night, they noticed a few lights that looked like stars but seemed to move across the sky. They believed that each of these moving heavenly objects traveled around the Earth in complicated loops. They named these strange objects the *planetes*, a Greek word meaning "wanderers."

The belief that the wanderers moved around the Earth persisted until 1543, when Nicolaus Copernicus (1473–1543), a Polish astronomer, suggested a bold new idea. He proposed that the Earth and all the other planets traveled in orbits around the sun. Together, the sun and all the bodies that orbit it are now called the solar system. The acceptance of the idea that the sun is at the center of the solar system came to be known as the Copernican theory.

Galaxies

The Copernican theory was an important step in our present understanding of the universe. Although the size of the universe is still unknown, evidence suggests that its age may be 15 billion years or older! What's more, scientists now believe that the universe contains millions or, more likely, billions of widely separated galaxies. Each of these galaxies is a group of hundreds of millions or even hundreds of billions of stars.

THE MILKY WAY GALAXY

Sun's position

Our own galaxy is called the Milky Way. The Milky Way contains the sun and about 100 billion other stars. The distance across the Milky Way is estimated to be about 100,000 light-years. The distance between the Milky Way and the nearest similar galaxy is about 2 million light-years. (A *light-year* is the distance that light travels in 1 year, about 6 trillion miles.)

The Solar System

The solar system contains the sun, nine planets, numerous comets, and a large number of asteroids—small planetlike rock fragments that orbit the sun. Many of the nine planets have one or more of their own natural moons, called satellites. For example, the Earth has a single moon, while the planet Jupiter has fifteen.

The largest planets include Jupiter, Saturn, Uranus, and Neptune. Four of the smaller planets—Mercury, Venus, Earth, and Mars—are also those closest to the sun. Not much is known about the smallest planet, Pluto. It is the outermost planet, and its eccentric orbit sometimes crosses the orbit of Neptune.

OUR SOLAR SYSTEM

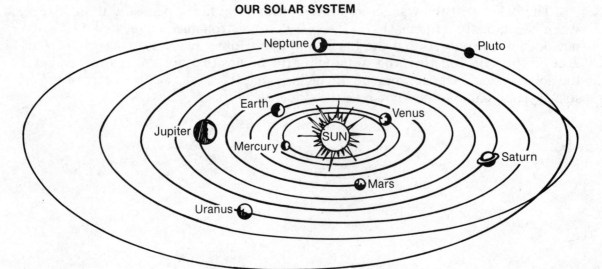

The Force of Gravity

The structure of both the Milky Way galaxy and our solar system results from the force of gravity. Although scientists do not know what causes gravity, they do know that it holds the objects in the universe together.

- Gravity holds stars together in galaxies.

- Gravity holds each planet in its orbit around the sun.

- Gravity holds the moon and human-made satellites in orbit around the Earth.

- Gravity holds objects onto the surface of the Earth.

Exercise 3: The Earth in Space

Directions: Answer each question in the exercise below.

1. Match each item on the left with the phrase that best describes it on the right. Write the letter of the phrase on the line before the correct number.

   _____ **a.** Milky Way

   _____ **b.** solar system

   _____ **c.** moon

   _____ **d.** galaxy

   _____ **e.** gravity

   (1) a group of millions or even billions of stars

   (2) a strong force of attraction between any two objects

   (3) the sun and the objects in orbit around it

   (4) the galaxy that contains the sun

   (5) a natural satellite in orbit around a planet

2. Complete each sentence by filling in the blanks with the correct word from the reading passage or illustrations.

   a. The closest planet to the sun is _____.

   b. The Earth is the _____ farthest planet from the sun.

   c. The outermost planet is named _____.

   d. One light-year is a distance of _____ miles.

   e. The Milky Way contains about _____ stars.

★ **GED PRACTICE** ★

Exercise 4: The Solar System

Directions: Choose the best answer to each question below.

1. Which statement below best expresses the idea for which Nicolaus Copernicus is now remembered?

   (1) The sun orbits the Earth and other planets.
   (2) The sun is only one of billions of stars in the Milky Way.
   (3) The Earth is at the center of a system of orbiting planets.
   (4) The sun is at the center of a system of orbiting planets.
   (5) The universe contains billions of galaxies.

2. Planets are seen as faint lights that move across the night sky. Yet, unlike stars, planets do not give off their own light. Knowing this, decide which of the following facts are needed in order to explain how we are able to see the other planets while standing on Earth.

   A. Planets that are close to the sun have higher surface temperatures than planets farther away.
   B. Five planets are at a greater distance from the sun than the Earth, while only three are closer.
   C. Planets reflect part of the sunlight that strikes them.

   (1) A only
   (2) B only
   (3) C only
   (4) A and C only
   (5) B and C only

3. The ancient Greeks made the following observations.

   A. The sun appears to rise in the morning and set at night.
   B. The sun and the moon appear to be about the same size.
   C. The moon appears to change shape during different times of each month.
   D. Standing on Earth, you get the impression that the Earth is motionless.

   Which of the above observations could have been used by the ancient Greeks to support their incorrect belief that the sun moved in an orbit around the Earth?

   (1) A and B only
   (2) A and C only
   (3) B and C only
   (4) B and D only
   (5) A and D only

ANSWERS AND EXPLANATIONS START ON PAGE 298.

Writing Activity 1

In January of 1986, the space shuttle *Challenger* exploded after takeoff, killing the seven people on board. This accident caused many people to reevaluate their stand on a controversial issue: whether or not to continue to send astronauts into space.

If you were in charge of the space program, would you support manned or unmanned flights? Write a paragraph explaining your decision. Be sure to give examples to support your choice.

SAMPLE ANSWERS START ON PAGE 298.

Seasons on the Earth

Key Words

axis—an imaginary line about which the Earth turns
North and South Poles—points where the Earth's axis passes through
the Earth's surface
rotation—the turning of the Earth around its axis
revolution—the movement of the Earth along its orbit around the sun

---

You may not realize it, but as you're sitting here reading this sentence you are racing through space at a speed of 66,000 miles per hour! As incredible as it may seem, this is the speed at which the Earth travels in its orbit around the sun. It takes 365 days (one year) to make one complete trip (revolution). During this time, the only clue you have to the Earth's orbital motion is the changing of the seasons.

As it moves along its orbital path, the Earth also turns (rotates) on its axis—the imaginary line running through the North and South Poles. You can think of the Earth as slowly spinning like a top around this axis. It makes one complete turn during each twenty-four hour period (one day). Because the Earth turns from west to east, the sun appears to rise over the eastern horizon each morning and set below the western horizon each evening. The Earth's rotation is what causes day and night.

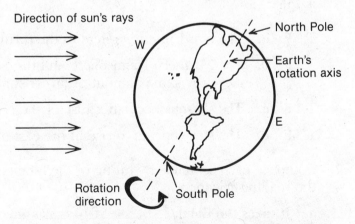

The Earth rotates from west to east on its rotation axis. One complete turn takes twenty-four hours (one day).

As you can see from the illustration on page 159, the Earth's axis is not vertical. Seasons are caused by the tilt in the Earth's axis. In summer, the Northern Hemisphere is tilted toward the sun, so it receives more direct rays of sunlight. Direct rays produce more heat and light. In winter, the Northern Hemisphere is tilted away from the sun. It receives slanting rays from the sun, which are not as strong and result in colder temperatures and longer nights. The diagram below shows the position of the Earth in relation to the sun at different times of year.

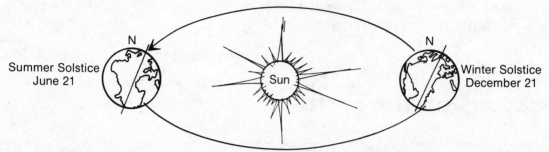

Seasons are caused by the tilt in the Earth's axis. The first day of summer and winter for countries in the Northern Hemisphere is shown above.

The situation in the Southern Hemisphere is exactly the opposite. When the northern half of the world receives more light and heat from the sun, the southern half receives less. Therefore, when it is summer in the Northern Hemisphere, it is winter in the Southern Hemisphere, and vice versa. While July is a warm month in the United States, it is a cold month in Australia.

Exercise 5: Seasons on Earth

Directions: Answer each question below.

1. Circle *T* for each statement below that is true and *F* for each statement that is false.

   T F **a.** The word *rotation* refers to the turning of the Earth on its axis.

   T F **b.** The Northern Hemisphere and the Southern Hemisphere each receive the same amount of direct sunlight in January.

   T F **c.** The seasons occur because of the Earth's rotation.

   T F **d.** The sun appears to rise in the east and set in the west.

2. Complete each sentence by filling in the blanks with the correct word(s) from the reading selection.

   a. It takes the Earth _____ to make one rotation.
            (time)

   b. It takes the Earth _____ to make one revolution.
            (time)

★ GED PRACTICE ★

Exercise 6: The Earth's Rotation

Directions: Choose the best answer to each question below.

1. In which of the following months are people most likely to be sunbathing in coastal cities in southern Brazil?

    (1) February
    (2) April
    (3) July
    (4) August
    (5) September

Questions 2 and 3 refer to the following passage and diagram.

At any instant, people in different parts of the world see the sun in a different position in the sky. For example, while people in San Francisco are watching the sun come up, people in Moscow (Russia) are watching the sun go down.

To avoid confusion in telling time, scientists have divided the Earth into twenty-four time zones. As you move from west to east, you add one hour to your clock for each new time zone that you enter. For example, when it is 2:00 P.M. in San Francisco, it is 5:00 P.M. in New York City. As shown on the time zone map at right, you cross into three new time zones as you go from San Francisco to New York City.

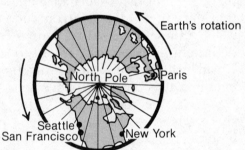

THE WORLD TIME ZONES

2. While vacationing in Paris, France, James calls his home in Seattle, Washington. If he places the call at 6:00 A.M. on Saturday, July 9, Paris time, what time and day will it be in Seattle when the call is received?

    (1) 2:00 P.M. Friday, July 8
    (2) 10:00 P.M. Friday, July 8
    (3) 2:00 P.M. Saturday, July 9
    (4) 10:00 P.M. Saturday, July 9
    (5) 2:00 A.M. Sunday, July 10

3. If an airplane leaves San Francisco at 8:00 A.M. and flies nonstop to New York, what time will the airplane arrive in New York City (New York City time), assuming that the trip takes five hours of actual flying time?

    (1) 1:00 A.M.
    (2) 10:00 A.M.
    (3) 1:00 P.M.
    (4) 4:00 P.M.
    (5) 10:00 P.M.

ANSWERS AND EXPLANATIONS START ON PAGE 298.

The Structure of the Earth

Key Words

continents—the seven large land masses on the Earth

islands—small land masses that are surrounded by water

oceans—the five large bodies of salt water that cover most of the Earth's surface

crustal plates—twelve to twenty rigid, separate plates that are believed to make up the Earth's crust

plate tectonics—the theory that the Earth's surface is made up of slowly moving crustal plates

Imagine for a moment that you're a sailor living in the fifteenth century. You're about to sail due west from the shore of Europe, out onto a vast unknown sea. Many of your friends say that the ocean leads to the edge of the flat Earth. Others tell of sailors who ventured out past the horizon and never returned. Still others warn of giant sea monsters swallowing up ships—like yours—that dare to sail too far from land.

Do these ideas sound funny? Sure, they do today, but you probably wouldn't be laughing if you were about to set sail with Columbus in search of a "new world"! During those adventurous days, when very little was known about our planet, it was normal to have fears about the nature of the Earth.

Today we have a much better understanding of the Earth. We know that its surface is mostly water (about 71 percent) divided into several large oceans. The land portion (about 29 percent) is divided into seven continents and numerous islands. The oceans and land masses are the visible part of the outer skin of the Earth known as the *crust*. The crust varies in size, being about six miles thick under the oceans and as much as forty miles thick under high mountain ranges on the continents.

Beneath the crust is a very thick layer called the *mantle*. The mantle is about 1,800 miles thick and is made up mainly of heavy rock.

Beneath the mantle, and running to the center of the earth, is the core. The core is divided into two parts: a solid *inner core*, made up of iron, and a liquid *outer core* that is composed mainly of melted iron. The inner core is shaped like a ball. The radius (distance from the center to the edge) is about 800 miles. The outer core surrounds the inner core and is about 1,400 miles thick.

THE STRUCTURE OF THE EARTH

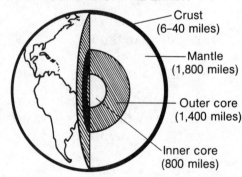

Crust
(6–40 miles)

Mantle
(1,800 miles)

Outer core
(1,400 miles)

Inner core
(800 miles)

Plate Tectonics

Looking at a world map, you can't help but notice that the east coasts of North and South America look like pieces of a jigsaw puzzle of which Greenland, Europe, and Africa are also a part. It appears that, if you could slide the Americas over next to Europe and Africa—placing Greenland in the opening at the top—the coastlines would neatly fit next to one another. Although this fit has been noticed for centuries, it has only been in recent years that geologists have come to understand this remarkable circumstance.

There is now evidence to indicate that the continents may have actually sat side by side at one time, perhaps 200 million years ago. In fact, geologists have given the name *Pangea* to this possible supercontinent. According to the most recent theory, called plate tectonics, the Earth's crust is made up of from twelve to twenty separate rigid plates that slowly move around on the surface of the mantle. Although each crustal plate moves only about two inches per year, 200 million years would have been enough time for Pangea to separate into today's continents.

 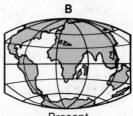

200 million years ago   Present

The theory of plate tectonics does more than describe the possible movement of continents—often called **continental drift**. It also helps geologists understand earthquakes and volcanoes. Both of these natural phenomena occur along the boundary lines where two plates collide with each other. When slippage occurs between two plates, an enormous amount of energy is released. This energy results in one or more earthquakes, felt mostly by those around the plate boundary. For example, California experiences thousands of small quakes each year along the plate boundary known as the San Andreas fault. Volcanoes can be caused by the tremendous pressure that develops as one plate actually moves under a second plate at the collision boundary. The group of islands that now make up Japan is an example of a whole string of volcanoes formed at the boundary of two plates.

Exercise 7: Structure of the Earth

Directions: Answer each question below.

1. Complete each sentence by filling in the blanks with the correct word(s).

   a. Approximately _____ percent of the surface of the Earth is covered by water and _____ percent by land.

   b. The large land masses on the Earth's surface are called _____.

   c. The large bodies of water that cover the surface of the Earth are called

   _____.

d. The thin surface of the Earth is called the _____.

e. The three interior regions of the Earth are called the _____, _____, and _____.

2. Briefly tell what is meant by each of the following:

a. Pangea _____

b. continental drift _____

3. Name two natural phenomena that can occur at the boundary between two moving plates: _____ and _____

★ **GED PRACTICE** ★

Exercise 8: Plate Tectonics

Directions: Choose the best answer to each question below.

1. Which of the following best summarizes the main idea of the theory of plate tectonics?

    (1) The Earth's crust varies in thickness, being much thicker beneath mountain ranges than beneath bodies of water.
    (2) The Earth's crust is made up of rigid plates that slowly move along the Earth's surface.
    (3) The Earth's continents are slowly being pushed apart by the movement of the oceans.
    (4) The coasts of several continents are similar in shape, giving the Earth the appearance of a jigsaw puzzle.
    (5) The Earth is round and not flat as was once widely believed.

2. Which of the following is a hypothesis?

    (1) In the fifteenth century, no one knew for sure that the Earth was round.
    (2) Seismic measurements (measurement of shock waves from earthquakes) indicate that the Earth's crust tends to be thicker beneath the continents than beneath the oceans.
    (3) Seventy-one percent of the Earth's surface is covered by water and 29 percent by land.
    (4) The Earth's continents look like a jigsaw puzzle because they were once part of a huge supercontinent that split apart.
    (5) The Earth is the only planet in the solar system that looks blue when seen from space.

3. Which of the following would *not* be important to a geologist interested in predicting the possibility of a volcanic eruption from a peak in the Appalachian Mountains?

(1) the history of volcanic activity in all parts of the eastern United States
(2) the average amount of yearly rainfall received in the Appalachian Mountains
(3) the location of the nearest boundary between two crustal plates
(4) the history of any earthquake activity in or near the Appalachian Mountains
(5) the age and structure of the Appalachian Mountains

ANSWERS AND EXPLANATIONS START ON PAGE 298.

 Writing Activity 2

As you know, earthquakes occur when the plates of the Earth's crust shift and cause the ground to move. Should the public be told about a predicted earthquake if scientists are not certain that the earthquake will occur?

Some people say that earthquake warnings are necessary to prevent death and destruction. Others point to cases where people were needlessly evacuated from their homes on the basis of an erroneous prediction.

List three reasons why it may be wise to inform people and three problems that informing them can cause.

SAMPLE ANSWERS START ON PAGE 299.

Reading a Topographical Map

> ## Key Words
>
> *topographical map*—a map that shows the details of a part of the Earth's surface
> *elevation*—height above sea level
> *contour line*—a line that connects points of equal elevation

Details about the Earth's surface, such as the location and height of mountains, are called *topography*. A map that is drawn to show these details is called a topographical map. These maps are produced by the government for use by all segments of society. Hikers, campers, and hunters use them by the millions each year.

A topographical map shows elevation (height of land above sea level) by using contour lines. A contour line is a line that connects points that are at the same elevation. Most often, contour lines are drawn at twenty-foot intervals. This means that as you move from one line to the next you either gain or lose twenty feet of elevation. Every fifth contour line is drawn darker than the others and includes a number that gives the elevation of that line.

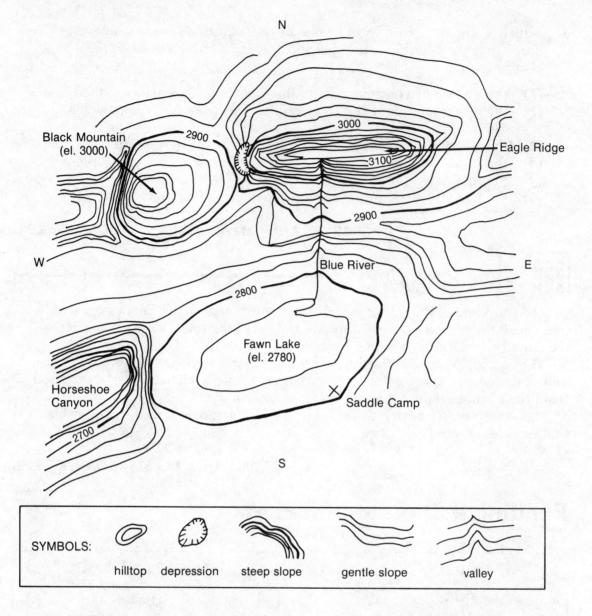

As you look at the topographical map above, see how the general ideas below apply.

- The space between contour lines gives you an idea of the slope of the land. Lines that are spaced widely apart indicate land that is almost flat. Lines that are spaced closely together indicate a steep slope.

- Contour lines that form a closed loop indicate a hilltop.

- Contour lines that cross a valley bend to form a *V* shape. The point of the *V* points uphill (toward increasing elevation).

- A depression (low place) is indicated by short, straight lines pointing in the direction of the depression. A depression is just the opposite of a hilltop.

Exercise 9: Map Symbols

Directions: Match each symbol on the left with the phrase that best describes it on the right. Write the letter of the phrase on the line before the correct number.

_____ 1.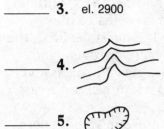

_____ 2.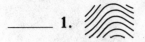

_____ 3. el. 2900

_____ 4.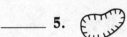

_____ 5.

_____ 6.

a. a depression

b. a steep slope

c. a hilltop

d. an elevation reading

e. a gentle slope

f. a valley

★ **GED PRACTICE** ★

Exercise 10: Reading a Topographical Map

Directions: The following questions refer to the topographical map on page 166.

1. The point of greatest elevation shown on the map is

   (1) Fawn Lake
   (2) Eagle Ridge
   (3) Black Mountain
   (4) Horseshoe Canyon
   (5) Saddle Camp

2. On which side of Black Mountain is there a steep slope?

   (1) north side
   (2) southeast side
   (3) west side
   (4) east side
   (5) northeast side

ANSWERS AND EXPLANATIONS START ON PAGE 299.

The Earth's Atmosphere

Key Words

air—the mixture of gases found in the lower atmosphere
atmosphere—the blanket of air that surrounds the Earth
ozone—a type of oxygen gas that absorbs ultraviolet sunlight

Unless it's raining or the wind is blowing, we don't usually pay much attention to the atmosphere, the blanket of air that surrounds the Earth. Yet, without the atmosphere, the Earth would be a desolate planet with no signs of life!

The atmosphere plays several roles in helping to make life possible. First, the atmosphere provides the three gases necessary for life: oxygen, nitrogen, and carbon dioxide. All animals, including ourselves, breathe oxygen. Nitrogen and carbon dioxide are both needed for plant growth. Less important atmospheric gases include argon, neon, helium, and hydrogen.

Second, the atmosphere also protects us from most of the sun's high-energy ultraviolet light rays, which are harmful to life. Although these rays are only a small part of the sunlight striking the Earth, they are known to be very dangerous. However, 99 percent of all ultraviolet rays are absorbed before they reach the Earth's surface. They are absorbed by an atmospheric gas called ozone, a type of oxygen gas. The ozone layer surrounds the Earth but is much thinner over the North and South Poles than over other regions of the Earth.

The 1 percent of the ultraviolet light in the atmosphere that does reach the Earth's surface is known to cause sunburn and is now believed to cause skin cancer in many people. Because of this, doctors recommend that people limit the amount of time they spend in direct sunlight. They also recommend that people who like to sunbathe wear a suntan lotion that blocks the ultraviolet rays.

Finally, the atmosphere gives us weather, both clear blue skies and storms. It acts as a huge energy machine, changing sunlight into other forms of energy such as heat and wind. As part of this role, the atmosphere regulates the temperature at the Earth's surface. First, it allows only 46 percent of the sunlight striking it to pass through and actually reach the Earth's surface. Second, carbon dioxide gas in the atmosphere controls the amount of sunlight warmth on the Earth's surface that is allowed to radiate back into space. By these two controlling devices, the atmosphere regulates the Earth's surface temperature.

When meteorologists talk about the atmosphere, they usually divide it into four (or sometimes five) layers:

- The *troposphere* is the layer closest to the ground. Most of the gas in the atmosphere is in this layer. In fact, more than half of all atmospheric gas is within an altitude, or height, of 3½ miles. It is in the troposphere that almost all weather occurs. Under normal conditions, the temperature decreases about 10°F for each mile you gain in altitude in the troposphere. The carbon dioxide gas in this layer regulates the Earth's surface temperature.

- The second layer is called the *stratosphere*. The temperature is about the same throughout the stratosphere; it no longer decreases with increasing altitude. The stratosphere is especially important to us because it contains the ozone gas that protects us from harmful sunlight.

- Above the stratosphere is the *mesosphere*, a layer of atmosphere in which air temperature again drops with increasing altitude.

- The top layer of atmosphere is called the *thermosphere*, a region where the temperature rises with altitude. The thermosphere, together with the upper mesosphere, is often called the *ionosphere*, a region that reflects radio waves back toward the ground. The ionosphere can be thought of as a layer of atmosphere that is made up of parts of two other layers. The ionosphere makes it possible for a radio station to broadcast over hundreds or even thousands of miles.

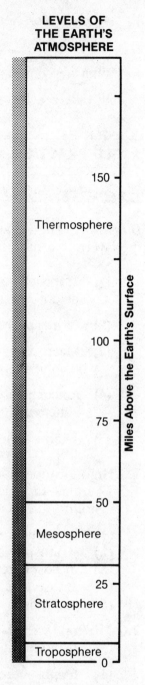

LEVELS OF THE EARTH'S ATMOSPHERE

Miles Above the Earth's Surface

150

Thermosphere

100

75

50

Mesosphere

25

Stratosphere

Troposphere

0

Exercise 11: The Earth's Atmosphere

Directions: Write a brief answer to each of the following questions.

1. Define what is meant by the word *atmosphere*.

_____

2. Why is ozone an important gas in the atmosphere?

_____

3. Which atmospheric gas prevents sunlight warmth from radiating back out into space? _____

4. What percent of the energy from the sun gets through the atmosphere and actually reaches the land? _____

★ **GED PRACTICE** ★

Exercise 12: Layers of the Atmosphere ━━━━━━━

Directions: The questions below are based on the following information about the layers of atmosphere.

(1) **Troposphere**—closest layer to Earth; weather conditions occur here; height: ground level to about eight miles

(2) **Stratosphere**—contains ozone gas; height: about eight miles to thirty miles

(3) **Mesosphere**—region of decreasing temperature with increasing altitude; height: about thirty miles to fifty miles

(4) **Ionosphere**—region that reflects radio waves; made up of top of mesosphere and bottom of thermosphere

(5) **Thermosphere**—top of atmosphere; height: fifty miles and up

1. High-altitude clouds, called *cirrus clouds*, form at altitudes of between 5 and 7½ miles. In which layer of atmosphere must pilots be concerned about poor visibility due to cirrus clouds?

   (1) troposphere
   (2) stratosphere
   (3) mesosphere
   (4) ionosphere
   (5) thermosphere

2. The top layer of the atmosphere that the space shuttle must pass through as it leaves its orbit (above the atmosphere) to return to Earth is the

   (1) troposphere
   (2) stratosphere
   (3) mesosphere
   (4) ionosphere
   (5) thermosphere

3. Disturbances in the atmosphere often affect radio reception. In which layer of the atmosphere are such disturbances most likely to affect the reception in Seattle, Washington, of stations broadcasting from Tokyo, Japan?

   (1) troposphere
   (2) stratosphere
   (3) mesosphere
   (4) ionosphere
   (5) thermosphere

4. A high-altitude balloon is sent up to take measurements of the ozone layer in the atmosphere. After rising through the ozone layer, the balloon records that the temperature is falling as the balloon continues to move upward. At this point the balloon is entering the layer of atmosphere known as the

    (1)   troposphere
    (2)   stratosphere
    (3)   mesosphere
    (4)   ionosphere
    (5)   thermosphere

5. In recent years, man-made chemicals called *fluorocarbons* have been banned from use as propellants in aerosol sprays such as spray paint. Scientists believe that these chemicals get into the atmosphere and wear away the layer of protective ozone gas. In which layer of atmosphere are the fluorocarbons believed to be causing the damage?

    (1)   troposphere
    (2)   stratosphere
    (3)   mesosphere
    (4)   ionosphere
    (5)   thermosphere

ANSWERS AND EXPLANATIONS START ON PAGE 299.

The Earth's Weather

Key Words

air pressure—the weight of the atmosphere
humidity—the water vapor content of air
temperature—a measure of heat content
wind—the movement of air

How often have you begun a conversation with "Nice day out, isn't it?" or "Cold enough out there for you?" Like it or not, we spend a lot of time talking about the weather. Weather is the one topic of earth science that everybody cares about on a daily basis! We choose what to wear because of it, and we sometimes have to make our plans around it. Even our moods—the way we feel—can be affected by it.

The study of weather is the study of the changes that take place in the Earth's atmosphere, the layer of gases that surrounds the Earth. A local weather report usually includes four features of the atmosphere:

- Temperature is a measure of how warm the air is.

- Humidity is a measure of how much water vapor is in the air. Humidity readings are usually given as percents. A humidity reading of 90 percent means that the air contains 90 percent of the water vapor it can possibly hold at that particular temperature.

- Wind refers to air movement and is usually given as a wind speed and a wind direction (the direction from which the wind is blowing).

- Air pressure (most often called barometric pressure) refers to the weight of the atmosphere. Air pressure depends on atmospheric temperature, humidity, and air movement. A high pressure reading usually indicates clear, pleasant weather, while a low reading indicates wet or stormy weather.

Although the exact causes of weather changes are not completely understood, meteorologists have discovered several characteristics of weather. For instance, they know that most changes in weather are caused by movements of large masses of air. Air masses are bodies of air at a certain temperature and with a certain moisture content.

Air masses that form over the polar regions tend to be very cold and dry, while air masses that form over tropical oceans tend to be warm and moist. An air mass takes on the characteristics of the region where it originated.

The movement of air masses is caused by temperature and pressure differences. Warm air masses tend to rise over cold ones, and air tends to flow from regions of high pressure to regions of low pressure. As an air mass moves, its direction of motion is also greatly affected by the rotation of the Earth.

Stormy or turbulent weather conditions tend to form along a line called a *front*, the boundary line where a warm air mass collides with a cold air mass. Because the moisture in the warm air will condense into water droplets when it cools, clouds, rain, sleet, hail, or snow occurs along the front. The actual weather you get depends on the air temperatures and moisture contents of the two colliding air masses. Because weather changes take place along a front, you'll often hear a weather forecaster talk about a "front that's moving in and bringing the weather with it!"

Exercise 13: The Earth's Weather —————————————

Directions: Answer each question below.

1. Match each item on the left with the phrase that best describes it on the right. Write the letter of the phrase on the line before the correct number.

    _____ **a.** air mass   **(1)** moisture content of air

    _____ **b.** front   **(2)** movement of air

    _____ **c.** air pressure   **(3)** weight of the Earth's atmosphere

    _____ **d.** humidity   **(4)** body of air at equal temperature and humidity

    _____ **e.** wind   **(5)** boundary line of warm air mass against a cold air mass

2. What kind of weather is indicated by each of the following barometric pressure readings?

    a. a high pressure reading _____

    b. a low pressure reading _____

Exercise 14: Weather Forecasting

Directions: Choose the best answer for each question below.

1. Which of the following is *not* mentioned in the reading selection as a standard feature of a weather report?

   (1) humidity
   (2) air pollution level
   (3) wind speed and direction
   (4) barometric pressure
   (5) temperature

2. The type of air mass that forms over a region depends on the region's climate. An air mass that forms over northern Canada will most likely have temperature and moisture characteristics similar to an air mass that forms over

   (1) the Gulf of Mexico
   (2) the Mediterranean Sea
   (3) the Sahara Desert
   (4) Antarctica
   (5) Australia

Questions 3 and 4 are based on the following passage and diagram.

Probably the most common science diagram you'll ever see is a weather map. A weather map gives a brief summary of the weather conditions in a certain location. Most United States newspapers carry a daily weather map that shows the weather conditions over the continental United States.

Weather maps use symbols to stand for certain weather conditions. Most often, a brief definition of these symbols accompanies the map. An example of a weather map is shown below. Following the map are definitions of the map symbols.

FORECAST

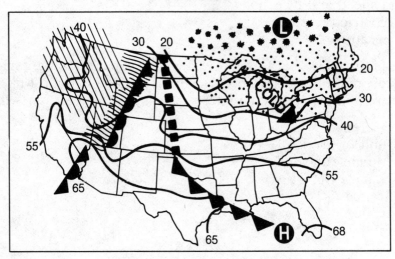

SYMBOLS USED ON THE MAP

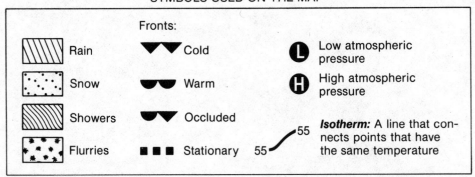

As seen on the map above, the weather in the southern states was cool (55 to 68° F) while the weather in the northern states was cold (20 to 40° F) and wet. Rain is shown over the northwestern states, while snow is shown over the northern part of the central and eastern United States.

3. Cities that lie on the same isotherm could expect to have the same

   (1) weather
   (2) type of precipitation
   (3) temperature
   (4) humidity
   (5) wind speed

4. Which month is most likely represented by the weather map above?

   (1) April
   (2) June
   (3) August
   (4) October
   (5) December

ANSWERS AND EXPLANATIONS START ON PAGE 299.

 Writing Activity 3

   People's moods are often affected by the weather. Three or four days of rain can cause some people to feel depressed just as a week of sun and warm temperatures can raise spirits. Have you ever noticed that your feelings, or those of someone close to you, are connected to what's going on outside?

   If so, describe in one or two paragraphs how weather influences your emotions and behavior. If you don't believe that changes in the weather can cause changes in mood, explain why not.

ANSWERS WILL VARY.

The Changing Earth

Key Words

weathering—the natural breaking of large rocks into smaller rocks
soil—a mixture of tiny rock fragments and organic materials
erosion—the natural movement of rock fragments, soil, and sand along the
   Earth's surface

The Earth is often compared to a gigantic sculpture, slowly being shaped by the forces of nature. This comparison is especially meaningful to anyone who has seen the awe-inspiring canyons in the southwestern United States or other natural wonders such as Niagara Falls in New York.

The land on the Earth's surface looks solid and unchanging. But while we don't notice the effects on a daily basis, changes are continually taking place in the land's features. The Grand Canyon itself was once just a highland plateau that was crossed by the Colorado River. Then, over millions of years, the river, wind, and rain combined to carve and shape this mile-deep canyon.

The two most important natural processes involved in sculpturing the earth are weathering and erosion.

Weathering

Weathering is the breaking down of large rocks into smaller pieces by natural processes. It is because of weathering that soil is produced. Soil is just a mixture of tiny rock fragments and organic materials produced by living things. Most organic materials in soil are simply the decaying remains of plants and animals.

There are several types of weathering. The most common is called *physical weathering*, also referred to as *mechanical weathering*. Physical weathering causes the rocks to break apart without changing the chemicals within the rocks. One main form of physical weathering is from the action of freezing water. Water from rain, rivers, or streams may flow over a rock and fill any small cracks in the rock's surface. Then, as the water freezes in cold weather, the ice tends to widen the cracks in the rock and split it into pieces. Nothing has been added to or taken from the rock; it has just been broken apart.

A second type of weathering is called *chemical weathering*. In this process, chemical changes cause a rock to become soft and crumble. These chemical changes occur because rock is exposed to water and atmospheric gases. For example, when iron in a rock is exposed to water, it forms rust. Rust is created from the combination of the iron in the rock and the oxygen gas that is present in water.

Sometimes plants and animals can cause physical and chemical weathering. For example, the roots of plants may grow in small cracks in rocks. As the plants increase in size, they push the rocks apart and cause them to split. Chemicals present in the plant root may help dissolve the rock. Burrowing animals such as gophers and worms also add to the weathering process. Their tunnels allow water and atmospheric gases to penetrate more easily into surface soil.

Erosion

Erosion is defined as the natural movement of rock fragments over the surface of the Earth. The three main causes of erosion are gravity, wind, and water.

Because of the force of gravity, rock fragments always fall to the lowest point they can. This effect is called *gravity erosion*. If small rock pieces break off from solid rock high on a cliff, they will fall until other rocks stop them. Hillsides covered with loose rock are often the result of the gravity erosion of rocks higher up.

Wind erosion acts mainly on small rock fragments such as loose soil and sand. An important part of wind erosion occurs when fine, hard rock particles are carried in a strong wind. This stream of particles can act like a sand-blaster when they strike other rock formations. Thus, wind erosion can add to the effects of both weathering and gravity erosion.

The most powerful of all types of erosion is caused by running water. A river tends to move rock fragments along the direction of its flow. As shown in the diagram below, water erosion produces a river canyon.

Exercise 15: The Changing Earth

Directions: Write the answer to each question below.

1. What is soil made from? _____ and _____

2. In what way do small ground animals play a part in the process of

   weathering? _____

   _____

3. After a new concrete slab is poured for a driveway, what tends to occur first,

   weathering or erosion? _____

Exercise 16: Weathering and Erosion

Directions: Choose the best answer to each question below. Questions 1–5 are based on the following definitions:

(1) Physical weathering—weathering (the breaking up of rocks) that does not involve chemical change

(2) Chemical weathering—weathering that does involve chemical change

(3) Wind erosion—rock movement caused by wind

(4) Water erosion—rock movement caused by water

(5) Gravity erosion—rock movement caused by gravity

1. When ocean waves move sand from the north end of a beach to the south end, what process is occurring?

    (1) physical weathering
    (2) chemical weathering
    (3) wind erosion
    (4) water erosion
    (5) gravity erosion

2. In a landslide, tons of rocks slide from the top of a cliff down to the bottom. This is an example of

    (1) physical weathering
    (2) chemical weathering
    (3) wind erosion
    (4) water erosion
    (5) gravity erosion

3. Trapped carbon dioxide gas in a mineral reacts with water washing over the mineral and forms an acid that causes the mineral to crumble. This is an example of

    (1) physical weathering
    (2) chemical weathering
    (3) wind erosion
    (4) water erosion
    (5) gravity erosion

4. Rainwater seeps into a crack in a piece of granite, and the granite breaks apart when the water later freezes. Which of the following processes has happened to the granite?

    (1) physical weathering
    (2) chemical weathering
    (3) wind erosion
    (4) water erosion
    (5) gravity erosion

5. Which of the following processes is most important in the continually changing shape of land features now characteristic of the Sahara Desert?

   (1) physical weathering
   (2) chemical weathering
   (3) wind erosion
   (4) water erosion
   (5) gravity erosion

6. When a river goes round a bend, the river tends to erode the outside curve more than the inside curve. Because of this, a river that contains a slight bend can actually create a small lake that ends up cut off from the river. The small lake that is formed is called an *oxbow lake* because its *U* shape resembles the shape of an oxbow. In the illustration below, the four steps in the formation of an oxbow lake are not arranged in order.

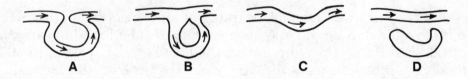

In what order should the drawings above be placed to show how an oxbow lake might develop from a bend in a river?

   (1) A, C, B, D
   (2) C, B, A, D
   (3) B, A, C, D
   (4) D, A, B, C
   (5) C, A, B, D

ANSWERS AND EXPLANATIONS START ON PAGE 300.

 Writing Activity 4

Think about the land features of the area where you live. If you live in a city, you might be able to see the effects of weathering and erosion on sidewalks, buildings, and small patches of grass or dirt. People who live in rural areas might see some of these effects on roads, hillsides, rivers, and fields.

Choose one instance of weathering or erosion in your environment and write a paragraph describing it. If you can determine the cause, include that as well.

ANSWERS WILL VARY.

The Earth's Past

Key Word

fossil—preserved remains or traces of ancient life forms

If the history of the Earth could be compressed into the span of one year's time, the story of the human race would be written as the last two hours of the final day! This fact gives you an idea of just how old the Earth is. Its age is estimated to be between four and five billion years. Although there is no written record to tell us about the Earth's geological past, the Earth itself has left a record in the form of fossils.

The Fossil Record

A fossil is the preserved remains or traces of an ancient living thing. Fossils are most often found buried in rock, but they may also be found in caves, ancient tar beds, and the solid ice that covers the Earth's polar regions. In all these places, fossils are protected from the damaging effects of weathering and erosion.

Usually only the hard parts of a dead plant or animal are preserved. The hard parts can include bones, shells, and woody tissues. The soft parts, like flesh, either decay or are eaten by animals before they can be preserved. One exception is when an organism is subjected to extreme cold. Then the entire body may be preserved in ice. For example, the frozen bodies of extinct woolly mammoths have been found in Siberia.

Sometimes the remains of an organism are preserved after having been changed into a completely different form. For instance, coal deposits on Earth are actually the fossil remains of plants. When plants decompose, eventually only deposits of carbon remain. When the carbon is under extreme pressure for a long period of time, it is slowly transformed into coal. Coal is called a "fossil fuel" because of the way it is created.

Another type of fossil contains only the traces of an organism, not its remains. One common example is footprints left in mud that later hardened into solid rock. Geologists have found dinosaur footprints that are over 100 million years old.

Fossils can help geologists learn about how animal and plant species have changed over time. Since geologists can date the rocks that the fossils are in, they can also tell during what time period in the past a species lived. For example, on the geologic calendar on page 181, you can see that fish first appear in the era labeled *Paleozoic*. This means that the oldest rocks discovered to contain fish fossils are between 225 million and 600 million years old. We can assume that fish existed in the world at least 225 million years ago.

Fossils are also used to study extinct species. For example, there are no longer any living woolly mammoths on Earth, but we can know what a woolly mammoth looked like by studying the frozen bodies found in Siberia.

ERAS	YEARS BEFORE PRESENT	LIFE FORMS

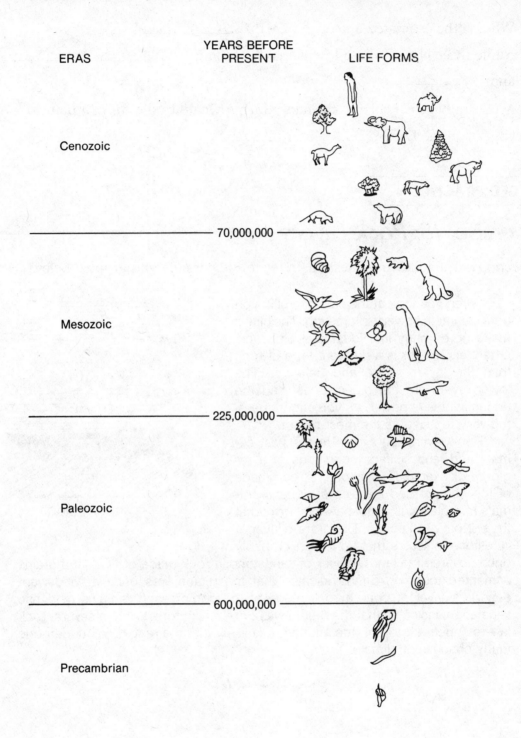

Cenozoic

70,000,000

Mesozoic

225,000,000

Paleozoic

600,000,000

Precambrian

Exercise 17: The Earth's Past

Directions: Write the answer to each question below.

1. What is the estimated age of the Earth? _____

2. Name three places where fossils may be found: _____, _____, and _____.

3. According to the geologic calendar, during what era did human beings appear on the Earth? _____

★ **GED PRACTICE** ★

Exercise 18: Rock Layers

Directions: The following questions refer to the passage and graphic below.

When you look at the side of a cliff, you notice something very interesting. The cliff is made up of many individual layers of rock. Often, each layer is a different type of rock than the layers above and below it. The lower layers are the oldest ones, and the upper layers are newer. As you might guess, the very top layer is the most recent.

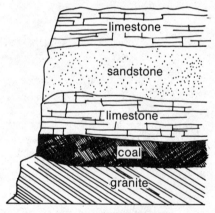

ROCKY RIDGE

Rock layers are a clue to the past climate and land surface conditions of a region. For example, limestone, a rock made of the compressed remains of aquatic animals and plants, is almost always formed at the bottom of an ocean. Therefore, a layer of limestone indicates that an ocean probably once covered the land. A layer of sandstone, a rock made of fine sand grains cemented together, often indicates that the region was once a windswept desert. A layer of coal, a rock made of the compressed remains of dense vegetation, indicates that the region was once a lush forest. When several rock layers appear on top of one another, it is likely that the region has undergone many changes of climate.

1. Which two layers of rock indicate the possibility that a lush tropical forest was covered by a rising ocean in the area that is now called Rocky Ridge?

    (1) the granite layer and the coal layer
    (2) the sandstone layer and upper limestone layer
    (3) the coal layer and the lower limestone layer
    (4) the lower limestone layer and the sandstone layer
    (5) the granite layer and the upper limestone layer

2. Which of the following fossils would most likely be found in the upper limestone layer of Rocky Ridge?

    (1) a dinosaur footprint
    (2) a woolly mammoth
    (3) the leaf of an ancient redwood tree
    (4) a thorn from an extinct desert cactus
    (5) an impression of a small sea worm

3. Which of the following fossils would most likely be found in the sandstone layer of Rocky Ridge?

    (1) an impression of a fin of an ancient fish
    (2) a bone fragment from the wing of an extinct type of penguin
    (3) a leg bone from an extinct type of camel
    (4) a jawbone from an extinct animal, similar to a gorilla, that ate mainly vegetables and fruit
    (5) a wing print from an extinct flying tropical insect

4. By looking at the order of rock layers, it is possible to form a hypothesis about the history of this location. It seems likely that this region

    (1) was a desert that later was covered by a tropical forest
    (2) has experienced many changes of climate
    (3) has always been a hot, dry desert
    (4) has mainly been under an ocean
    (5) has been under ice for much of its past

ANSWERS AND EXPLANATIONS START ON PAGE 300.

8
CHEMISTRY

Have you ever wished that you could take a piece of iron, say an old nail, and turn it into gold? What an idea! Think of how different your life would be! Untold riches would be as close as the nearest old scrap pile. Can you believe that anyone would ever take this idea seriously? Well, early chemists once did, and the idea persisted for 1,100 years!

The idea of turning iron into gold was more than just a fanciful wish to alchemists, the chemists of the Middle Ages (A.D. 500–1600). These early scientists searched for a way to change metal into gold and tried to create a medicine that would keep people from aging. Unfortunately for all of us, the alchemists did not achieve their goals. However, their experiments revealed a lot about the metals and other substances they worked with.

Modern chemistry has come a long way since the days of alchemy. Today's chemists seek to understand the structure, composition, and properties of all matter. *Matter* is anything that has weight and takes up space. Matter can be a solid like gold, a liquid like water, or a gas like oxygen.

By learning about the properties of matter, chemists have been able to improve traditional medical remedies. A well-known example is the development of aspirin. During the seventeenth and eighteenth centuries, American Indians used the bark of willow trees as a treatment for fever. Later, chemists discovered that the salycylic acid in the bark was the chemical responsible for the pain-relieving effect. They began to produce this acid in their laboratories. The drug proved to be helpful in easing pain, but it had unpleasant side effects, including stomach irritation. Chemists were able to reduce this irritation by adding another element to salicylic acid. The resulting drug, acetylsalicylic acid, is what we know today as aspirin.

In addition to improving traditional remedies, chemists are also developing new products at an ever-increasing rate. In fact, more than 90 percent of all the medicinal drugs now being used were not available in any form before World War II.

Chemists have also been able to create materials not found in nature. One example is plastic. Plastic has proven to be one of the most durable, inexpensive, and versatile materials known. Milk jugs, telephones, automobile parts, and clothes are just some of the products that can now be made of plastic. Yet, only a few decades ago, plastic was mainly a novelty material used to make children's toys.

Our study of chemistry in this chapter will involve three major topics: the structure of matter, the behavior of matter, and the chemistry of life.

Exercise 1: Overview of Chemistry

Directions: Match each item on the left with the phrase that best describes it on the right. Write the letter of the phrase on the line before the correct number.

_____ **1.** alchemy

_____ **2.** plastic

_____ **3.** willow bark

_____ **4.** matter

_____ **5.** aspirin

a. anything that has weight and takes up space

b. a natural source of salicylic acid

c. a medicinal drug

d. chemistry of the Middle Ages

e. a material not found in nature

★ **GED PRACTICE** ★

Exercise 2: Studying Chemistry

Directions: Choose the best answer to each question below.

1. According to the fourth paragraph of the passage on page 184, aspirin owes its beginnings to the

   (1) plastics industry
   (2) American Eskimos
   (3) American Indians
   (4) alchemists
   (5) early American pioneers

Questions 2 and 3 refer to the information below.

Chemistry is the study of the structure, composition, and properties of matter. In a classroom discussion, students made the following statements about the study of chemistry.

   A. Chemistry is the most difficult science to learn.
   B. There are many practical applications of chemistry.
   C. Much of the knowledge gained from chemistry is also useful in both geology and biology.

2. Which of the above statements is (are) most likely fact and not opinion?

    (1) A only

    (2) B only

    (3) C only

    (4) A and B only

    (5) B and C only

3. Which of the above statements is an opinion?

    (1) A only

    (2) B only

    (3) C only

    (4) A and B only

    (5) B and C only

ANSWERS AND EXPLANATIONS START ON PAGE 300.

 Writing Activity 1

Chemical companies make everyday products like batteries, plastic bags, pesticides, and cleaners. Though such products are valuable to modern society, the chemicals used to manufacture them are often extremely hazardous. Although chemical companies have the best safety record in manufacturing, a series of accidents in 1984 and 1985 caused many people to question safety standards in the chemical industry.

The worst of these accidents occurred in December 1984 in Bhopal, India. Over 2,500 people died when a toxic cloud of methyl isocyanate gas leaked from the Union Carbide plant there.

In one or two paragraphs, explain what you think a chemical company should do in response to a serious accident like this one.

SAMPLE ANSWERS START ON PAGE 300.

The Structure of Matter

The Atomic Theory of Matter

Key Words

element—a pure substance that cannot be broken down into other substances
atom—the smallest unit of an element having the properties of the element
nucleus—the core of an atom
mass—amount of matter

Long before scientists were able to prove it, the ancient Greek philosophers had an idea of what an atom was. They believed that any substance could be divided only so far before you reached the smallest possible piece of that substance. Democritus (460-370 B.C.) called this smallest particle an atom, from the Greek word meaning "indivisible." He believed in the existence of only four types of atoms or elements. Each type accounted for the properties of earth, air, water, and fire. Today our understanding of both elements and atoms is very different from that of Democritus.

We now know that all matter in the world is formed from one or more of ninety-two naturally occurring chemical elements. Each element is a pure substance that cannot be broken down further. You can think of elements as the building blocks of matter. Elements combine to form all known substances in the same way that the letters of the alphabet combine to form words.

Surprisingly, most of the natural elements are very rare. Only fifteen elements make up more than 99 percent of all matter on Earth. You may already know some of these common elements, which include the gases oxygen, hydrogen, and nitrogen, and the metals aluminum, iron, and nickel.

If we divided a gold coin into the smallest unit that still had the properties of gold, we would end up with a single atom of gold. That atom, like the atoms of all other elements, is made up of three types of particles: protons, neutrons, and electrons.

Protons are particles with a positive electric charge, while ***neutrons*** have no electric charge at all. The protons and neutrons make up the nucleus, the core of the atom. They are almost exactly the same size, and each is more than 1,800 times as massive as an electron. Because of this size difference, almost all the mass (amount of matter) of an atom is concentrated in the nucleus.

In their natural state, all atoms have the same number of electrons as protons. The negatively charged ***electrons*** move in orbits around the nucleus. Although the exact path followed by an electron is not known, it is often illustrated as shown in the diagram of a helium atom below.

THE HELIUM ATOM

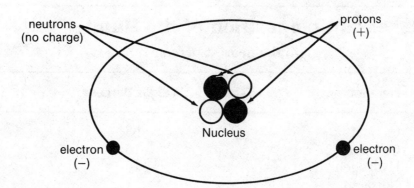

Exercise 3: The Atomic Theory of Matter ━━━

Directions: Answer each question below.

1. Complete each sentence by filling in the blanks with the correct word from the reading passage.

    a. Oxygen and iron are examples of _____.

    b. The only three particles that are found in atoms are _____,

        _____, and _____.

    c. The _____ is the only uncharged particle found in an atom.

2. The statements below refer to the atomic theory of matter. Circle *T* for each statement that is true and *F* for each statement that is false.

    T F a. Almost the entire mass of an atom comes from its electrons and protons.

    T F b. Electrons, protons, and neutrons are found in an atom's nucleus.

    T F c. More than 99 percent of all matter on Earth is made up of only fifteen out of ninety-two naturally occurring elements.

    T F d. Electrons are the only negatively charged particles found in an atom.

★ **GED PRACTICE** ★

Exercise 4: The Elements ━━━

Directions: Questions 1 and 2 refer to the following tables.

| **Elemental Composition of the Human Body** ||
| (to the nearest percent) ||
Element	**Weight Percent**
Oxygen	65
Carbon	18
Hydrogen	10
Nitrogen	3
Calcium	2
Phosphorus	1
Traces of other elements	1

Elemental Composition of the Earth's Crust, Seawater, and Atmosphere

(to the nearest percent)

Element	Weight Percent
Oxygen	49
Silicon	26
Aluminum	8
Iron	5
Calcium	3
Sodium	3
Potassium	2
Magnesium	2
Hydrogen	1
Traces of other elements	1

1. According to the first table, which two elements together make up almost exactly 75 percent of the weight of a human body?

    (1) oxygen and carbon
    (2) oxygen and hydrogen
    (3) carbon and hydrogen
    (4) carbon and nitrogen
    (5) oxygen and nitrogen

2. Which conclusion below can be correctly drawn from the data shown in the two tables?

    (1) Although sodium is present on the Earth, the human body contains no sodium at all.
    (2) The largest single source of oxygen on or near the Earth is the atmosphere.
    (3) Though not present in the human body in a great amount, iron is very important in a healthy diet.
    (4) Carbon is an element that is found in all forms of life that exist on Earth.
    (5) Although carbon is the second most abundant element in the human body, there is little carbon on or near the surface of the Earth.

ANSWERS AND EXPLANATIONS START ON PAGE 300.

The Periodic Table

Do you ever wonder what makes one element different from another? Why is helium different from gold? Helium is a colorless, odorless gas used to fill balloons. But gold is another story! This shiny yellowish metal is valuable in jewelry and in dentistry, and it is the basis of much of the world's money. Who hasn't seen a movie about the Gold Rush in California that took place in the mid-1800s? Can you imagine anyone getting excited about a "Helium Rush"?

Gold in a ring or a tooth differs from helium in a balloon because the atomic structure of gold differs from that of helium. A gold atom has more electrons, protons, and neutrons than a helium atom.

Every element has a unique atomic structure. In other words, no two elements have exactly the same combination of protons, neutrons, and electrons. We can use this uniqueness to identify an element by its mass number and its atomic number.

The mass number is the sum of the protons and neutrons in the nucleus. Aluminum, shown below, has a mass number of 27: it has 13 protons and 14 neutrons. The atomic number is the number of protons in an atom. A neutral atom has an equal number of protons and electrons. Later in this chapter, you'll learn about what happens when an atom is not neutral.

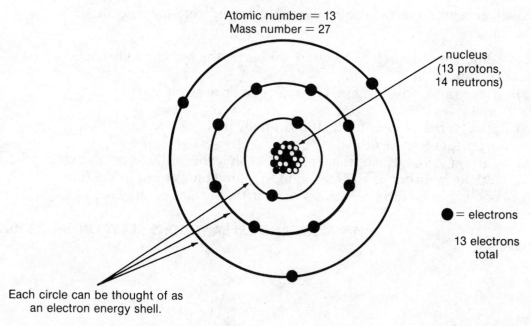

ALUMINUM

Atomic number = 13
Mass number = 27

nucleus
(13 protons,
14 neutrons)

● = electrons

13 electrons
total

Each circle can be thought of as
an electron energy shell.

In each atom, the electrons orbit in energy levels called shells. Each shell can hold only a set number of electrons. Atoms with larger atomic numbers have electrons in several energy shells.

Reading the Periodic Table

Differing shell structure is the basis of the design of the periodic table shown on page 192. Each row (read from left to right and called a ***period***) contains elements that have the same number of shells that are at least partially filled with electrons. Each column (read from top to bottom and called a ***group***) lists elements that have the same number of electrons in their outermost shell.

For example, potassium (K) and calcium (Ca) are both in the fourth period (row), so they have the same number of electron shells. Potassium and lithium (Li) are both in the first column, so they have the same number of electrons in their outermost shells.

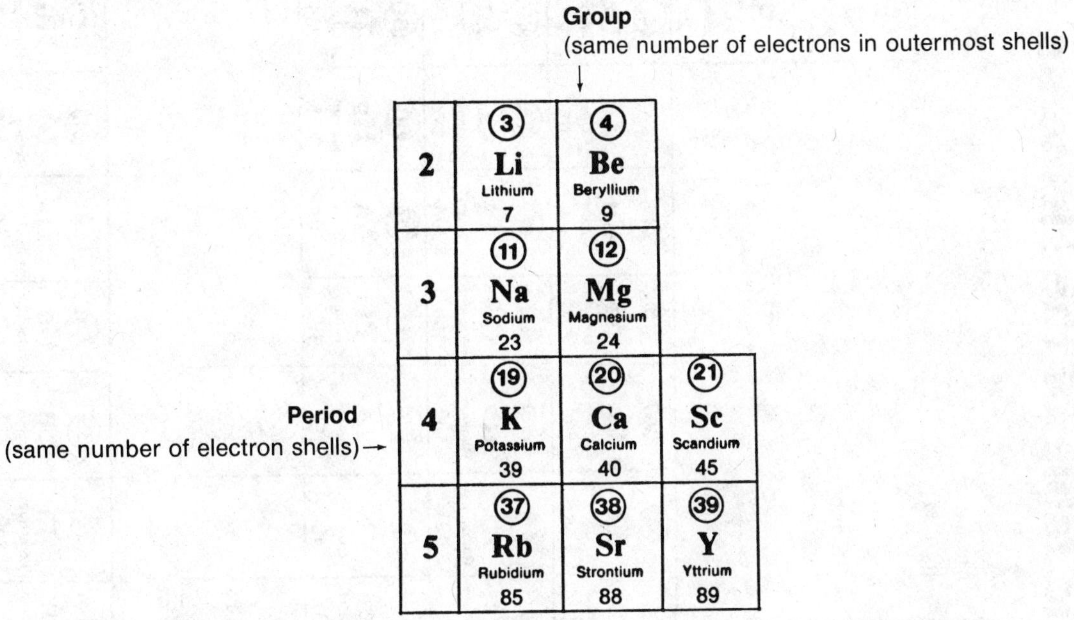
Group
(same number of electrons in outermost shells)
Period
(same number of electron shells)
2
③ Li Lithium 7
④ Be Beryllium 9
3
⑪ Na Sodium 23
⑫ Mg Magnesium 24
4
⑲ K Potassium 39
⑳ Ca Calcium 40
㉑ Sc Scandium 45
5
㊲ Rb Rubidium 85
㊳ Sr Strontium 88
㊴ Y Yttrium 89

Reading from left to right, elements are listed in order of atomic number. Each element in the table is shown with its name, symbol, atomic number, and mass number.

Periodic Table of the Elements

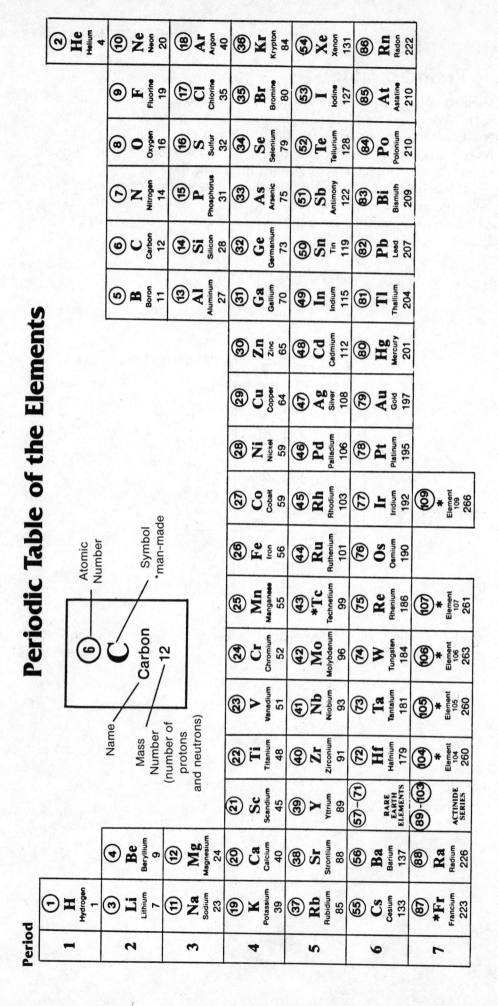

Exercise 5: Protons, Neutrons, and Electrons

Directions: Answer each of the questions below.

1. Complete each sentence by filling in the blanks with the correct word(s) from the reading passage.

    a. The number of protons in an atom is known as that atom's

        _____.

    b. An atom's mass number is the sum of the number of that atom's

        _____ and _____.

2. Sodium (atomic number 11) has a mass number of 23.

    a. How many protons does sodium have in its nucleus? _____

    b. How many neutrons does sodium have in its nucleus? _____

    c. How many electrons does a neutral sodium atom have? _____

★ **GED PRACTICE** ★

Exercise 6: The Periodic Table

Directions: Use the reading passage on pages 190–191 and the periodic table to answer questions 1–3 below.

1. The elements are listed in the periodic table according to

    (1) the number of neutrons in an atom
    (2) the alphabetical order of the atoms' symbols
    (3) the number of protons in an atom
    (4) the sum of the number of neutrons and protons in an atom
    (5) the difference between the number of neutrons and protons in an atom

2. Calcium (atomic number 20) has two electrons in its outermost electron shell. Which of the following elements also has two electrons in its outermost shell?

    (1) potassium (K)
    (2) carbon (C)
    (3) magnesium (Mg)
    (4) helium (He)
    (5) scandium (Sc)

3. Which of the following has the same number of shells as oxygen (atomic number 8)?

    (1) sulfur (S)
    (2) lithium (Li)
    (3) phosphorus (P)
    (4) selenium (Se)
    (5) helium (He)

ANSWERS AND EXPLANATIONS START ON PAGE 301.

Elements in Combination

Key Words

molecule—formed by the combination of two or more atoms
chemical formula—an expression used to indicate the kind and number of atoms in a molecule

Look around you and notice the variety of things in your everyday life. You might see chairs, tables, curtains, windows, water, people, and much, much more. It's hard to believe that this incredible variety is made up almost entirely of combinations of fifteen elements.

When two or more atoms combine, a molecule is formed. For example, a molecule of water is formed when one atom of oxygen combines with two atoms of hydrogen. As this example shows, two elements can combine to form a completely new substance. The newly created substance—in this case, water—is called a *compound*.

Chemical Formulas

To show which elements are contained in a molecule, chemists write a chemical formula. They use symbols to show which elements (from the periodic table) are present. They use small numbers to show how many atoms there are of each molecule.

For example, H_2O is the formula for water. The subscript *2* (small number 2) tells us there are two atoms of hydrogen in one molecule of water. The *O*, written without a subscript, tells us that one atom of oxygen is in each molecule of water.

Similarly, in the formula for the gas fuel propane, C_3H_8, each propane molecule contains three atoms of carbon and eight atoms of hydrogen.

When a number is written in front of a formula, it indicates that more than one molecule is represented. The formula $4H_2O$ represents four molecules of water. Notice that four molecules of water contain eight atoms of hydrogen ($4 \times 2 = 8$) and four atoms of oxygen ($4 \times 1 = 4$).

Exercise 7: Chemical Formulas

Directions: Answer each of the following questions.

1. **a.** In the formula Al_2O_3, how many atoms of aluminum (Al) are represented?

   _____

   b. In the formula $5C_3H_8$, how many molecules of propane are represented?

   _____

   c. In the formula $3H_2O$, how many atoms of hydrogen are represented?

   _____

2. The drawing at the right shows the molecular structure of isobutane. Each *H* stands for a hydrogen atom, and each *C* stands for a carbon atom. Write a formula to represent this molecule. Write carbon as the first element shown in the formula.

_____

Isobutane Molecule

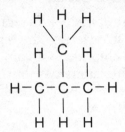

★ **GED PRACTICE** ★

Exercise 8: Elements in Combination

Directions: Choose the best way to complete each statement below.

1. One molecule of the iron oxide commonly called *rust* contains two atoms of iron (Fe) and three atoms of oxygen (O). The formula that represents two molecules of rust is written

   (1) Fe_2O_32
   (2) $2Fe_3O_2$
   (3) Fe_4O_6
   (4) $2Fe_22O_3$
   (5) $2Fe_2O_3$

2. Glucose is a sugar that is made by green plant cells. From its chemical formula, $C_6H_{12}O_6$, you can tell that one molecule of glucose contains

   (1) six atoms of hydrogen and twelve atoms of oxygen
   (2) six atoms of carbon, twelve atoms of hydrogen, and six atoms of oxygen
   (3) six atoms of carbon, twelve atoms of oxygen, and six atoms of hydrogen
   (4) one atom of carbon, six atoms of hydrogen, and twelve atoms of oxygen
   (5) six atoms of carbon, twelve atoms of helium, and six atoms of oxygen

ANSWERS AND EXPLANATIONS START ON PAGE 301.

Chemical Bonding

Key Word
ion—an atom that has either gained or lost an electron

The combining of atoms is a process called ***chemical bonding***. Chemical bonding results from either the transfer or the sharing of electrons between atoms.

Ionic Bonds

An *ionic bond* is formed when an electron in the outermost energy shell of one atom transfers to the outermost shell of a second atom. Ordinary table salt, sodium chloride, is a compound formed by the ionic bonding of sodium atoms to chlorine atoms. As illustrated below, a sodium atom has one electron in its outer shell, while a chlorine atom has seven electrons in its outer shell.

SODIUM AND CHLORINE ATOMS

(Only the electrons in the outermost
energy shells are shown.)

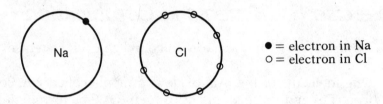

● = electron in Na
○ = electron in Cl

When the two atoms combine, the outer electron of the sodium atom transfers to the chlorine atom. After the transfer, neither atom is electrically neutral any longer. Each is an ion, an atom that has either lost or gained an electron.

SODIUM CHLORIDE

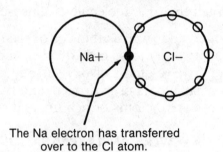

The Na electron has transferred
over to the Cl atom.

Having lost an electron, the sodium atom now has a positive charge, while the chlorine atom has a negative charge because it has gained an electron. Since unlike charges attract, the positive sodium ion is bonded to (attracted by and held close to) the negative chlorine atom.

Covalent Bonds

In a *covalent bond*, electrons are not transferred from one atom to another. Instead, electrons are shared by the bonded atoms.

This is how a molecule of water is formed: by the covalent bonding of two hydrogen atoms to one oxygen atom. As illustrated below on the left, an oxygen atom has six electrons in its outermost shell. As shown in the diagram on the right, each hydrogen atom in a water molecule shares its one electron with the oxygen atom and also shares one of the oxygen atom's electrons. This means that four electrons are shared in a water molecule, two in each of the covalent bonds.

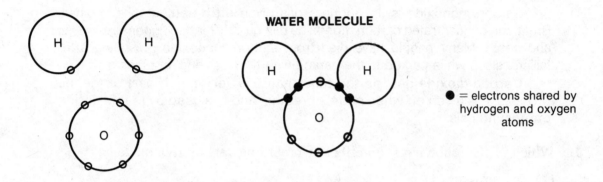

Exercise 9: Chemical Bonding

Directions: Answer each question below.

1. Match each item on the left with a phrase that best describes it on the right. Write the letter of the phrase on the line before the correct number.

   _____ **a.** chemical bonding   **(1)** an atom that has either a positive or negative charge

   _____ **b.** water   **(2)** a compound formed by ionic bonding

   _____ **c.** ion   **(3)** the chemical combining of two or more atoms

   _____ **d.** sodium chloride   **(4)** a compound formed by covalent bonding

2. Write a brief definition for each of the two types of chemical bonds:

   ionic bond: _____

   covalent bond: _____

★ GED PRACTICE ★

Exercise 10: Different Combinations of Elements————

Directions: Questions 1–4 refer to the following reading selection.

Two different elements may combine in more than one way and form compounds with very different properties. For example, the elements carbon and oxygen can combine to form carbon monoxide, CO, or carbon dioxide, CO_2.

Carbon monoxide is an odorless gas given off by automobile engines. Breathing concentrated carbon monoxide can quickly lead to unconsciousness and death. Many people have died from carbon monoxide poisoning after falling asleep while parked in the garage with their car engine running.

Carbon dioxide gas, on the other hand, is very much part of the life process. It is given off when people breathe, and it is used by plants during photosynthesis.

1. Which of the following is an effect of breathing carbon monoxide gas?

   (1) respiration
   (2) unconsciousness
   (3) photosynthesis
   (4) breathing
   (5) running

2. What is the most important safety consideration in an automobile repair shop?

   (1) a separate lunch room away from the working area
   (2) CPR training for all employees
   (3) properly designed tools
   (4) a safe level of ventilation
   (5) up-to-date repair manuals

3. Assume your car is parked in your garage on a freezing morning and that you can enter your garage from a door in the kitchen. Now read the following four steps, which are not in any particular order:

   A. Let the car warm up.
   B. Start the car.
   C. Drive out onto the driveway.
   D. Open the garage door.

   If you want to go for a drive and hope to emerge alive from your garage, what is the safest order of steps to follow after entering the garage and shutting the kitchen door?

   (1) B, A, D, C
   (2) D, B, C, A
   (3) B, A, C, D
   (4) C, A, B, D
   (5) D, B, A, C

4. Runners often complain of feeling light-headed or dizzy while running on or near busy city streets. A possible cause of the dizziness is that, near busy streets, there tends to be a high level of

   (1) carbon dioxide
   (2) oxygen
   (3) carbon monoxide
   (4) traffic noise
   (5) very dry air

ANSWERS AND EXPLANATIONS START ON PAGE 301.

 Writing Activity 2

Imagine being enveloped in a cloud of yellowish-white dust or stumbling across a strange white substance that looks like paint. Your eyes begin to burn, your vision fades, and you choke trying to get a breath of air.

Scenes like this result from such chemical weapons as mustard gas, yellow rain, and nerve gas. Even though chemical warfare is illegal all over the world, experts are worried that this method of fighting is occurring in the Persian Gulf, Southeast Asia, and Afghanistan.

Why do you think the United Nations has tried to forbid the use of chemical weapons but has not banned guns or nuclear weapons? Think about how chemical weapons are different from guns or tanks. Explain and support your opinions in one or two paragraphs.

SAMPLE ANSWERS START ON PAGE 301.

Behavior of Matter

Phases of Matter

Key Words

solid—matter that has definite shape and definite volume
liquid—matter that has definite volume but not definite shape
gas—matter that has neither definite shape nor definite volume

A chemical formula tells us a lot about a substance, but it doesn't tell us everything. For example, when you see the formula H_2O, you know that it stands for a water molecule. But what form of water: ice, liquid water, or steam? If you say, "All three," you're right! The formula H_2O identifies a water molecule, and it can be water in any of its three forms: solid water (ice), liquid water, or water vapor (steam).

These three forms of substances—solid, liquid, and gas—are called the three *phases of matter.* To understand the properties of each phase, you need only examine some common, everyday objects.

- *Solids:* Pick up a piece of wood or a metal spoon. Though they don't look at all alike, they do share the two common properties of solids: all solids have definite size and shape. Place a spoon in a dish, and the spoon will be unchanged in size or shape.

- *Liquids:* Pour a glass of water into a dish. Notice how the water takes the shape of the dish. Also notice that the volume of the dish that is filled is equal to the volume of the glass that was filled. This simple experiment indicates that liquids have a definite volume, but not a definite shape. A liquid will take the shape of any container that holds it.

- *Gases:* Add a little more air to a soft, but not flat, football. Observe that the ball does not change shape. The entering gas easily takes the shape of the ball and crowds in as necessary without noticeably affecting the ball's shape. From this, we can see that gases, such as those in air, have neither definite shape nor definite volume. A gas will spread out or contract as needed to fill uniformly any container that encloses it.

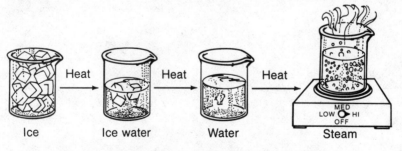

The three phases of water: ice, liquid, and steam

Changing from One Phase to Another

All substances change from one phase to another when their temperature is raised or lowered to certain points. Raise the temperature of ice (a solid) to its melting point temperature, and the ice turns into liquid water. With enough heat, even solid iron can be made to liquefy.

In a similar way, a liquid can be changed to a gas. If the temperature of water is raised to its boiling point, water becomes steam or vapor—the gaseous phase of a substance that's normally a liquid.

A gas becomes liquid when its temperature is lowered to its condensation point. Steam from a shower immediately condenses as water droplets on cool mirrors and cold-water pipes. Similarly, when the temperature of a liquid drops to its freezing point, a liquid hardens into a solid. Droplets of water, placed in a freezer, quickly turn to ice.

For many common substances, the melting point is the same as the freezing point, and the boiling point is the same as the condensation point. Because they appear so often in science, it's useful to remember these values for water at sea level. The freezing point of water (melting point of ice) is 32°F (Fahrenheit) or, equivalently, 0°C (Celsius). The boiling point of water (condensation point of steam) is 212°F or, equivalently, 100°C.

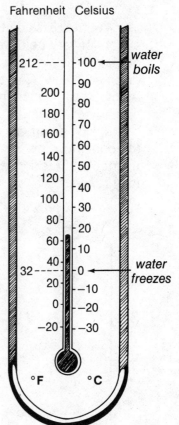

Exercise 11: Phases of Matter

Directions: Complete each sentence by filling in the blanks with the correct word(s) from the reading selection.

1. The temperature at which a liquid turns into a gas is called the liquid's

   _____.

2. The temperature at which a liquid turns into a solid is called the liquid's

   _____.

3. The freezing point of water is _____°F or _____°C, and the boiling point of water is _____°F or _____°C.

Exercise 12: Freezing Point

Directions: Questions 1–4 are based on the reading passage and graph below.

Antifreeze is added to a car's cooling system to protect the engine from the effects of very cold weather. Without antifreeze, a car's cooling system would contain only water. The water would freeze solid when the air temperature dropped below 32°F, the freezing point of water, and the car was not running. As many car owners have discovered, a frozen coolant can crack the block of an engine.

Mixing antifreeze with the radiator water lowers the freezing temperature of the coolant below 32°F. With the proper amount of antifreeze, you can reduce the coolant freezing temperature to well below any temperature the outside air may reach.

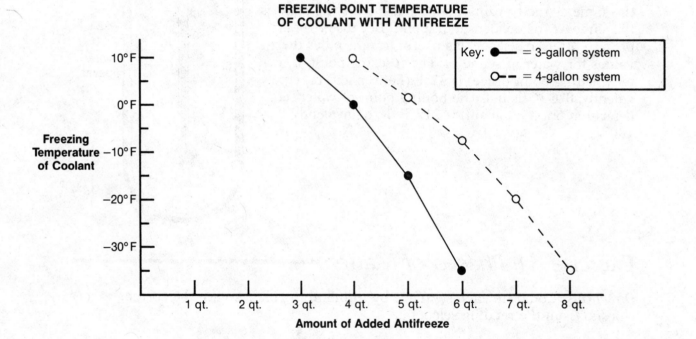

FREEZING POINT TEMPERATURE OF COOLANT WITH ANTIFREEZE

Key: ●— = 3-gallon system
O-- = 4-gallon system

1. For a car with a three-gallon cooling system, how many quarts of antifreeze are needed to protect the engine down to a temperature of −15°F?

   (1) 3
   (2) 4
   (3) 5
   (4) 6
   (5) 7

2. Assume you have a car with a four-gallon cooling system that is now protected to about 0°F. How many more quarts of antifreeze should you buy to add enough to lower the protection temperature to about −20°F?

  (1) 1
  (2) 2
  (3) 3
  (4) 4
  (5) 5

3. The graph on page 202 provides no information about antifreeze for temperatures

  (1) between 10°F and −35°F
  (2) below 10°F
  (3) above −35°F
  (4) above −10°F and below 10°F
  (5) above 10°F and below −35°F

4. From the information presented in the graph, you can conclude that a car with a larger cooling system

  (1) requires more antifreeze than a car with a smaller system
  (2) requires less antifreeze than a car with a smaller system
  (3) requires the same amount of antifreeze as a car with a smaller system
  (4) does not require antifreeze for temperatures above 10°F
  (5) does not require antifreeze for temperatures below −35°F

ANSWERS AND EXPLANATIONS START ON PAGE 301.

Physical and Chemical Changes

Key Words

physical change—a change that does not produce a new substance
chemical change—a change in which a new substance is created

In nature, change is continually taking place. We don't usually pay attention to changes like the evaporation of water into steam. Some changes, like babies growing, we welcome; while others, like cars rusting, we don't. But all changes in nature, welcome or not, are interesting to chemists.

When ice cream melts, it changes from a solid to a liquid. Yet we still recognize it as ice cream. We know it by its color and taste, even though it may not be as cold as we'd like. What's more, by simply putting the melted ice cream in the freezer, we can change it back to its more solid texture.

Melting ice cream is an example of a physical change. During a physical change, a substance may change shape, size, or state, but the qualities by which you identify that substance don't change. In other words, the substance may look different, but it has not turned into a new substance. Melting, boiling, freezing, condensing, and cutting are all examples of physical changes.

On the other hand, burning wood is an example of a chemical change. During a chemical change, a substance breaks down or combines with another substance to become something different, with different qualities from the original substance. While burning, wood changes to ashes, carbon dioxide gas, and water. No simple act, like placing the ashes in the freezer, can change the ashes back to wood. Other examples of chemical change include milk souring, iron rusting, paint oxidizing, and glue hardening.

Exercise 13: Physical and Chemical Changes ───

Directions: Answer each question below.

1. Write a brief definition for each of the two types of change, stressing their differences:

   physical change: _____

   chemical change: _____

2. Write the type of change (physical or chemical) that is taking place in each action described below.

   _____ **a.** An iron nail, left in the rain, rusts.

   _____ **b.** A board is sawed into three smaller pieces.

   _____ **c.** Gasoline burns in a car's engine.

   _____ **d.** A glass vase drops and shatters as it crashes on the floor.

★ **GED PRACTICE** ★

Exercise 14: Observing Physical Changes ───

Directions: Choose the best answer for each question below.

1. Suppose that a quart of frozen ice cream is taken out of the freezer and left at room temperature for thirty minutes. Which of the following would be most important in determining whether all the ice cream melts?

   (1) the type of ice cream
   (2) the room temperature
   (3) the outdoor temperature
   (4) the size of the freezer
   (5) the shape of the ice cream container

2. Melting a cube of ice and sanding a rough board are both examples of physical changes. Thinking about these two examples, which of the following statements is (are) true?

    A. A physical change in a substance can always be reversed, and the substance returned to its original form.

    B. A physical change in a substance can never be reversed.

    C. Some types of physical changes are reversible, while other types are not.

    D. Both a change of phase and a change of shape are examples of physical changes.

    (1) A only
    (2) B only
    (3) C only
    (4) A and D only
    (5) C and D only

ANSWERS AND EXPLANATIONS START ON PAGE 302.

Chemical Reactions

Key Words

chemical reaction—the combining of two or more substances to form a new substance

chemical equation—expression used to show a chemical reaction

reactants—substances that combine in a chemical reaction

products—substances formed by chemical reactions

Chemists spend most of their time investigating chemical changes. In a chemical change, two or more substances combine to form one or more new substances. This process is called a chemical reaction.

To describe what happens in a chemical reaction, chemists use a kind of shorthand known as a chemical equation. The equation shows the formulas of the reactants (the substances combining) and the products (the new substances formed). An arrow shows the direction in which the reaction proceeds.

For example, the equation for the formation of a water molecule is written as follows:

$$2H_2 + O_2 \longrightarrow 2H_2O$$

Reading from left to right, the equation says that two molecules of hydrogen combine with one molecule of oxygen to form two molecules of water. The formulas $2H_2$ and O_2 indicate that both hydrogen and oxygen molecules are made up of two atoms.

A second example of a chemical reaction is the formation of ammonia, $2NH_3$. Ammonia is formed when nitrogen (N) reacts with hydrogen. The chemical equation for the ammonia reaction is as follows:

$$N_2 + 3H_2 \longrightarrow 2NH_3$$

In words, one molecule of nitrogen combines with three molecules of hydrogen to produce two molecules of ammonia.

The Law of Conservation of Matter

In studying chemical reactions, chemists have observed that new atoms neither appear nor disappear during a chemical reaction. If there are two atoms of nitrogen on the left side of the equation, there must be two atoms of nitrogen on the right side of the equation. And, if there are six atoms of hydrogen on the left side, there must be six atoms of hydrogen on the right side. The Law of Conservation of Matter says that matter is neither created nor destroyed during a chemical reaction.

Exercise 15: Chemical Reactions

Directions: Answer each question below.

1. Complete each sentence by filling in the blanks with the correct word(s).

    a.   A _____ _____ is used to describe a chemical reaction.

    b.   The _____ are the substances that combine during a chemical

    reaction, and the _____ are the substances that are formed.

2. Respiration takes place in your body's cells to provide the energy necessary for all of your activities. During respiration, glucose reacts with oxygen obtained from your breathing. The products of the reaction are carbon dioxide gas, water, and energy. The chemical equation for respiration can be written as follows:

    $$C_6H_{12}O_6 + 6O_2 \longrightarrow 6CO_2 + 6H_2O$$

    The following questions refer to the equation for respiration.

    a.   How many molecules of glucose are represented in the equation? _____

    b.   How many total molecules result when one molecule of glucose combines with six molecules of oxygen? _____

    c.   How many atoms of hydrogen appear on each side of the equation? ____

★ GED PRACTICE ★

Exercise 16: Chemical Reactions in a Greenhouse——

Directions: Questions 1–3 are based on the following paragraph.

Photosynthesis is a chemical reaction that naturally takes place in plant cells when they're exposed to sunlight. During photosynthesis, carbon dioxide gas reacts with water to produce glucose, oxygen gas, and water. The chemical equation for photosynthesis can be written as follows:

$$6CO_2 + 12H_2O \longrightarrow C_6H_{12}O_6 + 6O_2 + 6H_2O$$

This reaction is needed for a plant to live and grow. If photosynthesis does not occur, a plant will die.

1. In the equation for photosynthesis, how many molecules of water are produced in the formation of one molecule of glucose?

   (1) one
   (2) six
   (3) seven
   (4) twelve
   (5) eighteen

2. For commercial purposes, great numbers of flowers are grown in sunlit buildings, called *greenhouses*, that have clear plastic or glass walls and roofs. Using controlled ventilation and watering, the greenhouse temperature and humidity are kept at levels that provide the best growing climate for the enclosed plants.

   If the attendant forgets to water a row of flowers during a hot summer month, the flowers might die. Without water, the flowers could not

   (1) keep their temperature at a safe level
   (2) produce the glucose they use as a source of life energy
   (3) get oxygen from the soil
   (4) reflect harmful sunlight that damages glucose
   (5) produce the carbon dioxide needed to capture the sun's energy

3. Many greenhouse operators believe that burning natural gas year-round in their greenhouses will shorten the growing time needed for plants to mature.

   Which of the following facts about natural gas best supports what these growers believe?

   (1) Burning natural gas produces heat.
   (2) Burning natural gas places chemical impurities in the air.
   (3) Burning natural gas produces light.
   (4) Burning natural gas uses up oxygen gas.
   (5) Burning natural gas produces carbon dioxide gas.

ANSWERS AND EXPLANATIONS START ON PAGE 302.

Solutions

Key Words

solution—uniform mixing of one substance with another
solute—substance that is dissolved in a solution
solvent—substance that dissolves the solute

If we had to choose a single word to describe the mix of elements that appear on and within the Earth, that word would be solution. Solutions are everywhere in nature. The air we breathe is a solution of gases. The water in the ocean is a solution of salt and other minerals, as anyone who's tasted it unhappily realizes. The fiery liquid interior of the Earth is believed to be one gigantic solution, a molten sea of elements and compounds.

To understand what a solution is, think of what happens when you drop a cube of sugar into a glass of water. While you watch, the sugar disappears. But is it really gone? If you taste the water, you'll find that it has a sweet taste. This lets you know that the sugar is still there, even if you don't see it.

When the sugar disappears in the water, we say that the sugar has dissolved. As it dissolves, the molecules of sugar become evenly distributed among the molecules of water. Because of this, the water is equally sweet everywhere. This even mixing of one substance with another is what defines a solution.

Two words used to describe a solution are solvent and solute. The substance that is dissolved is called the solute. The solvent is the substance that dissolves the solute. In a sugar solution, sugar is the solute and water is the solvent: the water dissolves the sugar.

Though solutions are very common, not every mixture forms a solution. For example, when sand is mixed with water, it appears at first to go into solution. But if you wait a few minutes, the sand will settle to the bottom. Sand does not dissolve in water.

Exercise 17: Solutions

Directions: Match each item on the left with the phrase that best describes it on the right. Write the letter of the phrase on the line before the correct number.

_____ **1.** solution   **a.** a solution made up of numerous gases

_____ **2.** solute   **b.** a dissolving agent

_____ **3.** solvent   **c.** a dissolved substance

_____ **4.** air   **d.** an even mixture of one or more substances

★ GED PRACTICE ★

Exercise 18: Types of Solutions

Directions: Read the selection below and then answer the questions that follow.

We usually think of a solution as a solid dissolved in a liquid or as a liquid dissolved in a liquid, but other kinds of solutions are also common. For example, air is a solution of gases that includes nitrogen, oxygen, hydrogen, and helium.

Gases can also be dissolved in a liquid. In carbonated soft drinks, carbon dioxide gas is dissolved in the water along with sugar and flavor additives.

Finally, solids can also be dissolved in solids. For example, metal alloys are made by dissolving one metal in another. To form an alloy, both metals are melted and then mixed as liquids. The solution of liquid metal is then cooled back to a solid. As an example, brass is an alloy made by dissolving zinc in copper. As an alloy, brass has qualities that are a mixture of the qualities of zinc and copper. Because of the presence of zinc, brass is much stronger than copper but it is less flexible.

1. Cola drinks are examples of carbonated soft drinks. What type of solution do they represent?

    (1) liquid dissolved in liquid
    (2) solid dissolved in liquid
    (3) gas dissolved in gas
    (4) gas dissolved in liquid
    (5) solid dissolved in solid

2. Paint thinner is added to paint in order to make the paint easier to work with. Water is a common paint thinner that is used in latex house paints. Which type of solution is represented by paint thinner and paint?

    (1) liquid dissolved in liquid
    (2) solid dissolved in liquid
    (3) gas dissolved in gas
    (4) gas dissolved in liquid
    (5) solid dissolved in solid

3. Many people make punch at home by adding powdered punch mix to water. How would you classify this punch mixture?

    (1) liquid dissolved in liquid
    (2) solid dissolved in liquid
    (3) gas dissolved in gas
    (4) gas dissolved in liquid
    (5) solid dissolved in solid

ANSWERS AND EXPLANATIONS START ON PAGE 302.

The Chemistry of Life

Properties of Carbon

Key Word

organic—produced by a living thing

On the morning of July 20, 1976, the *Viking I* lander slowly drifted, with parachutes open, down to the dusty, red surface of the plain of Chryse. The *Viking* would soon begin its mission to look for life on Mars, the planet that would now be its home. To aid in this search, *Viking II* would touch down on the Martian plain of Utopia on September 3. Disappointingly, neither landing craft was able to find any organic molecules, the fingerprints of life, on the windy, rust-colored surface.

Organic, from the word *organism*, refers to compounds produced by living things. All organic compounds contain the element carbon. Organic molecules form easily in environments that are rich in carbon and water. Scientists knew that water was present on Mars (in its polar ice caps) and that the Martian atmosphere consisted mostly of carbon dioxide gas, so it seemed likely that organic molecules could be found there. But no sign of life has yet been found on our distant neighbor.

Carbon is now thought to be so important to the life process that chemists have named the study of carbon **organic chemistry** and refer to it as the "chemistry of life." Several properties of carbon make it such an important element.

Carbon atoms can form covalent bonds with four other atoms at the same time. One or more of these other atoms can be another carbon atom. By linking with each other, carbon atoms can form closed rings or can stretch out in long chains. Each carbon atom in line can then combine with atoms of other elements. In this way, very large organic molecules can form. Below is an example of both a carbon chain molecule and a carbon ring molecule.

Organic Molecules

Butane

```
    H   H   H   H
    |   |   |   |
H—C—C—C—C—H
    |   |   |   |
    H   H   H   H
```

carbon chain

Benzene

carbon ring

Exercise 19: The Chemistry of Life

Directions: Write the answer to each question below.

1. **a.** What two substances are present on Mars that gave scientists hope that there might be life on Mars?

   _____ and _____

   b. What element do all organic compounds contain?

   _____

2. What is the proper name for that branch of chemistry that is often referred to as the "chemistry of life"?

   _____

★ **GED PRACTICE** ★

Exercise 20: Types of Fats

Directions: The questions on page 212 refer to the following reading selection and graph.

Fats are organic compounds made up of carbon, hydrogen, and oxygen. Fats are a large part of most people's diets. However, eating too much fat may cause heart disease and other ailments. Recent research in nutrition and health has led the American Heart Association to conclude that the average American diet is too high in saturated fats (fats found mainly in animal products) and too low in unsaturated fats (oils found mainly in vegetable sources). As the graph below shows, fats from vegetable sources contain different amounts of both unsaturated and saturated fats.

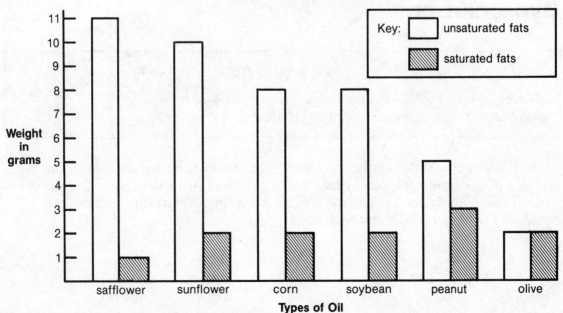

FAT CONTENT OF 1 TABLESPOON OF SELECTED VEGETABLE OILS

1. According to the graph, which vegetable oil contains the greatest amount of unsaturated oil compared to saturated oil?

   (1) safflower oil
   (2) corn oil
   (3) soybean oil
   (4) peanut oil
   (5) olive oil

2. One serving of which oil would give you approximately an equal amount of both saturated and unsaturated fats?

   (1) soybean oil
   (2) safflower oil
   (3) corn oil
   (4) olive oil
   (5) corn oil

3. In a TV commercial, the announcer makes these three statements:

   A. Smitty's oil and vinegar salad dressing contains only oil taken from vegetables grown in America.
   B. Smitty's oil and vinegar salad dressing is the best dressing you've ever tasted.
   C. Smitty's oil and vinegar salad dressing contains only one gram of saturated fat per tablespoon.

   Which of the above statements could be proven to be either true or false by doing a chemical analysis of Smitty's dressing?

   (1) A only
   (2) B only
   (3) C only
   (4) A and C only
   (5) B and C only

ANSWERS AND EXPLANATIONS START ON PAGE 303.

Hydrocarbons

Key Words

hydrocarbon—compound made only of carbon and hydrogen
polymer—hydrocarbon containing a long chain of atoms

Carbon atoms link together so easily that there is almost no limit to the number of different molecules that may be possible. At present, over 3 million carbon compounds are known. Most of these are hydrocarbons, compounds composed of only carbon and hydrogen.

The main sources of hydrocarbons found in nature are coal, natural gas, and petroleum (oil). Natural gas fuels you may be familiar with are methane (CH_4) and propane (C_3H_8). Distillation of petroleum gives us other fuels such as kerosene ($C_{12}H_{26}$) and gasoline, a mixture of hydrocarbons. From petroleum we also get hydrocarbon compounds that are used to make perfumes, pesticides, medicines, and many other consumer products.

Methane   **Propane**   **Kerosene**

The word *polymer* is commonly used to refer to any long-chain hydrocarbon, a hydrocarbon containing a large number of carbon atoms. Most of the modern-day synthetic polymers have been made within the last fifty years. An example is polyethylene, a type of plastic. Polyethylene is a polymer that often contains between 2,500 and 25,000 carbon atoms in each molecule. Polyethylene and other synthetic polymers are used to produce textiles, shoes, toys, plastics, construction materials, medical supplies, cooking utensils, recreational equipment, and synthetic rubber and leather.

Exercise 21: Hydrocarbons ━━━━━━

Directions: Briefly define each of the following words:

1. hydrocarbon: _____

2. polymer: _____

━━━━━━━━━━━

★ **GED PRACTICE** ★

Exercise 22: Products That Contain Hydrocarbons━━

Directions: Choose the best answer to each question below.

1. Which one of the following is *not* a common property of the fuels methane, propane, and kerosene?

   (1) Each fuel contains only carbon and hydrogen atoms.
   (2) In each fuel, every carbon atom links together with more than one hydrogen atom.
   (3) Each fuel is an example of a polymer.
   (4) Each fuel has more hydrogen atoms than carbon atoms.
   (5) Each fuel is in the class of compounds called *hydrocarbons.*

Questions 2 and 3 refer to the circle graph below.

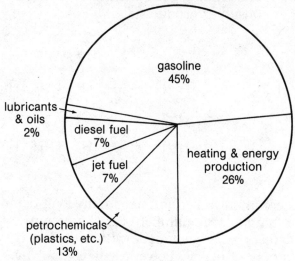

**PERCENT BREAKDOWN OF PETROLEUM
USE IN THE UNITED STATES**

gasoline
45%

lubricants
& oils
2%

diesel fuel
7%

jet fuel
7%

heating & energy
production
26%

petrochemicals
(plastics, etc.)
13%

2. According to the graph above, what is the main petroleum product used in the United States?

    (1) petrochemicals
    (2) diesel fuel
    (3) heating and energy production
    (4) gasoline
    (5) jet fuel

3. What total percentage of petroleum is used for the production of transportation fuels?

    (1) 7 percent
    (2) 14 percent
    (3) 59 percent
    (4) 72 percent
    (5) 98 percent

ANSWERS AND EXPLANATIONS START ON PAGE 303.

Plastic Trash, An Environmental Concern

Key Word
plastic—a commonly used polymer

With the invention of polymers, chemists gave us plastic, an almost ideal material. As a consumer product, plastic is strong, versatile, and durable. It can hold up under heat and pressure and can be subjected to total submersion in water (even ocean water) and not be affected. You can even leave it outside, and it remains almost as good as new, despite the weather. Unlike most other materials, plastic doesn't naturally decay.

For useful consumer products, this remarkable durability is a blessing. Plastic bottles are light and unbreakable; plastic bags don't leak or tear as easily as paper bags do. But when these items are ready for the garbage, it's an environmental nightmare! Millions of tons of plastic garbage litter our highways and beaches.

Plastic trash even affects marine life in the oceans. According to the National Academy of Sciences, more than 600,000 plastic containers and bags are tossed into the oceans every day. Fishermen lose or discard an estimated 150,000 tons of plastic fishing gear each year. At least forty-two species of seabirds are known to snack on plastic, a habit that is often fatal. In addition, tens of thousands of seals, sea lions, and turtles die each year after becoming entangled in bits of fish netting.

What should we do with the hundreds of millions of tons of plastic and other polymer products that end up in the garbage each year? We could burn it. However, that creates a thick, black smoke that is not only intolerable but is also a dangerous form of air pollution. We could bury it, but solid-waste dumps pose their own pollution problems. Too often, trash in the dumps is not buried for a long period of time and becomes a health hazard for birds and other land animals, including nearby human residents. What's more, highly populated countries with limited land may find that land is far too valuable to use as a dump site.

Obviously, a large-scale solution to the plastic trash problem is not yet in sight. However, individuals can help by keeping some of that plastic out of the garbage for as long as possible. For example, people who get plastic bags from the grocery store could save them and reuse them. Some people may choose not to buy plastic products when the same item is available in paper or glass. Of course, these are only small steps, but they could eventually be part of a larger solution.

Exercise 23: Pros and Cons of Plastic———

Directions: Answer each question below.

1. Name three properties of plastic that make it such a useful consumer product. _____ _____ _____

2. Name three types of animals that are known to be harmed by plastic trash.
_____ _____ _____
_____

★ GED PRACTICE ★

Exercise 24: An Environmental Concern———

Directions: Choose the best answer to each question below.

1. What is the main property of plastic that makes it such an environmental concern?

   (1) the ease with which it can be broken
   (2) its use in such a wide range of consumer products
   (3) that it can be manufactured anywhere in the world
   (4) its resistance to weathering or to decay
   (5) its light weight compared to steel

2. Following are four methods of disposing of polymer trash:

   A. dumping it in the ocean miles from shore
   B. recycling (reusing) polymer consumer products
   C. burning polymer trash on disposal ships far out at sea
   D. burying polymer trash in a properly designed and carefully regulated solid-waste dump

   Which of the above methods are environmentally unsound?

   (1) B and C only
   (2) C and D only
   (3) A and C only
   (4) A, B, and D only
   (5) A, C, and D only

ANSWERS AND EXPLANATIONS START ON PAGE 303.

Writing Activity 3

One possible solution to the plastic trash problem is recycling. In the past decade, communities across the United States have begun recycling plastic, glass, newspaper, and some metal waste. Do you think that recycling can help solve our garbage problems? Write a paragraph or two explaining your opinion.

ANSWERS WILL VARY.

The Greenhouse Effect

Key Word

greenhouse effect—a warming of the Earth's atmosphere as a result of pollution

Life on Earth is made possible by a delicate balance of many biological and chemical factors. If this balance is upset, the results can be disastrous. You already know how the disposal of garbage can affect the lives of many land and marine animals. In this section, we'll discuss how another form of pollution can affect all life on Earth simply by causing a slow increase in the temperature of our planet.

Our close neighbor, the planet Venus, has experienced such a temperature increase. Because it is the closest planet to the Earth and appears to be made up of the same minerals, you might think that Venus is a place where living organisms could develop and grow. Not so. In fact, the surface temperature of Venus is about 900°F—so hot that no form of life could hope to exist there.

The reason that Venus is so hot is that its atmosphere contains a large amount of carbon dioxide. Because of this gas, Venus can't cool the way other planets cool, by sending heat energy back out into space. Instead, the heat energy is absorbed by the carbon dioxide.

This natural heating of the atmosphere of Venus is commonly called the greenhouse effect. The greenhouse effect gets its name from the glass-sided and glass-roofed buildings that you see in plant nurseries. In a nursery greenhouse, sunlight freely passes though the glass and warms the soil, plants, and air inside. The glass prevents the heat from leaving. The result is that the greenhouse stays warm enough for plant growth even though the temperature outside may be below freezing. On Venus, the dense carbon dioxide atmosphere traps heat and keeps surface heat energy from escaping back into space. Unfortunately, unlike a real greenhouse, the high temperature on Venus can't be controlled simply by opening a few windows!

On Earth, the current level of carbon dioxide gas in the atmosphere keeps the Earth's temperature in the range it is in now. However, the burning of wood, coal, oil, and other hydrocarbons is adding an abnormal amount of carbon dioxide to the atmosphere. The result is that the level of this gas has been slowly increasing since at least 1958, when scientists started to follow carefully atmospheric levels of carbon dioxide. The Earth's temperature has been gradually going up as well. Most probably, the increases have taken place since the beginning of the Industrial Revolution in the late eighteenth century.

CONSTANT CO₂ IN ATMOSPHERE

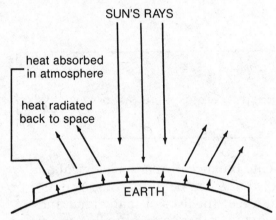

With a constant level of carbon dioxide in the atmosphere, the Earth cools by radiating excess heat back into space.

INCREASED CO₂ IN ATMOSPHERE

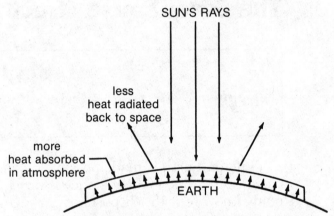

As the high level of carbon dioxide in the atmosphere increases, the Earth's average temperature also increases.

Consequences of the Greenhouse Effect

No one is sure just what the consequences of the greenhouse effect will be in the long run. However, many scientists feel that, if the addition of carbon dioxide to the atmosphere continues unchecked, several things could eventually happen:

- The average surface temperature of the Earth will increase, perhaps by as much as 6°F to 10°F in the next fifty years.

- The warming effect will cause a lot of glacial ice to melt. This will result in the oceans rising by a couple of feet during the same fifty years. Over a period of a couple of hundred years, ocean levels could rise by as much as twenty or more feet. Cities like San Francisco and New York would find themselves under water!

- A rising surface temperature will also probably change world rainfall patterns. The United States, now the breadbasket of the world, could become an arid, parched wasteland.

Though no one is sure just how serious these effects may be and how soon they may occur, one thing is certain: all the countries on Earth live together under a single shared atmosphere. People are now coming to see that proper care of this atmosphere is a must if the Earth's environment is to remain capable of sustaining human life.

Exercise 25: The Greenhouse Effect

Directions: Write an answer to each question below.

1. What name is given to the glass-sided, glass-roofed buildings you see in plant nurseries? _____

2. What role does carbon dioxide gas play in the greenhouse effect? _____

_____

★ **GED PRACTICE** ★

Exercise 26: Consequences of the Greenhouse Effect

Directions: Choose the best answer to each question below.

1. Which of the following is most similar to the heating that takes place inside a nursery greenhouse?

   (1) warming yourself by standing in front of a fireplace in a closed room
   (2) being warmed by sunlight while sitting inside a car with all the windows closed
   (3) becoming suntanned while lying on the beach on a warm summer day
   (4) warming yourself after a shower by standing under a sunlamp
   (5) keeping warm on a cold day by wearing a wool sweater and a heavy overcoat

2. Which of the following is given as the cause of the greenhouse effect that's starting to occur on Earth?

   (1) the increasing average temperature of the Earth
   (2) the success of the Industrial Revolution
   (3) the fact that a single atmosphere covers the whole planet
   (4) the slow rising of the ocean levels
   (5) the increasing levels of carbon dioxide in the atmosphere

3. Which of the following items would be of *least* importance to someone studying the greenhouse effect?

   (1) any change in the average thickness of the ice covering the polar ice caps
   (2) any change in the average air temperature off the coast of Alaska
   (3) the success of efforts designed to protect Arctic polar bears from extinction
   (4) a comparison of summer and winter conditions on the planet Venus
   (5) any change in the average levels of high and low tides in San Francisco Bay

4. Which of the following would be the *most* effective solution for the problem known as the greenhouse effect?

    (1)   reducing our dependence on all forms of hydrocarbon fuels
    (2)   placing restrictions on the use of wood stoves
    (3)   developing new cars that get extremely high mileage
    (4)   carefully managing forests in order to prevent lightning fires
    (5)   placing high taxes on all hydrocarbon fuels

ANSWERS AND EXPLANATIONS START ON PAGE 303.

 Writing Activity 4

    Many scientists believe that a global campaign to reduce chemical pollution is the only way to stop the greenhouse effect. In the U.S., emissions from coal plants are regulated to some extent. However, in many developing countries, no such regulations exist.

    In view of the urgency of the problem, would it be possible to get all the countries of the world to agree to cut down on chemical pollution? What might be some of the objections raised by developing countries? Who should pay for cleaning up the Earth's atmosphere?

    Write two or three paragraphs describing the positive and negative aspects of a worldwide campaign to stop the greenhouse effect.

SAMPLE ANSWERS START ON PAGE 303.

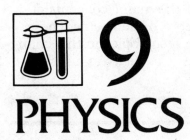

9 PHYSICS

Imagine that you wake up tomorrow and nothing seems to work. There's no hot water, so you can't shower. The stove doesn't work, so you can't cook a hot breakfast. The refrigerator is off, and your TV won't turn on! Sound like a world gone crazy? Maybe so. But that's what life would be like if the world ran out of energy.

Because the world's population is increasing and worldwide standards of living are rising, more people can now afford energy-consuming products like cars, stereos, and air conditioners. Since 1940, the total amount of energy used in the world has doubled almost every 20 years. Many people are worried that we are headed for a serious energy shortage, a situation in which there would not be enough energy for everyone who needed it. The challenge currently facing physics is to develop new sources of safe energy.

The Science of Energy

When most people think about energy, they think about the gasoline that powers their car and the electricity or natural gas that heats their home. Besides these, though, there are many other important forms of energy. Sound and light are two examples. Energy carried by water and wind are two more.

Physicists study how energy is produced and how it can be used most efficiently. They try to learn as much as possible about each form of energy. The results of their research often lead to the development of new types of consumer products. For example, physicists have helped develop and improve entertainment products like television, video recorders, and cameras; kitchen appliances like microwave ovens and electronic dishwashers; and medical equipment like digital thermometers, CAT scanners (used to see inside the human body), and ultrasonic sound monitors (used to observe a growing fetus).

Processes that involve energy also play important roles in other areas of science. Because of this, several new fields have developed in recent years that link physics directly with these other sciences. For example, *biophysicists* apply the techniques and results of physics research to questions in biology. *Astrophysicists* study the birth and death of stars and planets. *Physical chemists* try to determine the atom-by-atom details of the structure of molecules.

Physics, more than any other science, uses the language of mathematics to describe its theories and experiments. However, many of the major concepts of physics can be understood without the aid of either algebra or geometry. These are the major concepts that appear on the GED Science Test. Topics in this chapter will include properties of motion, properties of waves, electricity and magnetism, and nuclear physics.

Exercise 1: Overview of Physics

Directions: Match each item on the left with the phrase that best describes it on the right. Write the letter of the phrase on the line before the correct number.

_____ **1.** biophysics

_____ **2.** physical chemistry

_____ **3.** physics

_____ **4.** astrophysics

a. the application of physics to problems in chemistry

b. often called "the science of energy"

c. the application of physics to research in astronomy

d. the application of physics to research in biology

★ **GED PRACTICE** ★

Exercise 2: The Science of Energy

Directions: Choose the best answer to each of the following questions or statements.

1. Which of the following is given in the reading passage as a cause of the worldwide increase in energy use this century?

   (1) the possibility of a serious energy shortage
   (2) the production of alternative energy sources
   (3) worldwide rising standards of living
   (4) the fact that energy use has doubled in the past 20 years
   (5) the importance of processes involving energy in other areas of science

2. It can be concluded from the reading passage that physicists

    (1) rely on observation but not on mathematical analysis
    (2) support the development of more nuclear power plants
    (3) have little interest in other areas of science
    (4) are involved in work that often has practical applications
    (5) support worldwide family planning efforts

**ENERGY PRODUCTION IN THE
UNITED STATES (1985)**

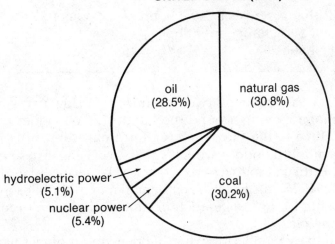

oil
(28.5%)

natural gas
(30.8%)

hydroelectric power
(5.1%)

nuclear power
(5.4%)

coal
(30.2%)

3. According to the circle graph above, approximately what total percent of the energy produced in the United States comes from fossil fuels (coal, oil, and natural gas)?

    (1) 30 percent
    (2) 50 percent
    (3) 75 percent
    (4) 82 percent
    (5) 90 percent

ANSWERS AND EXPLANATIONS START ON PAGE 304.

 Writing Activity 1

Applications of physics have produced the technology to create many machines and consumer products, including computers. In some respects, computers have made our lives much easier, enabling us to do things we wouldn't even dream of trying if we didn't have a machine to organize the information for us. However, sometimes computers cause inconveniences.

Write two to three paragraphs explaining how computers have affected our daily lives. You may want to focus on either the positive aspects or the negative aspects. Be sure to use examples to support your point of view.

SAMPLE ANSWERS START ON PAGE 304.

Properties of Motion

Newton's Laws of Motion

Key Words

force—any push or pull that can affect the motion of an object
inertia—natural resistance to change in motion
acceleration—increase of speed

How would you answer the following two questions? (1) How many angels does it take to keep the moon moving around the Earth? (2) Why does an arrow, when shot into the sky, return to the Earth looking for a natural resting place?

If these questions seem a little odd to you, it's not surprising. These questions aren't often asked today! But such matters were taken very seriously in the time of Sir Isaac Newton (1642–1727), an English mathematician and philosopher. Newton spent his life looking for an explanation of motion that didn't require angels' help or natural resting places!

Newton began his study by wondering what happens to an object like a ball when a force acts upon it. (As used by Newton, a force is any push or pull that can affect an object either in motion or at rest.) By doing careful experiments, Newton made several discoveries that today are written as three laws of motion that still bear his name. Newton's Laws of Motion are now known to apply to all types of objects and all types of forces.

Newton's First Law: The Law of Inertia

Newton realized that, unless some force stopped it, a rolling ball would roll forever. He also realized that, without a force to start it rolling, a ball that was not moving would sit forever.

With these two ideas in mind, Newton wrote his first law: **If no force is applied, an object at rest will remain at rest, and an object in motion will continue to move in a straight line at the same speed.** You've seen this principle in action if you've ever watched children slide along an icy sidewalk. Because there is only a very slight force to slow them down, they are able to slide a long distance.

This property of matter, a natural resistance to any change in motion, is called inertia. Every object, whether sitting or moving, has inertia.

Newton's Second Law: The Law of Acceleration

Newton's second law, most easily written in two parts, is based on two observations that he made. First, Newton noticed that a ball can be thrown faster and farther simply by throwing it harder (applying more force). In other words, **an object's speed will increase in proportion to the amount of force applied.**

Second, Newton noticed that, using as much force as your muscles can apply, you can throw a one-pound ball much faster and farther than you can throw a ten-pound ball. From this second observation Newton noted that **for the same amount of applied force, a lighter object will accelerate—change its speed—at a greater rate than a heavier object.** To see how this works, think of how much easier it is to throw a baseball across a yard than it would be to throw a bowling ball the same distance.

Newton's Third Law: The Law of Interaction

Finally, Newton thought about what happens when one object exerts a force on a second object. For example, imagine what happens when a child kicks a door shut. At the instant his foot strikes the door, it exerts a force that slams the door. At the same instant, though, the foot feels a reaction force from the door. Needless to say, the child would be painfully aware of this reaction force if he were barefoot!

Newton stated his third law as follows: **For every action, there is an equal and opposite reaction.** When one object exerts a force on a second object, the second object exerts an equal and opposite force on the first object.

A reaction force can also act on an object that is not moving. As an example, think about a telephone sitting on a desk. Due to gravity, the phone exerts a force (its weight) on the desk. At the same time, the desk exerts an upward reaction force on the phone. To explain why the phone remains motionless, Newton would simply say that the reaction force pushing the phone up exactly balances the force of gravity pulling the phone down.

Exercise 3: Newton's Laws of Motion

Directions: Answer each question below.

1. Briefly define each of the words below:

    a. force: _____

    b. inertia: _____

2. Each of the four facts below demonstrates one of Newton's laws of motion. On the line preceding each fact, write *1, 2,* or *3* to indicate which law is being demonstrated.

   1—The law of inertia: an object's motion will not change unless a force acts on the object.
   2—The law of acceleration: an object's speed increases when more force is applied.
   3—The law of interaction: for every action, there is an equal and opposite reaction.

_____ **a.** When a gun is fired, the exploding gunpowder forces the bullet through the barrel and pushes the gun back against the shooter.

_____ **b.** Because the force of gravity is less on the moon than on the Earth, a rock dropped on the moon would fall more slowly than an equal-size rock dropped on Earth.

_____ **c.** A fast-moving barrel, rolling on a level floor, will roll until a force is applied to stop it.

_____ **d.** Using equal amounts of force, a track athlete can toss a twelve-pound shot farther than she can toss a sixteen-pound shot.

★ GED PRACTICE ★

Exercise 4: Properties of Motion

Directions: Choose the best answer for each question below.

1. The property of inertia accounts for the fact that

   (1) a car without brakes is difficult to stop
   (2) a telephone on a desk is acted upon by a reaction force
   (3) a basketball rebounds off a backboard
   (4) light reflects off a glass
   (5) the effect of air friction is to slow a moving vehicle

Questions 2 and 3 on the next page refer to the sprinkler shown below.

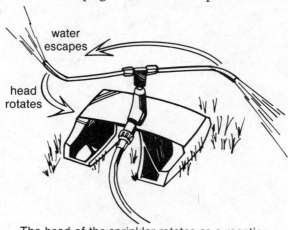

The head of the sprinkler rotates as a reaction to the force of escaping water.

2. The action of the sprinkler illustrates

    (1) Newton's first law of motion, the law of inertia
    (2) Newton's second law of motion, the law of acceleration
    (3) Newton's third law of motion, the law of interaction
    (4) an exception to Newton's laws of motion
    (5) Newton's law of gravity

3. Which of the three actions listed below would cause the sprinkler to rotate more quickly?

    A. Oil the sprinkler parts to enable the sprinkler to turn more easily.
    B. Hang one-ounce weights at the end of each sprinkler nozzle.
    C. Increase the amount of water flowing through the hose.

    (1) A only
    (2) B only
    (3) C only
    (4) A and B only
    (5) A and C only

4. The graph below shows the rate at which an object's speed increases as it falls due to the force of gravity. For example, if an object is dropped from a tall building, it reaches a speed of 96 feet per second after falling for three seconds.

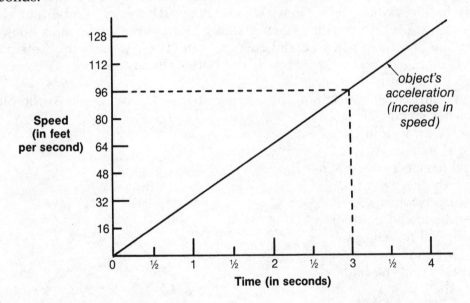

    Under the action of gravity, how much does an object's speed increase each second it falls?

    (1) 10 feet per second
    (2) 16 feet per second
    (3) 32 feet per second
    (4) 64 feet per second
    (5) 100 feet per second

ANSWERS AND EXPLANATIONS START ON PAGE 304.

The Law of Conservation of Energy

Key Words

kinetic energy—energy of motion
potential energy—stored energy
friction—a force that tends to slow down a moving object

You can't actually see the process, but every time you turn on a lamp, energy changes from one form to another. Electrical energy flows through the light bulb and is changed into light energy and heat energy: the bulb glows brightly and gets very hot.

By studying how energy changes from one form to another, physicists discovered the *Law of Conservation of Energy*. This law says that, although energy changes from one form to another, no energy is lost. The total amount of energy present remains constant.

Kinetic Energy and Potential Energy

Two basic types of energy that an object may have are kinetic energy and potential energy. Kinetic energy is energy of motion, such as the energy that a bowling ball has while rolling down a lane. Potential energy can be thought of as stored energy, energy capable of being changed into another form. A book sitting on the edge of a table has potential energy. If the book is pushed off, its potential energy is changed to kinetic energy as the book falls to the floor. The energy changes form but is not lost.

Now think about what happens when a little girl is swinging. At the highest point of her swing, she stops moving for an instant as she reverses direction. At this point, all her energy is potential (stored) energy. A few seconds later, when she reaches the lowest point of her swing, all her energy is kinetic (motion) energy. As she swings from the highest point to the lowest point, her potential energy is changed to kinetic energy. Then, as she swings back up, her kinetic energy changes once again to potential energy. At all points between the highest and lowest points, her energy is partly potential and partly kinetic.

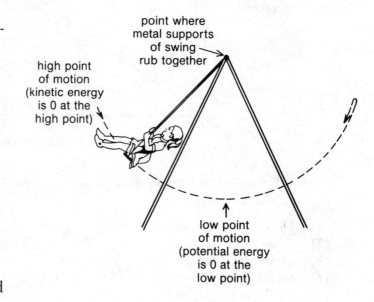

point where
metal supports
of swing
rub together

high point
of motion
(kinetic energy
is 0 at the
high point)

low point
of motion
(potential energy
is 0 at the
low point)

The Force of Friction

Friction is a force that opposes the motion of one object rubbing against a second object. Friction tends to slow down a moving object. If it weren't for friction acting on the swing, the girl could swing back and forth effortlessly, each time reaching the same height as before. But because there is friction, the girl will slowly lose energy and come to a stop unless she is pushed or unless she pumps the swing herself.

Friction slowly changes the kinetic energy of the swing to heat energy. Heat energy is produced mainly where the metal supports of the swing rub together. You can observe a similar warming effect when you rub your hands together.

In addition, a small amount of heat is produced in the air because the girl's motion is opposed by air friction, commonly called air resistance. You can most easily feel air resistance when you're traveling down a highway and stick your hand out of the car window.

The heat produced by friction must be taken into account in the conservation of energy law. The girl stops moving, but her kinetic energy is not lost; instead, it has been changed into heat energy—heat that warms the metal supports of the swing and heat that is in the air.

Exercise 5: The Law of Conservation of Energy────

Directions: Complete each sentence by filling in the blanks with the correct word(s) from the reading passage.

1. According to the Law of Conservation of Energy, the amount of energy in

   any given situation is _____.

2. Energy of motion is called _____, while stored energy is

   called _____.

3. _____ is a force that opposes the motion of any object that is

   rubbing against a second object.

Exercise 6: Energy and Motion

Directions: Questions 1–3 are based on the following paragraph and illustration.

A pendulum consists of a suspended object that can swing freely back and forth. A wrecking ball swung by a crane is an example of a practical use of a pendulum. The wrecking ball illustrated at right rises to its high point, A, before swinging back through its low point, C, and then over to the right side as indicated.

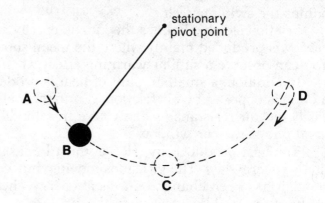

1. At which point is the energy of the wrecking ball partly kinetic and partly potential?

    (1) point A only
    (2) point B only
    (3) point C only
    (4) points A and B only
    (5) points B and C only

2. A crane operator must position a wrecking ball to strike a building. In which position will the wrecking ball have the greatest amount of force?

    (1) point A
    (2) point B
    (3) point C
    (4) point D
    (5) point A or point B

3. After impact, the wrecking ball hangs motionless, having lost the total kinetic and potential energy it had while swinging.

Which conclusion below is supported by the above observation and is consistent with the Law of Conservation of Energy (which states that energy is never lost)?

(1) The lost energy will be recovered when the crane operator swings the ball up again.
(2) The lost energy cannot be recovered.
(3) Because it was being swung by the crane, the ball never did have its own energy.
(4) The ball will continue moving on its own after a short time.
(5) The lost energy has been changed into the energy used to break apart the building.

ANSWERS AND EXPLANATIONS START ON PAGE 304.

The Nature of Heat

Key Words

heat—the energy of motion of an object's atoms
temperature—a measure of heat

Bill lives in a third-floor apartment in the city. In the summer, his apartment is stiflingly hot, even when he keeps the windows open all the time. In the winter, the landlord keeps the heat turned down, and Bill is freezing!

A physicist might describe Bill's predicament in terms of heat energy. Heat energy is the motion of atoms. When the atoms in an object move faster, the object gets hotter; when the atoms move more slowly, the object gets colder. So when Bill is suffering in the heat, the atoms in the air are moving very fast. When his teeth are chattering from the cold, the atoms in the air are moving more slowly.

Temperature is a measure of heat energy. When an object absorbs heat, its temperature rises. For example, room-temperature water in a pan on a lighted range will quickly come to a boil when you turn up the flame. Similarly, when an object gives off heat, its temperature falls. When put in a freezer, room-temperature water loses heat and rapidly falls to its freezing point.

When two objects of different temperature are brought together, heat energy flows from the warmer object to the cooler object. This heat flow continues until both objects reach the same temperature. When you put a package of frozen food in a sink full of hot water, the food will warm up and start to thaw. At the same time, the water will become cooler, until both the food and the water are the same temperature. The heat flows from the hot water to the package of frozen food.

Expansion and Contraction

As an object is heated up, it expands. When the object gets hotter, its atoms move faster and are farther apart. You may have noticed that doors sometimes stick in the summer. This is because the door expands more than the door frame. Most objects expand so little that you hardly notice it. For instance, a pan heated on a stove expands a small fraction of an inch.

As objects cool down, they lose heat energy. The atoms slow down, and the object contracts. For example, after you take a cake out of the oven, you need to let it cool for a while before taking it out of the pan. As it cools, the cake will contract and come farther away from the sides of the pan.

For an equal amount of heating, a gas will expand more than a liquid, and a liquid will expand more than a solid. For instance, when the outdoor temperature rises, the liquid mercury inside a thermometer expands more than the glass—a solid—containing it.

These properties of expansion and contraction hold true for solids (like doors), liquids (like water), and gases (like air).

Exercise 7: Expansion and Contraction

Directions: Each statement below refers to the effect of heat on matter. Circle *T* for each statement that is true and *F* for each statement that is false.

T F **1.** If a penny is placed in the sunshine, it will expand as it becomes warmer.

T F **2.** If a helium-filled weather balloon is released at ground level, it will expand when it reaches the cold upper atmosphere.

T F **3.** If car tires are filled with air at the beginning of a day-long drive, the pressure in the tires will increase during the heat of the afternoon.

T F **4.** As the hot water in a bathtub cools, the water expands and may flow over the sides of the tub.

★ **GED PRACTICE** ★

Exercise 8: The Nature of Heat

Directions: Choose the best answer for each question below.

1. When a piece of hot iron (temperature 380°F) is thrown into a barrel of cold water (temperature 50°F), which of the following will occur?

    (1) Heat will flow from the water to the iron until both are the same temperature.
    (2) Heat will flow from the iron to the water until both are the same temperature.
    (3) The water will be heated to 380°F.
    (4) The iron will be cooled to 50°F.
    (5) Nothing, because heat can't flow from iron to water.

2. When engineers design bridges and overpasses, they purposely place gaps between the points where large metal beams are to meet end-to-end. The purpose of these gaps is to

   (1) allow for water drainage during rainstorms
   (2) provide room for the beams to contract in cold weather
   (3) prevent rust from forming at the point where the beams might rub together
   (4) allow for errors in measurement during construction
   (5) provide room for the beams to expand in hot weather

Questions 3–5 are based on the following reading selection and diagram.

Your body temperature is a measure of the heat produced within your body. Most of the time, your temperature is regulated and remains about the same. However, during illness, your temperature goes up as your body attempts to fight off infection or disease.

One of the first signs of illness in a child is an unusual increase in body temperature. A temperature rise can be a symptom of a cold, the flu, or even a much more serious illness such as meningitis, a disease that requires immediate medical attention. Also, extreme fever itself can be very harmful. A fever higher than 105.8°F (41°C) can cause permanent damage to a person's nervous system.

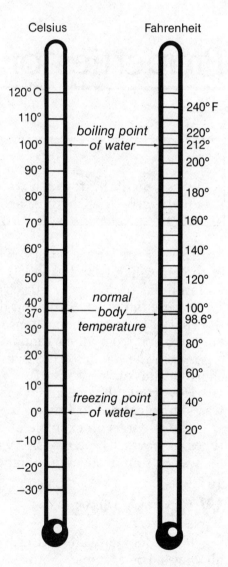

3. According to the diagram, what is the normal human body temperature?

   (1) 33°C or 91.4°F
   (2) 37°C or 98.6°F
   (3) 39°C or 102.2°F
   (4) 40°C or 104°F
   (5) 44°C or 111.2°F

4. According to the diagram, which temperature below represents a slight fever?

   (1) 96°F
   (2) 37°C
   (3) 98.6°F
   (4) 38°C
   (5) 106°F

5. What is the best parental response to a child's waking in the middle of the night with a 104°F fever?

(1) Tell the child to go to sleep and see how the fever is in the morning.
(2) Cool the child with a damp cloth, call the "after hours" number at your doctor's office or hospital, report the child's symptoms, and receive good medical advice.
(3) Wait for a few hours and see if the temperature goes down by itself.
(4) Don't worry, because high temperatures in children are common.
(5) Call a friend with children and ask for advice.

ANSWERS AND EXPLANATIONS START ON PAGE 305.

Properties of Waves

Key Words

waves—the form in which water, light, and sound travel
wavelength—the length of one wave

During the afternoon of April 1, 1946, huge ocean waves pounded the shores of the Hawaiian Islands and left 173 people dead or missing, 163 people injured, and millions of dollars worth of property damage.

Where did the ocean along the normally peaceful Hawaiian shores get all the energy to cause such extensive damage? Believe it or not, this tremendous energy came from an earthquake only five hours earlier in the Aleutian Trench, a gorge in the Earth's crust that lies on the bottom of the Pacific Ocean off the shore of Alaska.

How could the ocean have moved so far so quickly? It didn't! The energy was simply carried to Hawaii by the wave motion on the ocean's surface.

The ocean is an example of the action of water waves, one of many common types of waves. Three types of waves we'll discuss on the next few pages are water waves, sound waves, and light waves.

Water Waves

If you look at water waves, you can see many of the properties common to all waves. For example, Picture A on page 235 shows what happens when you drop a stone into a pond. The waves move directly away in a circular pattern from the place where the stone was dropped. Like all other types of waves, water waves travel in a straight line away from their source.

Picture B is a cutaway drawing of the wave pattern. It illustrates the position of crests and troughs along the wave's surface. The distance between two crests (or two troughs) is called the wavelength.

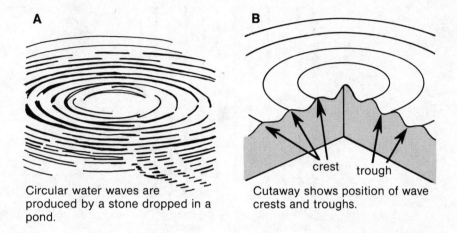

A

Circular water waves are produced by a stone dropped in a pond.

B

crest   trough

Cutaway shows position of wave crests and troughs.

When a wave hits a smooth surface, it *reflects*, or bounces off the surface. In Picture C, one series of waves spreads out away from the center. As the waves hit the barrier, they are reflected, causing the rainbow-shaped pattern.

As a wave crosses a boundary, it *refracts*, or bends, continuing its course but moving in a slightly different direction. A straight water wave refracts as it crosses from an area of deep water to an area of shallow water. Water waves tend to refract as they approach a beach.

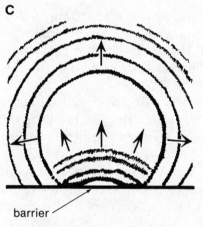

C

barrier

A circular water wave **reflects** as it strikes a solid barrier.

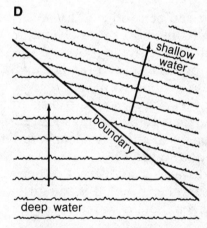

D

shallow water

boundary

deep water

A straight water wave **refracts** as it moves across a boundary between deep and shallow water.

Finally, all waves *diffract*—they spread out into a region behind or around a barrier. You can see water waves diffracting in Picture E below.

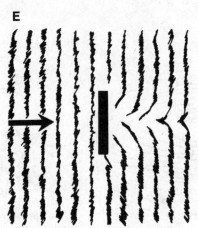

Waves **diffract** as they move around a barrier. A water wave diffracts, or spreads out, as it goes by an object.

Sound Waves

What does a cricket's shrill have in common with a rock concert? Your answer will depend upon your interest in rock music! One similarity between them is that both are forms of sound, a type of energy that travels to our ears as a wave.

Sound can be produced by any vibrating object. For example, when a vibrating guitar string moves to the right, it compresses the air molecules to the immediate right. As the string moves to the left, the air molecules just to the right of the string become spaced farther apart. The result of the string's vibrating back and forth is a sound wave.

Like other waves, sound travels in a straight line and will reflect off a smooth surface. Reflection is most easily demonstrated by honking a car horn in a tunnel or by shouting in a canyon. The echoes that you hear are simply reflected sound waves.

Sound waves also diffract. When you stand in one room and speak with a person in another room, it is the diffraction of sound that allows you to hear the second person. Sound waves easily spread around corners and through doorways.

Exercise 9: Water Waves and Sound Waves———

Directions: Read each statement below. Circle *T* if the statement is true and *F* if the statement is false.

T F **1.** Sound waves carry energy, but water waves do not.

T F **2.** The distance between two crests of a wave is called a wavelength.

T F **3.** Water waves on the ocean move along the ocean's surface.

T F **4.** Sound waves move in a straight line away from their source.

Exercise 10: Frequency and Hearing

Directions: The questions below refer to the following paragraph and table.

The frequency of sound is the number of complete waves produced each second. Frequency determines pitch. A high-frequency sound like the high note on the piano is said to have a high pitch. A low-frequency sound like a bass drum has a low pitch. Each type of animal life on Earth has one frequency range in which it can hear and another frequency range in which it can speak or make sound. Several common frequency ranges are listed in the table below.

Common Frequency Ranges (in cycles per second)	Hearing	Making Sound or Speaking
Human Being	20–20,000	85–1,100
Dog	15–50,000	452–1,080
Cat	60–65,000	760–1,520
Grasshopper	100–15,000	7,000–100,000
Dolphin	150–150,000	7,000–120,000
Robin	250–21,000	2,000–13,000
Bat	1,000–120,000	10,000–120,000

1. Of the animals listed in the table, which is the only animal that can hear sounds of a lower frequency than human beings can hear?

    (1) dolphin
    (2) dog
    (3) cat
    (4) bat
    (5) grasshopper

2. Of the animals listed in the table, which is the only animal that can "speak" at frequencies far greater than the highest frequencies it can hear?

    (1) dog
    (2) dolphin
    (3) grasshopper
    (4) robin
    (5) cat

3. Which of the following conclusions is best supported by the information given in the table?

    (1) In most cases, the smaller an animal is, the more sound frequencies it can hear.

    (2) Human beings can speak at higher frequencies than other animals can "speak."

    (3) The hearing range of most animals includes both lower and higher frequencies than their speaking range.

    (4) Human beings can hear at higher frequencies than other animals can.

    (5) Four-legged mammals such as dogs and cats can hear sounds of much higher frequencies than are heard by birds or sea animals.

ANSWERS AND EXPLANATIONS START ON PAGE 305.

Light Waves

Key Words

vacuum—space that contains no matter
prism—a triangular piece of glass

When you look into the sky on a clear, moonless night, the stars appear as little pinholes of light shining through a black canvas. Yet, seen through a telescope, starlight reveals distant galaxies—worlds that have existed billions of years longer than our own. Today, scientists look at this starlight with the hope of discovering how stars and planets are created.

Light is a special form of wave called an electromagnetic wave. Unlike other waves, electromagnetic waves can travel through a vacuum, space that contains no matter. In fact, all the light we receive from the sun, moon, and stars travels to us through the vacuum of space. This light moves in a straight line on its long journey to us. It is only because sunlight moves in a straight line that we have clearly defined shadows on Earth.

Light and Color

We usually think of sunlight as white, but it is actually made up of a spectrum of colors. You can see this spectrum beautifully displayed as a rainbow arching across the sky after a light rain. The same bands of color can also be created by passing sunlight through a prism, a triangular piece of glass.

As you already know, refraction occurs when a wave strikes a boundary and begins to move in a different direction. In this case, the prism acts as a boundary, and when the sunlight hits it, it bends, or refracts. The white light separates into its component colors because each color of light refracts by a different amount.

Each color of light can be thought of as a wave of a certain wavelength. In the spectrum of colors, red has the longest wavelength, and violet has the shortest wavelength. As the drawing below shows, red light refracts the least, and violet light refracts the most.

As we've seen, white light is made up of many colors. But why, when we look at most objects, do we see only a single color? The answer is that objects reflect some wavelengths of light and absorb others. For example, a leaf appears green because it reflects the wavelengths associated with green. This reflected light is what we see. The leaf absorbs all other wavelengths of light.

A black surface absorbs almost all the light that strikes it. A mirror or white surface reflects almost all light. During reflection, light changes its direction of travel much as a tennis ball changes direction after striking a solid wall.

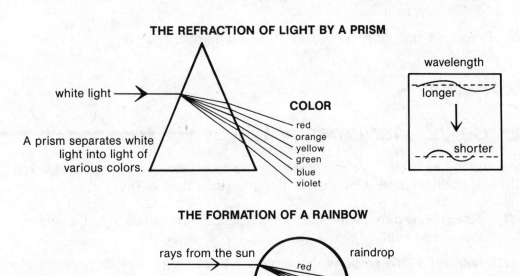

THE REFRACTION OF LIGHT BY A PRISM

white light →

A prism separates white light into light of various colors.

COLOR

red
orange
yellow
green
blue
violet

wavelength

longer

shorter

THE FORMATION OF A RAINBOW

rays from the sun   raindrop

red
violet
violet

violet
blue

green
yellow
red

red

Exercise 11: Light Waves

Directions: Answer the questions below.

1. Complete each sentence by filling in the blanks with the correct word(s) from the reading passage.

    a. Space that contains no matter is called a _____.

    b. Each color of light can be thought of as a wave that has a certain

    _____.

2. From the information given in the reading passage, determine if each of the following statements is true or false. Circle each answer choice.

   T F **a.** An asphalt road appears almost black because it reflects all the sunlight that strikes it.

   T F **b.** A red car appears red because it absorbs all wavelengths of light except wavelengths associated with red light.

   T F **c.** On a hot summer day, a green shirt will keep you cooler than a white shirt.

   T F **d.** A mirror reflects almost all the light that strikes it.

★ GED PRACTICE ★

Exercise 12: Properties of Waves

Directions: Below are five properties common to water, sound, and light waves. Read the definitions and then answer the questions that follow.

   (1) Straight-line movement—the property that a wave travels in a straight line from its source

   (2) Reflection—the property that a wave will reflect (reverse its direction of travel) after striking a smooth surface

   (3) Refraction—the property that a wave will bend (change the angle of its forward motion) as it moves across a boundary

   (4) Diffraction—the property that a wave will spread out into a region behind or around a barrier

   (5) Wavelength—the property that a wave can be described as a series of crests and troughs, the distance between two crests (or troughs) being the wavelength

1. When you hear a child shout from the other side of the house, the sound of the shouting must travel through doorways and around corners in order to reach you. This is an example of the wave property known as

   (1) straight-line movement
   (2) reflection
   (3) refraction
   (4) diffraction
   (5) wavelength

2. After a rainstorm, you can sometimes see the rainbow spectrum of colors displayed in a drop of oil on the street. What property is demonstrated by the light as it strikes the oil?

   (1) straight-line movement
   (2) reflection
   (3) refraction
   (4) diffraction
   (5) wavelength

3. The echo of a person walking down an empty alley demonstrates the property of

    (1) straight-line movement
    (2) reflection
    (3) refraction
    (4) diffraction
    (5) wavelength

4. Emilio, a fisherman, spends most of his day sitting in a boat on the ocean. His boat bobs up and down about every seven seconds. Which property of waves is most related to Emilio's up and down movement?

    (1) straight-line movement
    (2) reflection
    (3) refraction
    (4) diffraction
    (5) wavelength

ANSWERS AND EXPLANATIONS START ON PAGE 305.

Electricity and Magnetism

Electricity

> ### Key Words
>
> *electric current*—the movement of electrons
> *circuit*—a complete path in which an electric current flows
> *conductor*—a material in which an electric current can be made to flow

In 1877, when the famous physicist Hermann von Helmholtz was taking a few ladies of the Imperial Court on a tour of his laboratory in Berlin, one of the ladies looked at the electric wires and asked in amazement, "But, my dear professor, how is it possible for electricity to flow through these thin little tubes?"

History doesn't tell us how Helmholtz answered this question, but today we have a pretty good idea about the nature of electricity. According to the atomic theory of matter, all matter is composed of atoms. Each atom has an equal number of negatively-charged electrons and positively-charged protons. Electricity involves the motion of these electrons and can be either of two types: static electricity or electric current.

Static Electricity: Electric Charges at Rest

Because most objects in nature are electrically neutral, having the same number of electrons as protons, we usually don't notice the electrical properties of things. However, what do you suppose would happen if you could upset this balance of positive and negative charges?

Here are a couple of examples in which you do just that. When you rub a comb through dry hair, the comb picks up extra electrons. These electrons actually leave your hair and electrically stick to the comb. The charged comb can then make your hair stand on end, and it can pick up small pieces of paper. You can also see this effect when you walk across a woolen carpet. Your body becomes charged with excess electrons picked up from the wool, and you can get quite a shock by touching a metal door handle.

In each of these examples of static electricity, electrons are transferred from one object to another. This transfer of electric charge takes place because the outermost electrons in many atoms are held loosely by the nuclei and can be removed easily.

Electric Current: Electric Charges In Motion

In static electricity, you observe effects of the presence of excess electric charges at rest. Now, what about charges in motion?

You can make electrons flow in many materials, particularly metals, much the way water flows in a hose. This flow of electrons is called an electric current. A material in which electric current can flow is called a conductor. A material in which it can't flow is called a **nonconductor** or an **insulator**. You have probably seen electrical insulation, the rubber material that covers electric wires and cables. Electric current cannot flow through insulation. Insulation protects you from electric shock when you touch current-carrying wires.

Electric current that moves in one direction only is called **direct current (DC)**. You can set a direct current in motion by attaching a battery to the ends of a copper wire. The battery produces an electric force that pushes electrons away from the negative terminal and toward the positive terminal. But for a current to flow, you must set up a complete circuit. You must connect the wires so that there is an electrical path that electrons can move along from one side of the battery to the other. A break anywhere in the circuit will stop the current's flow.

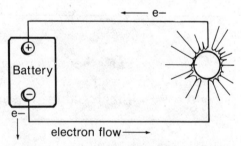

In a direct current circuit, electrons flow in a complete path from the negative terminal of the battery to the positive terminal.

The most common household power source is the wall socket. A wall socket provides an *alternating current (AC)*—a current in which the electrons flow first in one direction and then in the opposite direction. The current in most homes is called 60-cycle AC: the current goes back and forth in the wire 60 times in one second.

The amount of current that flows from any power source depends on the voltage. Commonly used batteries you see around home are the 1½-volt flashlight battery and the 9-volt radio battery. A wall socket, which produces a 120-volt signal, provides a much greater amount of current. This is why you can safely handle batteries but should not, under any circumstances, stick your finger in a wall socket!

Exercise 13: Electricity

Directions: Match each item on the left with the phrase that best describes it on the right. Write the letter of the phrase on the line before the correct number.

_____ **1.** alternating current

_____ **2.** voltage

_____ **3.** insulator

_____ **4.** electrons

_____ **5.** direct current

a. current that flows in one direction only

b. the moving particles that make up an electric current

c. a number that tells the strength of a battery

d. current that alternately flows each direction

e. a material in which electric current can't flow

6. Complete each sentence by filling in the blanks with the correct word(s) from the reading passage.

a. The two types of electricity are _____ and _____.

b. A _____ is a material in which an electric current can be made to flow.

★ **GED PRACTICE** ★

Exercise 14: Electric Circuits

Directions: Look at the circuit diagrams and then answer the questions that follow.

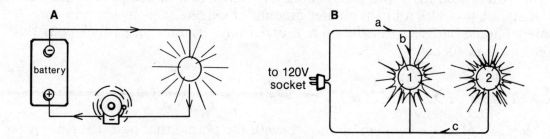

1. Below are three statements that refer to circuit **A** above.

    A. Direct current is flowing in circuit **A**.
    B. Electrons are flowing from the positive terminal of the battery to the negative terminal.
    C. Disconnecting the wire at the positive terminal of the battery will turn off the light but not the bell.

    Which of the statements above is *false?*

    (1) A only
    (2) B only
    (3) C only
    (4) A and B only
    (5) B and C only

2. When a switch in a circuit is opened, the flow of current stops. Referring to circuit **B** above, which one of the three switches (a, b, and c) could you open in order to turn off light 1 only?

    (1) a only
    (2) b only
    (3) c only
    (4) either a or c
    (5) either b or c

ANSWERS AND EXPLANATIONS START ON PAGE 305.

Superconductivity

Key Words

superconductivity—the disappearance of resistance in an electrical conductor
superconductor—a material that exhibits the property of superconductivity

Imagine trains that float on cushions of magnetic force and speed across the country at hundreds of miles per hour. Imagine computers only a fraction of the size they are now and powerful electric motors the size of your thumb. Will such devices be in our future? "Yes!" say many excited physicists today. In fact, they predict that these are just three of many consumer products that may result from one of the most exciting advances to take place in physics in decades: superconductivity.

Superconductivity is an amazing phenomenon that involves electric current—the flow of electrons through a conductor. In common conductors of electricity like copper wires, electrons bump into each other, so there is resistance to the flow of the current. Electrical resistance causes heat and results in a loss of energy. For example, about 20 percent of the electrical energy carried by high-voltage power lines is lost as heat.

In a superconductor, on the other hand, electrons do not collide with each other. There is no electrical resistance. No energy is lost when electrons flow, and no heat is created. Superconductors are perfect conductors of electricity.

No one knows exactly why superconductivity occurs. A popular hypothesis is that electrons in a superconductor have a way of pairing together and then moving in step with other electron pairs. This coordinated motion enables the electrons to avoid collisions. You can think of this motion as being similar to the organized movement of two-lane traffic on a very busy street.

Although superconductivity was first discovered in the element mercury in 1911, no practical applications were developed in the years that followed. The most important obstacle was that materials that become superconductors would do so only at extremely low temperatures. Mercury, for example, was found to become superconducting only when its temperature was lowered to −452°F (452 degrees below zero)! At any higher temperature, mercury is just as resistant as a regular conductor. What's more, cooling mercury to this temperature requires immersing it in a bath of liquid helium, a very expensive and scarce coolant.

Between 1911 and the early 1980s, only a few other superconducting materials were discovered. Each of these was either a metal or metal alloy, and each had to be cooled to hundreds of degrees below zero before superconductivity would occur. Then, in the mid-1980s, a major discovery was made. Physicists found that certain types of ceramics also become superconductors, and they do so at temperatures much higher than previously was believed possible. In fact, new types of superconducting ceramics are now being developed with the hope that room-temperature superconductors may someday be in common use.

Exercise 15: Superconductivity

Directions: Match each item on the left with the phrase that best describes it on the right. Write the letter of the phrase on the line before the correct number.

_____ **1.** helium

_____ **2.** mercury

_____ **3.** superconductivity

_____ **4.** conductor

_____ **5.** ceramic

a. the absence of electrical resistance

b. any material that will transmit electricity

c. a material recently discovered to have superconducting properties

d. the first known superconductor

e. a coolant when in liquid form

Exercise 16: Superconductor Research

Directions: Choose the best answer to each question below.

1. The important advantage that superconductors have over regular conductors is that they

   (1) can be used inside computers to carry electric current
   (2) cost less to make than regular conductors
   (3) use less electric current than regular conductors
   (4) don't produce heat when electricity flows through them
   (5) don't produce magnetic fields when electricity flows through them

2. When a certain low temperature is reached, superconductivity occurs in a superconductor. It is believed that this happens because

   (1) the magnetic field surrounding the superconductor becomes very strong as the electric current is increased
   (2) the superconductor's electrical resistance disappears
   (3) the superconductor's electrons become very small and move through the material very rapidly
   (4) the superconductor suddenly exhibits several new types of electron motion
   (5) the superconductor's electrons join in pairs and move through the material without colliding

3. The use of superconducting electric power lines could save utility companies billions of dollars each year. What assumption is made by scientists who claim that this will result in lower electricity costs to consumers?

   (1) After utility companies install superconducting power lines, consumers will use less electricity.
   (2) Consumers will get rebates for the installation of superconducting power lines.
   (3) Superconducting power lines will enable the construction of faster trains and result in lower train fares.
   (4) The money saved by utility companies using superconducting lines will be passed along as savings to consumers.
   (5) After superconducting power lines are installed, many people who presently heat by gas or oil will switch to electricity.

4. Most scientific research is undertaken with the goal of improving human life. Which of the following actions by research scientists is *not* based on that goal?

   (1) announcing research results promptly in scientific journals for all interested scientists to read
   (2) announcing research results only after a patent, which protects the commercial rights of the discoverer, has been filed
   (3) applying for a government research grant in order to find practical applications of superconductivity
   (4) working hard to discover a material that can be used as a room-temperature superconductor
   (5) attending scientific conferences in Europe to better learn about research done by European scientists

ANSWERS AND EXPLANATIONS START ON PAGE 306.

Magnetism

> ## Key Word
>
> *pole*—region of a magnet where the magnetic force is very strong

Centuries ago, the Greeks discovered that small pieces of a certain iron ore could both attract and repel other pieces of the same ore. Today this ore is called magnetite, and pieces of magnetite are referred to as **natural magnets**. The phenomenon the Greeks observed is called **magnetism**.

Have you seen magnets do these things?

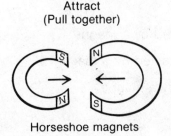

Attract
(Pull together)

Horseshoe magnets

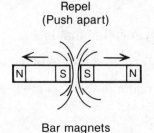

Repel
(Push apart)

Bar magnets

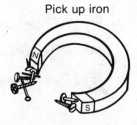

Pick up iron

Magnets have two poles, or regions, where the magnetic force is very strong. When magnets are brought close together, they act in a way that reminds you of electric charges. Opposite poles attract each other: the north pole of one magnet is strongly attracted to the south pole of a second magnet. Like poles repel each other: north poles repel each other, and so do south poles.

Two common magnets that you may have used at one time or another are the horseshoe magnet and the bar magnet. A horseshoe magnet, as its name implies, looks like a horseshoe. The poles are the two ends of the magnet. A bar magnet is in the shape of a straight bar. One end is the north pole, and the other end is the south pole. Horseshoe and bar magnets differ only in shape. Like all other magnets, each of these types always has only one north pole and one south pole.

When you use magnets, you will discover two more of their properties. First, you will find that a magnet can strongly attract metal such as iron, which itself is not a magnet, to either its north or south pole. And second, you will find that magnetic force, whether it attracts or repels, becomes less strong as you move farther away from a magnet.

Exercise 17: Magnetism

Directions: The statements below refer to magnetism. Circle *T* for each statement that is true and *F* for each that is false.

T F **1.** The north pole of any magnet is always attracted to the south pole of any other magnet.

T F **2.** A bar magnet differs from a horseshoe magnet because a bar magnet will not attract iron.

T F **3.** Magnetite is a name given to a type of natural magnet.

T F **4.** The strength of a magnet increases as you move farther from the magnet.

★ GED PRACTICE ★

Exercise 18: Types of Magnetic Materials

Directions: Read the definitions of types of magnetic materials and then answer the questions that follow.

(1) **Nonmagnetic**—substances that are not attracted to a magnet at all

(2) **Naturally magnetic**—any material that occurs in nature as a natural magnet

(3) **Ferromagnetic**—any material that is strongly attracted by a magnet

(4) **Paramagnetic**—any material that is only slightly attracted by a magnet

(5) **Diamagnetic**—any material that is weakly repelled by a magnet

1. While playing with a magnet and a box of thumbtacks, Laurie noticed that the tacks strongly clung to both poles of the magnet. These thumbtacks would be best classified as

   (1) nonmagnetic
   (2) naturally magnetic
   (3) ferromagnetic
   (4) paramagnetic
   (5) diamagnetic

2. The ancient Chinese used lodestone, a type of magnetic ore found in mountains and on sandy beaches, to make compasses for use in navigation. Lodestone can be classified as

   (1) nonmagnetic
   (2) naturally magnetic
   (3) ferromagnetic
   (4) paramagnetic
   (5) diamagnetic

3. When alchemists were trying to find a way to create gold, they knew that one property of gold was that it is weakly repelled by a magnet. Knowing this, you would classify gold as

   (1) nonmagnetic
   (2) naturally magnetic
   (3) ferromagnetic
   (4) paramagnetic
   (5) diamagnetic

4. Many gases such as helium are neither attracted to nor repelled by a magnet. These gases would be best classified as

   (1) nonmagnetic
   (2) naturally magnetic
   (3) ferromagnetic
   (4) paramagnetic
   (5) diamagnetic

5. Aluminum, which at first doesn't appear to be attracted by a magnet, is found to be slightly attracted to a very strong magnet. Aluminum is in a class of materials called

   (1) nonmagnetic
   (2) naturally magnetic
   (3) ferromagnetic
   (4) paramagnetic
   (5) diamagnetic

ANSWERS AND EXPLANATIONS START ON PAGE 306.

Nuclear Physics

Radioactivity

> ### Key Words
>
> ***atom***—smallest particle of an element that has the properties of that element
> ***nucleus***—the core of an atom
> ***nuclei***—more than one nucleus

What do dental X-rays and atomic bombs have in common? You may already know the answer: they both make use of radioactivity, a property of some types of atoms. The nuclei of radioactive atoms are unstable and break apart on their own. As an unstable nucleus breaks apart, it shoots out certain types of particles and rays. Nine of the elements are known to be radioactive.

There are three basic types of particles and rays given off by a radioactive nucleus:

1. Alpha particles. An alpha particle is made up of two protons and two neutrons bound tightly together.

2. Beta particles. A beta particle is an electron. It is identical to the electrons that orbit the nucleus of each atom.

3. Gamma rays. A gamma ray is a high-energy electromagnetic wave. A gamma ray differs from visible light in that its energy is much higher and its wavelength is much shorter.

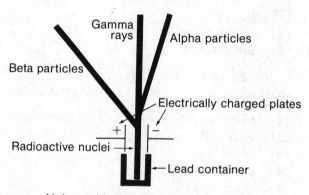

Alpha and beta particles and gamma rays are shot out as radioactive nuclei decay. Electrically charged plates can be used to separate these radiations.

A given amount of a radioactive substance will decay (change into other substances because its nuclei are splitting) over a period of time. The rate at which the substance decays is given as a number called a ***half-life***. During one half-life, one-half of the radioactive nuclei present will have split into smaller nuclei. Different radioactive elements have different half-lifes. For example, the half-life of uranium-238 is 45,000,000 years, while the half-life of polonium is less than one-thousandth of a second.

Below is an illustration of radioactive decay. It is a decay curve for a fictitious element that has a half-life of one day. The element starts with 1,000 nuclei. Notice how many nuclei remain as each day (half-life) passes.

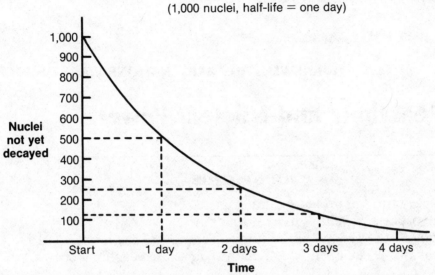

RADIOACTIVE DECAY CURVE
(1,000 nuclei, half-life = one day)

Notice that when one half-life (one day) has passed, only 500 nuclei have not yet decayed.

Exercise 19: Radioactivity

Directions: Answer each question below.

1. Name the three types of particles and rays given off by radioactive nuclei as they decay. _____, _____, _____

2. What is the name given to the length of time it takes one half of a group of radioactive nuclei to decay? _____

★ **GED PRACTICE** ★

Exercise 20: Half-life

Directions: Choose the best answer to each question or statement below.

1. Which of the following statements is false?

   (1) A radioactive element may emit one or more types of particles and rays.
   (2) Different radioactive elements have different half-lifes.
   (3) During radioactive decay, a nucleus breaks apart.
   (4) During one half-life, half of the radioactive nuclei will decay.
   (5) Radioactive decay occurs only when elements are X-rayed or blown up in atomic bombs.

2. According to the graph on page 251, the number of nuclei that remain when three half-lifes have passed is

   (1) 1000
   (2) 500
   (3) 250
   (4) 125
   (5) less than 100

ANSWERS AND EXPLANATIONS START ON PAGE 306.

Chain Reactions and Nuclear Power

Key Words

fission—the splitting of an atomic nucleus
fusion—the process of joining two atomic nuclei
chain reaction—the production of nuclear energy through fission of nuclei
nuclear reactor—a device in which controlled chain reactions occur

The discovery of radioactivity in 1896 was the first step toward a more complete understanding of atomic nuclei. Another discovery showed that many nuclei could be split into smaller nuclei if they were bombarded with particles such as protons or alpha particles.

The process of splitting a nucleus into two medium-sized nuclei is called fission. The fission of a nucleus causes the release of a large amount of nuclear energy. Scientists realized that a tremendous supply of energy could be released through the fission of very small amounts of elements such as uranium.

In 1942, Enrico Fermi, an Italian physicist working at the University of Chicago, produced the first controlled nuclear chain reaction. In a chain reaction, nuclei are split apart in a controlled way, and as a result a great quantity of nuclear energy is produced. (An example of an *uncontrolled* nuclear reaction is the explosion of an atomic bomb.)

By 1943, the first nuclear reactors were being built. A nuclear reactor is a device in which controlled chain reactions are carried out. Nuclear reactors are the heart of a nuclear power plant.

A nuclear power plant operates much the same way as a coal power plant. In each, heat energy is used to produce electrical energy. In the coal plant, heat is produced by the burning of coal in a boiler. In a nuclear plant, the heat comes from the fissioning of nuclei in a nuclear reactor. In each plant, the heat created is used to boil water to produce steam. The steam turns a turbine that is connected to an electric generator. The generator produces electrical power, which then flows down electric power lines on its way from each plant.

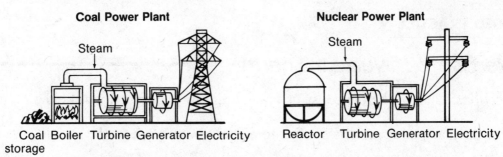

Coal Power Plant

Steam

Coal Boiler Turbine Generator Electricity
storage

Nuclear Power Plant

Steam

Reactor Turbine Generator Electricity

In both coal and nuclear power plants, water is heated to produce steam, which turns a turbine to create electricity.

Compared to other fuels, nuclear fuel produces an almost unbelievable amount of energy. At the present time, though, only one kind of atom found in nature can be used as nuclear fuel. This is U-235, a rare form of the element uranium. A piece of U-235 the size of a grain of rice can produce energy equal to that contained in three tons of coal or fourteen barrels of oil! One pound of U-235 can produce energy equal to that produced by 3,000,000 pounds of coal or 6,400 barrels of oil.

No one knows for sure how much U-235 is contained in the Earth's crust. However, it is fairly scarce. In fact, it is estimated that, with equal use, the known sources of uranium fuel would run out before fossil fuel sources (coal, oil, and natural gas) run out.

Nuclear Fusion

Someday it may be possible to obtain large amounts of power by a process called nuclear fusion. Nuclear fusion occurs when two nuclei are *fused*, or joined together. Nuclear fusion is the process that provides the energy given off by stars. On the sun, hydrogen atoms combine to form helium atoms, releasing tremendous energy in the process.

Unfortunately, fusion reactions can take place only in regions of extremely high temperature—near 100 million degrees Celsius! Because it is so difficult to produce this high temperature, nuclear fusion is not yet a practical energy source. Whether it ever will be is still a debated question. However, hydrogen—the fuel needed for nuclear fusion reactions—is available in abundance on Earth. It can be taken directly from ocean water.

Exercise 21: Nuclear Power

Directions: Briefly define what is meant by each of the following terms.

1. nuclear fission: _____

2. chain reaction: _____

3. nuclear reactor: _____

4. nuclear fusion: _____

★ GED PRACTICE ★

Exercise 22: Nuclear Energy

Directions: Choose the best answer to each question or statement below.

1. A nuclear power plant is similar to a coal power plant in the way it

    (1) uses an electric generator to turn a steam-driven turbine
    (2) produces nuclear waste
    (3) uses a steam-driven turbine to turn an electric generator
    (4) burns coal as a source of heat energy
    (5) uses nuclear fission as a source of heat energy

2. What is U-235?

    (1) a type of nuclear reaction
    (2) an electric generator in a nuclear power plant
    (3) a form of heat energy produced by nuclear fission
    (4) a type of fuel used in nuclear fusion
    (5) a type of fuel used in nuclear fission

3. All of the statements below were made by a scientist working at a nuclear power plant. Which statement is a prediction?

    (1) Nuclear fission produces radioactive by-products as waste materials.
    (2) By the year 2050, nuclear power plants will be the world's primary method of producing electrical power.
    (3) The reason that nuclear fusion power plants have not been developed is that no one knows how to build one.
    (4) When U-235 fissions, a tremendous quantity of energy is released.
    (5) Accidents like Three Mile Island and Chernobyl remind us just how dangerous nuclear power plants can be.

ANSWERS AND EXPLANATIONS START ON PAGE 306.

 Writing Activity 2

Nuclear power is also used in the manufacture of nuclear weapons. While some people support the continued build-up of nuclear arms, others are strongly opposed. Do you think that the U.S. should keep manufacturing nuclear weapons, or do you think we should stop?

Pick *one* side of the issue and write one or two paragraphs defending your point of view. Be sure to support your reasons with specific examples.

SAMPLE ANSWERS START ON PAGE 307.

Our Energy Future

Key Words

solar energy—energy from the sun
geothermal energy—energy from the earth's crust
hydroelectric power—energy from running water

In this chapter, we've discussed the major forms of energy currently available to us: fossil fuels (oil, coal, and gas) and nuclear energy. Each of these energy sources has its problems. The supply of fossil fuels is limited and will not last forever. In addition, the burning of fossil fuels creates a dangerous form of pollution.

Nuclear energy, seen by some as a promising source of energy, is also limited, and there is no known way of disposing of radioactive waste. Scientists are doing research on alternative forms of energy, hoping that one of these, or a combination of them, may someday fill our energy needs.

Solar Energy

The term *solar energy* refers to any of a number of uses of sunlight. The great advantage of energy from the sun is that it is unlimited and does not pollute the environment. Homes and office buildings can be heated using solar energy. Passive solar heating is achieved through the greenhouse effect—simply using captured sunlight to heat a glass-walled room. Active solar heating can be accomplished by using solar collectors. A solar collector (a device that is most often placed on a building's roof) uses sunlight to heat a fluid that slowly passes through it. The heated fluid is then pumped from the collector and is circulated through the pipes of a building's heating system.

Another mechanism that runs on energy from the sun is the solar cell, a device that produces electricity when sunlight strikes it. Solar cells have a wide range of possible uses. At present, though, solar cell use is pretty much limited to spacecraft and to a small number of low-energy consumer items such as watches and hand-held calculators. Large solar cells are expensive to make and cannot yet be considered a reasonable alternative to other methods of generating power. However, if technological advances can bring the costs down, you may one day see solar cells power automobiles, homes, and a wide range of consumer products.

Geothermal Energy

Geothermal energy is energy that comes from the Earth's hot interior. You already know about two forms of geothermal energy that aren't under our control: volcanoes and earthquakes. But some forms of geothermal energy can be controlled and used to our advantage.

In certain places, scientists can drill wells into the Earth's crust and tap into naturally occurring bodies of hot water or steam. This energy can then be used to turn turbines that produce electricity. Even now, some of San Francisco's electricity is produced in this way.

Though the amount of geothermal energy available in the Earth's crust is almost unlimited and nonpolluting, technical difficulties prevent it from seriously being considered a major energy source in the near future. Some of the hot springs are so far under the Earth's crust that it is very hard to get the heat up to the surface.

Wind and Water Energy

Wind energy has been used for several centuries to power windmills in Europe. Now windmills are being designed in many places in the world to provide a small amount of electricity to cities near strong wind areas. Although they are proving useful in some locations, windmills will probably not supply a very large share of the energy needed by future generations.

The most important form of water energy in the United States is the energy of flowing rivers. Flowing water can be used to turn turbines and produce electricity. At present, hydroelectric power provides about 5 percent of the energy used in the United States.

Ocean water also contains a great amount of energy, both as ocean waves and in the heat energy held in ocean water. But harnessing that energy has proven difficult. A machine large enough to capture a significant amount of energy from ocean waves would have to be more than a mile long. Many technical problems remain to be solved before the ocean could become a practical energy source.

Decisions About Energy Use

With all these energy sources available, the United States itself will not run out of energy in the near future. We have enough coal alone to last for several centuries. But, as you've seen, having energy sources isn't the whole story. Today's most immediate concern is not whether energy is available, but about the price we'll have to pay in order to continue to use those sources.

The dangers of air pollution, the greenhouse effect, and nuclear waste will not go away by themselves. These effects are only controlled by laws that regulate the industries that are responsible. What's more, the technological advances needed in order to develop safe, nonpolluting, affordable energy sources will cost a lot of money, much of which will probably be paid by taxpayers. For these reasons, the future of energy in the United States very much depends on what we citizens decide. In our society, pollution control and technological advances end up being as much political questions as scientific ones.

Exercise 23: Forms of Energy

Directions: Rushing water in a river is an example of uncontrolled energy. When river water is used to turn turbines and create electricity, we say that the energy is controlled. On each line below, write *controlled* or *uncontrolled* to indicate the use of energy being described.

_____ **1.** a raging house fire

_____ **2.** a race car being driven at 200 miles per hour

_____ **3.** a campfire

_____ **4.** an erupting volcano

_____ **5.** a telephone ringing

★ GED PRACTICE ★

Exercise 24: Our Energy Future

Directions: Choose the best answer to each question below.

1. Which of the following is *not* an advantage of the use of solar cells to produce electricity?

　(1)　the level of pollution produced
　(2)　the cost of producing the electricity
　(3)　the amount of space taken up by the cells
　(4)　the amount of sunlight energy available
　(5)　the versatility of solar cell use

2. What are the two main reasons that geothermal and solar energy are not being used more than they currently are?

　(1)　excessive cost and pollution control problems
　(2)　scarcity of the resource and excessive cost
　(3)　technical problems and pollution control problems
　(4)　technical problems and excessive cost
　(5)　scarcity of the resource and technical problems

3. Which of the following is *least* likely to be the main factor that determines which type of energy will provide most of the power used in the United States during the 21st century?

　(1)　potential profits made by power companies
　(2)　unforeseen natural disasters
　(3)　technological advances in energy production
　(4)　the supply of remaining fossil fuels
　(5)　industrial competition from foreign countries

ANSWERS AND EXPLANATIONS START ON PAGE 307.

Posttest Answer Grid

1 ① ② ③ ④ ⑤   23 ① ② ③ ④ ⑤   45 ① ② ③ ④ ⑤

2 ① ② ③ ④ ⑤   24 ① ② ③ ④ ⑤   46 ① ② ③ ④ ⑤

3 ① ② ③ ④ ⑤   25 ① ② ③ ④ ⑤   47 ① ② ③ ④ ⑤

4 ① ② ③ ④ ⑤   26 ① ② ③ ④ ⑤   48 ① ② ③ ④ ⑤

5 ① ② ③ ④ ⑤   27 ① ② ③ ④ ⑤   49 ① ② ③ ④ ⑤

6 ① ② ③ ④ ⑤   28 ① ② ③ ④ ⑤   50 ① ② ③ ④ ⑤

7 ① ② ③ ④ ⑤   29 ① ② ③ ④ ⑤   51 ① ② ③ ④ ⑤

8 ① ② ③ ④ ⑤   30 ① ② ③ ④ ⑤   52 ① ② ③ ④ ⑤

9 ① ② ③ ④ ⑤   31 ① ② ③ ④ ⑤   53 ① ② ③ ④ ⑤

10 ① ② ③ ④ ⑤   32 ① ② ③ ④ ⑤   54 ① ② ③ ④ ⑤

11 ① ② ③ ④ ⑤   33 ① ② ③ ④ ⑤   55 ① ② ③ ④ ⑤

12 ① ② ③ ④ ⑤   34 ① ② ③ ④ ⑤   56 ① ② ③ ④ ⑤

13 ① ② ③ ④ ⑤   35 ① ② ③ ④ ⑤   57 ① ② ③ ④ ⑤

14 ① ② ③ ④ ⑤   36 ① ② ③ ④ ⑤   58 ① ② ③ ④ ⑤

15 ① ② ③ ④ ⑤   37 ① ② ③ ④ ⑤   59 ① ② ③ ④ ⑤

16 ① ② ③ ④ ⑤   38 ① ② ③ ④ ⑤   60 ① ② ③ ④ ⑤

17 ① ② ③ ④ ⑤   39 ① ② ③ ④ ⑤   61 ① ② ③ ④ ⑤

18 ① ② ③ ④ ⑤   40 ① ② ③ ④ ⑤   62 ① ② ③ ④ ⑤

19 ① ② ③ ④ ⑤   41 ① ② ③ ④ ⑤   63 ① ② ③ ④ ⑤

20 ① ② ③ ④ ⑤   42 ① ② ③ ④ ⑤   64 ① ② ③ ④ ⑤

21 ① ② ③ ④ ⑤   43 ① ② ③ ④ ⑤   65 ① ② ③ ④ ⑤

22 ① ② ③ ④ ⑤   44 ① ② ③ ④ ⑤   66 ① ② ③ ④ ⑤

SCIENCE POSTTEST

Directions: This science posttest will give you the opportunity to evaluate your readiness for the actual GED Science Test.

This test contains 66 questions. Some of the questions are based on short reading passages, and some of them require you to interpret a chart, graph, or diagram.

You should take approximately 95 minutes to complete this test. At the end of 95 minutes, stop and mark your place. Then finish the test. This will give you an idea of whether or not you can finish the real GED Test in the time allotted. Try to answer as many questions as you can. A blank will count as a wrong answer, so make a reasonable guess for questions you are not sure of.

When you are finished with the test, turn to the evaluation and scoring charts on page 283. Use the charts to evaluate whether or not you are ready to take the actual GED Test, and if not, what areas need more work.

Questions 1 and 2 refer to the illustration below.

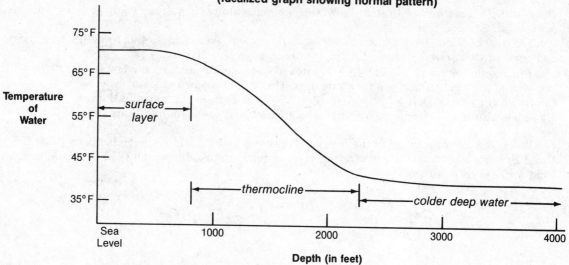

CHANGES OF OCEAN TEMPERATURE WITH INCREASING DEPTH
(Idealized graph showing normal pattern)

1. A thermocline can best be described as a

   (1) temperature distribution in the ocean
   (2) layer of warm water close to the surface
   (3) layer of cold water beneath the warm surface
   (4) transition region between the warm surface and the much colder deep water
   (5) region of nearly constant temperature just beneath the warm surface

2. Which of the following would be the *most likely* to upset the ocean's normal temperature distribution?

   (1) an earthquake near the ocean shore
   (2) an erupting volcano on the ocean bottom
   (3) a violent rainstorm on the ocean surface
   (4) a hot sunny day when there is no wind
   (5) a hurricane passing over the ocean surface

3. Any object that moves through air feels the effect of air resistance, a force that pushes against the object and slows it down. All of the following objects are designed to take advantage of air resistance except

   (1) a parachute
   (2) a kite
   (3) an electric fan
   (4) a golf club
   (5) a frisbee

Questions 4 and 5 refer to the following passage.

Did you ever wonder why, on a clear day, the sky appears so blue? What happens to the other colors of the rainbow that are also present in sunlight? The answer has to do with the scattering of sunlight by the atmosphere.

When you look at the daytime sky, you see only the light that travels to your eyes from the direction of your gaze. This light is blue, because only blue light is to a great degree scattered in all directions by atoms of nitrogen and oxygen, the main gases found in the earth's atmosphere. Other colors of light are less apt to be scattered, and they continue their straight-line movement through the atmosphere and away from your eyes.

4. According to the passage, scattering causes blue light to

   (1) change color
   (2) change its direction of movement
   (3) return to space instead of striking the Earth
   (4) lose its energy
   (5) become invisible

5. What information would scientists first need to know before they could determine the color of the daytime Martian sky as it is seen from the surface of Mars?

   (1) the amount of sunlight that strikes the Martian atmosphere
   (2) the types of gases that make up the Martian atmosphere
   (3) the color of the Martian surface
   (4) the average temperature on the Martian surface
   (5) the types of rocks and soil that make up the Martian surface

6. Two identical negatively charged spheres are suspended by string from support stands. Which of the drawings below correctly illustrates how the charged spheres will react when the stands holding them are moved close together?

(1)

(2)

(3)

(4)

(5)

Questions 7 and 8 refer to the following information.

Methane (CH_4), also called *natural gas*, is commonly used as fuel for heating and cooking. When methane burns, it combines with oxygen gas (O_2) and produces carbon dioxide gas (CO_2) and water (H_2O). The equation of this chemical reaction is written as:

$$CH_4 + 2O_2 \longrightarrow CO_2 + 2H_2O + energy$$

7. For each molecule of methane gas that burns, how many molecules of CO_2 gas form?

   (1) 1
   (2) 2
   (3) 3
   (4) 4
   (5) 6

8. Which of the following statements about the reaction equation above is true?

   (1) There are more atoms of oxygen on the left side of the arrow than on the right side.
   (2) There are fewer atoms of oxygen on the left side of the arrow than on the right side.
   (3) There is an equal number of molecules of oxygen gas on each side of the arrow.
   (4) There is an equal number of atoms of oxygen on each side of the arrow.
   (5) No oxygen gas is represented in the reaction equation.

Questions 9 and 10 are based on the information given below.

In a television commercial, an oil company salesman makes the following four statements about a synthetic car oil.

  A. Syn 1 is the most efficient oil you'll ever use in your car.
  B. Using Syn 1, you'll need to change your oil only once every 35,000 miles.
  C. The new Syn 1 oil costs only $4.49 per quart.
  D. Syn 1 is available wherever high-quality automotive products are sold.

9. Which of the statements above implies that scientific tests have determined the amount of wear received by an engine that uses Syn 1 oil?

   (1) A only
   (2) B only
   (3) C only
   (4) D only
   (5) B and D only

10. Which of the above statements are most likely based on opinion rather than facts?

   (1) A and B only
   (2) A and C only
   (3) A and D only
   (4) B and C only
   (5) C and D only

Questions 11 and 12 refer to the following illustration.

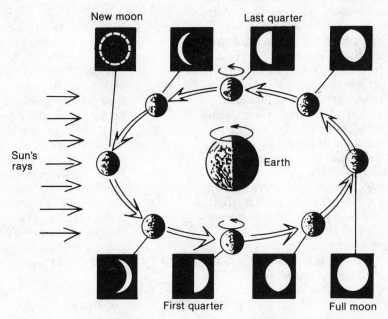

11. According to the illustration above, a full moon occurs when

    (1) the moon is between the sun and the Earth
    (2) the moon is not visible from the Earth
    (3) the sun is between the Earth and the moon
    (4) the moon and the Earth are the same distance from the sun
    (5) the Earth is between the sun and the moon

12. What can you conclude by observing the different shapes in which the moon appears to us on Earth?

    (1) Moonlight is light produced by the moon.
    (2) Moonlight is light from Earth that reflects off the moon's surface.
    (3) Moonlight is sunlight that reflects off the moon's surface.
    (4) The direction of the moon's rotation (spinning motion) is opposite to that of the Earth.
    (5) During a full moon, the entire surface of the Earth is lit by sunlight.

Questions 13–15 refer to the passage below.

Geologists believe that the Earth's surface is made up of many slowly moving rigid plates. Devastating earthquakes often occur along the boundary line where two plates meet. An example is the earthquake activity along the San Andreas fault in California. Along this fault, or collision boundary, the slowly moving Pacific plate pushes against the continental plate and causes a buildup of pressure. Occasionally a sudden slippage occurs, and a tremendous amount of earth-shaking energy is released. Such an earthquake destroyed the city of San Francisco in 1906.

The San Andreas fault can be drawn on a map as a line that runs throughout the length of California. This fault passes near San Francisco in the north and Los Angeles in the south, two major population regions on the West Coast. Slippage anywhere along the San Andreas fault can result in major earthquakes in nearby areas and smaller earthquakes throughout the entire state of California.

No one can predict for sure just where or when the next major earthquake will strike. Every point along the fault must be considered at equal risk. For this reason, most buildings in cities near the fault zone are specially designed to be earthquake-proof.

13. A fault can best be described as

   (1) a line drawn between two recorded earthquakes
   (2) a boundary line between two crustal plates
   (3) a boundary line that divides a state into two regions
   (4) a boundary line that separates a region of high population from a region of low population
   (5) a boundary line between two major population centers

14. Which of the following is *not* a conclusion that can be drawn from information given in the passage?

   (1) In California, some buildings are constructed with earthquake danger in mind.
   (2) The San Francisco earthquake of 1906 resulted from slippage along the San Andreas fault.
   (3) People living along the San Andreas fault are more likely to be injured in an earthquake than people living in other parts of California.
   (4) Major earthquake danger is less in San Francisco than in Los Angeles because San Francisco has already had a major quake in this century.
   (5) Because the islands of Japan also lie along a fault, Japan also faces the danger of earthquakes.

15. A geologist is trying to predict when an earthquake might occur in or near Redding, California. Each of the following will be important to this study *except*

   (1) the history of earthquakes in and around the city of Redding
   (2) the pattern of yearly weather conditions in and around the city of Redding
   (3) the distance Redding lies from the San Andreas fault
   (4) the types of land formations around Redding
   (5) the history of earthquake activity in other areas of California that are geologically similar to the Redding area

Questions 16–19 refer to the following passage.

Selective breeding is a method that's used to improve the traits of animals or plants that are commercially valuable. In selective breeding, only those plants and animals that have desirable traits are mated.

Hybridization is the selective breeding of two organisms that have distinct genetic differences even though they are members of the same species and are able to mate. The purpose of hybridization is to produce a new individual (a hybrid) that inherits desirable traits from each parent organism. However, hybrids may inherit undesirable traits as well.

An example of a hybrid animal is the mule, a cross between a female horse and a male donkey. The mule gets its size and strength from the horse. Its endurance and surefootedness come from the donkey. Like many hybrids, though, the mule is sterile—unable to produce offspring of its own.

Inbreeding, the opposite of hybridization, is the selective mating of plants or animals that have nearly identical genetic makeup. Inbreeding can produce generations of nearly identical offspring. In plants, inbreeding is done by self-pollination. Self-pollination insures that only the one parent-plant's genes are passed on. Inbreeding in animals is done by mating close relatives. The breeding of thoroughbred horses and purebred dogs are good examples of inbreeding.

16. If a pet store advertises that a dog is a purebred cocker spaniel, which of the following can you assume to be true about the dog?

    A. The dog will have traits that are very similar to the traits of other purebred cocker spaniels.
    B. The dog will have only the favorable traits of its parents.
    C. Both parents of the dog are purebred cocker spaniels.
    D. Only one parent of the dog is a purebred cocker spaniel.

    (1) A and B only
    (2) A and C only
    (3) A and D only
    (4) B and C only
    (5) B and D only

17. The main purpose of hybridization is to produce organisms that

    (1) are incapable of breeding
    (2) are gentically identical to each other
    (3) have a unique combination of desirable traits
    (4) have no inheritable traits
    (5) are genetically identical to their parents

18. From the information given in the passage, you can conclude that hybrid organisms are produced only when

    (1) the offspring of the mating organisms are sterile
    (2) organisms from two different species mate
    (3) an offspring inherits only desirable traits
    (4) genetically different members of the same species mate
    (5) genetically identical members of the same species mate

19. Which of the following is *not* a hybrid?

    (1) a pink rose, produced by crossing a red rose with a white rose
    (2) a tangelo, produced by crossing a grapefruit with a tangerine
    (3) a first-generation cockapoo, the result of breeding a purebred cocker spaniel with a purebred poodle
    (4) a golden retriever, the result of breeding a purebred golden retriever with its second cousin
    (5) popcorn, usually created by crossing two kinds of corn

Questions 20–22 refer to the following passage.

Potential energy is stored energy, energy available to be used. Four common forms of potential energy are gravitational, chemical, nuclear, and elastic.

When a rock simply sits on top of a mountain, it has gravitational potential energy. If the rock is knocked loose, it rolls down the mountain due to the pull of the force of gravity. As it rolls and gains speed, its gravitational potential energy is changed to kinetic energy—energy of motion.

Chemical potential energy is stored chemical energy such as that found in a flashlight battery. When a flashlight is turned on, the battery's stored energy is changed into light energy. Another example of stored chemical energy is glucose, the food sugar from which your body cells get their energy. During exercise, your muscles change the energy stored in this sugar into body heat and into the kinetic energy of body movement. A third example is the energy stored in coal. Coal's chemical potential energy is changed to heat when it is burned.

The energy stored in the nucleus of atoms is called nuclear potential energy. At a nuclear power plant, this energy is released and changed to heat. The heat is used to boil water and create the high-pressure steam needed to turn the electricity-producing turbines.

Elastic potential energy is energy that is stored in a stretched or compressed object such as a spring. A spring in a windup watch is an example. As the spring slowly unwinds, its stored energy is changed to the kinetic energy of the watch's moving hands.

20. Which of the following is the best restatement of information given in the passage?

(1) Potential energy and kinetic energy are both forms of stored energy.
(2) Potential energy and kinetic energy are both forms of energy of motion.
(3) Potential energy is energy of motion, while kinetic energy is stored energy.
(4) Potential energy is stored energy, while kinetic energy is energy of motion.
(5) Potential energy always changes into kinetic energy.

21. Of the following, which is the only object that is *not* designed to make practical use of stored chemical energy?

(1) boat oars
(2) a fireplace
(3) a bicycle
(4) a bathtub drain
(5) an automobile engine

22. Which of the following would be *least* relevant in determining whether a newly discovered source of potential energy might have great practical value?

(1) the amount of the new energy-containing material that is available for use
(2) whether the new source is a form of gravitational, chemical, nuclear, or elastic potential energy
(3) the cost of changing the potential energy of the new source into usable forms of energy such as heat
(4) whether there are technical problems that must be solved before the energy can be used
(5) whether use of the new source produces dangerous waste products

Questions 23–27 refer to the passage below.

An ecosystem is a community of plants, animals, and nonliving things. Ecosystems may be found in forests, grasslands, deserts, mountains, and bodies of water. Each type of ecosystem depends on three cycles that make community life possible.

In the carbon dioxide-oxygen cycle, plants take carbon dioxide gas from the atmosphere and use it for photosynthesis, the production of food sugar. As plants use carbon dioxide gas, they give off oxygen gas. Animals, on the other hand, breathe in oxygen and give off carbon dioxide as a waste product. The cycle is completed when plants and animals die and carbon dioxide gas forms from their decomposing bodies.

In the water cycle, both plants and animals take in water for life activities. To complete the cycle, plant leaves give off water vapor in a process called transpiration. While transpiring, a plant uses evaporating water to help eliminate waste products formed from plant activity. Animals give water back to the atmosphere when they exhale and when they perspire (sweat).

In the nitrogen cycle, plants get nitrogen, which they need in order to grow plant tissue, from nitrates (nitrogen compounds in the soil). Nitrates are produced in the soil by a two-step process. First, nitrogen-fixing bacteria break down the proteins of decaying plant and animal remains and produce ammonia. Then, nitrifying bacteria change this ammonia to nitrates. The nitrates are used to produce healthy plants that then become food for animals. With the death and decomposition of plants and animals, the nitrogen cycle is completed.

23. The animal that is well known for being adapted to an ecosystem in which the water cycle may be very unpredictable is a

(1) penguin
(2) swordfish
(3) camel
(4) frog
(5) duck

24. According to the passage, carbon dioxide gas is produced and returned to the atmosphere when

(1) animals exhale
(2) plants carry on photosynthesis
(3) animals perspire
(4) plants transpire
(5) water decomposes

25. Which of the following would be most disruptive to the balance of atmospheric carbon dioxide gas and oxygen gas?

(1) a huge forest fire
(2) a major earthquake
(3) a tidal wave on the ocean
(4) a volcanic eruption
(5) a major flood

26. In soil that is overwatered and does not drain well, a second type of bacteria, called denitrifying bacteria, thrives and breaks down ammonia before it is converted to nitrates. From this fact, you can conclude that overwatering a houseplant can

(1) speed up plant growth
(2) destroy denitrifying bacteria in the soil
(3) result in a breeding ground for small insects
(4) prevent the plant's roots from obtaining carbon dioxide
(5) inhibit normal plant growth

27. Which of the following items of information would be *least* important to a biologist who wants to determine whether certain farmland could be used to grow bok choy, an Oriental vegetable?

(1) the types of ammonia compounds in the soil
(2) the types of bacteria that live in the soil
(3) the types of crops previously grown on the land
(4) the amount of dead plant and animal remains in the soil
(5) the average amount of rain that falls on the land during the bok choy growing season

Questions 28–33 refer to the following passage.

Important characteristics of the six most familiar groups into which most animals can be classified are given below.

(1) **Fish:** Because they live only in water, most fish have two organs that no other animals have: gills and an air bladder. Fish use gills to take dissolved oxygen out of water. The air bladder, a thin-walled sac that acts as a float, controls the level at which they swim. To reproduce, fish lay soft eggs, depositing them on the bottom of the ocean or other body of water where they live.

(2) **Insects:** Insects are six-legged creatures whose bodies are divided into three distinct regions. Many insects have wings and fly. Other insects have neither legs nor wings. Most insects go through a four-stage development process in which the young look nothing like the adult. To reproduce, insects also lay eggs.

(3) **Amphibians:** Amphibians live for a time in water and for a time on land. Young amphibians live only in water. As they mature, though, they develop features that allow them to live on land. However, amphibians do not become total land animals. Like fish, amphibians must reproduce and lay eggs in water.

(4) **Reptiles:** Reptiles are land animals. Unlike fish and amphibians, they lay an *amniote egg*—an egg that is surrounded by a protective membrane and tough shell. Reptiles are also characterized by a dry body covering of some type of horny scales or plates.

(5) **Birds:** Birds are the only type of animals that are well adapted to life in the air, in the water, and on land. Bird flight is accomplished by the movement of a pair of feather-covered wings. Birds, like reptiles, lay amniote eggs.

(6) **Mammals:** Of all the animals, mammals have the most highly developed organ systems and brains. Most mammals give birth to live young, offspring that look similar to their parents from the moment of birth. Young mammals are nourished with milk from the mammary glands of their mother.

28. Chameleons are best known for their ability to change color in order to match their environment. A chameleon's scaly skin may turn green, yellow, white, brown, or black. Since it lays an amniote egg, the chameleon is best classified as a

(1) fish
(2) insect
(3) amphibian
(4) reptile
(5) mammal

29. Although a bat has eyes, it does most of its flying and hunting at night. The offspring of a bat are born live and receive nourishment from the glands of the mother bat. Knowing this, you would classify the bat as a

(1) fish
(2) amphibian
(3) reptile
(4) bird
(5) mammal

30. A salamander is a timid, harmless animal that has a thin, elongated body and a long tail. Most species have four short legs. Salamanders live near streams and ponds in which the female lays her soft eggs. The larvae (young form of the salamander) grow in the water, and they eventually develop lungs that allow them to live on land. A salamander would be placed in the class of animals known as

(1) fish
(2) amphibians
(3) reptiles
(4) birds
(5) mammals

31. The killdeer gets its name from the sound it makes—it seems to be saying, "Killdeer." Killdeers build their nests in fields, where the female usually lays four spotted eggs. They are often seen flying around fields where they feast on crop-destroying insects. Killdeers belong to the class of animals known as

(1) fish
(2) amphibians
(3) reptiles
(4) birds
(5) mammals

32. A whale spends all of its life in the ocean. But unlike almost all other marine animals, whales do not lay eggs. Instead, they give birth to live young. After birth, whales are nourished from milk obtained from the glands of the mother whale. A whale is best classified as a

(1) fish
(2) insect
(3) amphibian
(4) reptile
(5) mammal

33. The seahorse gets its name from the shape of its head, which looks very much like a tiny horse. This five-inch-long animal lives only in water. It uses its tail to cling to plants or floating vegetation. The female lays about 200 eggs, which she deposits in a pouch on the underside of the male seahorse's body. A seahorse can best be classified as a

(1) fish
(2) amphibian
(3) reptile
(4) bird
(5) mammal

34. A new roller coaster in an amusement park travels in a loop as shown in the illustration below.

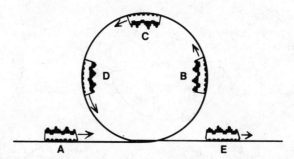

In which of the five indicated positions is the potential energy (stored energy) of the passenger car the greatest?

(1) A
(2) B
(3) C
(4) D
(5) E

Questions 35–38 refer to the passage and illustrations below.

From person to person, differences exist in the surface proteins found in red blood cells. Because of these differences, each person can have any one of four types of blood. These four blood types are named A, B, AB, and O. The circle graphs below contain information about the blood types of three ethnic groups in the United States. The chart shows which kinds of blood transfusions are possible. (A transfusion is the use of one person's donated blood in the body of a second person who has suffered a blood loss.)

Blood Types and Transfusion Possibilities

Blood Type	Can Recieve Blood from	Can Donate Blood to
A	O, A	A, AB
B	O, B	B, AB
AB	A, B, AB, O	AB
O	O	A, B, AB, O

**BLOOD TYPES IN THREE
UNITED STATES ETHNIC GROUPS**

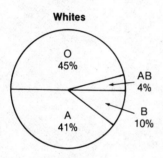

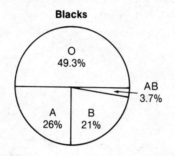

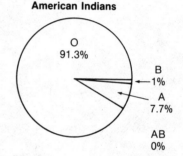

35. Referring to the three circle graphs above, in which ethnic group(s) is one blood type far more common than the other three types?

(1) whites
(2) blacks
(3) American Indians
(4) blacks and whites
(5) whites and American Indians

36. In each ethnic group, the hierarchy of blood types is the same. One blood type is the most common, another is second most common, and so on. Writing the most common blood type first, which of the following correctly lists the blood types in the order of their presence in all three ethnic groups shown in the circle graphs?

(1) O, A, B, AB
(2) A, B, O, AB
(3) B, O, AB, A
(4) AB, B, A, O
(5) O, B, A, AB

37. According to the chart above the graphs, a person with blood type B can give blood only to people of blood type

(1) B
(2) O or B
(3) AB or B
(4) O or A
(5) A or AB

38. A person who can give blood to any other type is called a universal donor. A person who receives blood from all types is called a universal recipient. With these definitions in mind, let A, B, AB, and O each stand for a person with that particular blood type. Which of the following conclusions can be drawn from the chart above the graphs?

(1) A is a universal donor and AB is a universal recipient.
(2) B is a universal donor and O is a universal recipient.
(3) AB is both a universal donor and a universal recipient.
(4) O is a universal donor and AB is a universal recipient.
(5) AB is a universal donor and O is a universal recipient.

Question 39 refers to the following graphs.

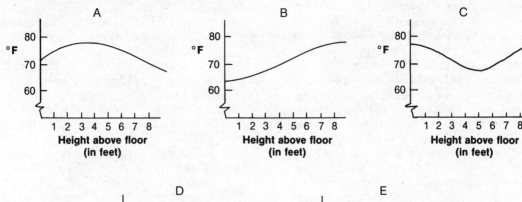

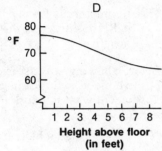

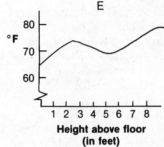

39. Remembering that warm air tends to rise above cold air, which of the following readings most likely represents the temperature readings taken in a room in which the doors and windows are closed?

(1) A
(2) B
(3) C
(4) D
(5) E

40. The pressure of a gas in a closed container can be increased by increasing the temperature of the gas or by adding more gas to the container. Which of the following *does not* utilize these properties of gas pressure?

(1) an automobile tire
(2) a sail on a sailboat
(3) a pressure cooker for use in home cooking
(4) a basketball
(5) a pressure-relief valve on a car radiator

41. An important principle of science is that matter is neither created nor destroyed during physical or chemical changes. Rather, the matter is changed from one form to another. Which of the following is *not* an example of *matter* changing from one form to another?

(1) boiling water changing into steam
(2) burning wood changing into ashes
(3) sugar dissolving in water
(4) the energy of a plucked guitar string changing into sound
(5) gasoline in a car engine changing into a mixture of hot exhaust gases

Questions 42–46 refer to the following passage.

It is standard medical procedure to check a pregnant woman's blood Rh factor. The Rh factor is a protein found in the blood of about 85 percent of all people. Those who have the Rh factor are said to be Rh positive, while those who don't are said to be Rh negative.

If an Rh-negative person receives Rh-positive blood, he or she develops Rh-positive antibodies that will attack Rh-positive blood. This is usually not a problem the first time it happens because the Rh-positive blood mixes thoroughly with the Rh-negative blood before the antibodies form. However, if the person receives Rh-positive blood a second time, the result may be serious and possibly fatal. This is because antibodies are already present and attack the new blood immediately. The antibodies cause the unmixed Rh-positive blood to form clumps that can block small blood vessels.

A difficult situation may arise when a pregnant woman is Rh negative and her partner is Rh positive. Since their child inherits genes from both parents, the fetus can be either Rh positive or Rh negative. If the fetus is Rh positive, the mother's blood may develop Rh-positive antibodies, and some of these antibodies may pass into the fetus's blood. This condition occurs only when there are tiny tears in the membranes that normally keep the mother's blood completely separate from the blood of the fetus. Fortunately, this seepage of blood from mother to fetus does not occur in every pregnancy.

If Rh-positive antibodies do enter the blood of an Rh-positive fetus, the fetus becomes anemic and jaundiced and may die before (or shortly after) birth. To save the child's life at birth, his or her blood is almost entirely replaced by transfused blood. On rare occasions, blood transfusions have even been done to an endangered fetus before birth.

Even if an Rh-negative mother delivers a healthy Rh-positive baby the first time, a second baby born at a later time may be in danger. This is because the mother's blood may now contain Rh-positive antibodies produced during the first pregnancy. To avoid this problem, doctors can give a woman a shot at the time of her first delivery that will prevent her blood from developing Rh-positive antibodies during future pregnancies.

42. According to the passage, a problem pregnancy can develop when

   (1) the mother is Rh positive, the father is Rh negative, and the fetus is Rh positive
   (2) the mother is Rh negative, the father is Rh negative, and the fetus is Rh negative
   (3) the mother is Rh positive, the father is Rh positive, and the fetus is Rh positive
   (4) the mother is Rh negative, the father is Rh positive, and the fetus is Rh positive
   (5) the mother is Rh negative, the father is Rh positive, and the fetus is Rh negative

43. Before allowing a transfusion of Rh-positive blood to an Rh-negative patient, a doctor will want to check to see if the patient

   (1) has ever had a blood transfusion before
   (2) has ever had a problem pregnancy
   (3) is married to an Rh-negative person
   (4) has an Rh-negative mother and an Rh-positive father
   (5) has Rh-positive antibodies in his or her blood

44. The discovery of the importance of the Rh factor during pregnancy has most likely resulted only in

   (1) fewer pregnancies in which Rh-positive babies are born to Rh-negative mothers
   (2) a decrease in early deaths of babies born in countries where modern medical care is available
   (3) a method of stopping Rh-positive antibody production during any pregnancy
   (4) the careful screening of marriage partners by Rh-negative women
   (5) a better understanding of the effectiveness of birth control methods

45. A man who is Rh-negative is given a transfusion of Rh-positive blood. The transfusion would probably cause the man's blood to

    (1) become Rh-positive
    (2) become Rh-negative
    (3) become neutral
    (4) produce Rh-positive antibodies
    (5) produce Rh-negative antibodies

46. Suppose a doctor's patient is pregnant and has Rh-negative blood. Which of the following additional items of information would the doctor need in order to plan to protect the health of the developing fetus?

    (1) whether the patient has other children
    (2) whether the father of the fetus she is carrying is also the father of her other children
    (3) whether either of the patient's parents has Rh-positive blood
    (4) whether the father of the fetus she is carrying is Rh positive
    (5) whether the fetus is male or female

47. Ancient alchemists used a process called calcination to convert limestone ($CaCO_3$) into lime (CaO). The same process, which is simply the controlled heating of limestone, is still used today in the cement industry. By comparing the chemical formulas of limestone and lime, determine which of the following formulas represents the gas given off during calcination.

    (1) O_2
    (2) CO
    (3) C_2O
    (4) CO_2
    (5) C_2

Questions 48–51 are based on the passage below.

The discovery that the Earth acts as a giant magnet led to the development of the magnetic compass, a useful direction-finding device. The most popular type of compass consists of a magnetized needle that is in a case and is free to rotate around its center point. The needle is a type of bar magnet and has both a north pole and a south pole. You simply hold this compass in your hand and watch the needle naturally line up with the direction of the Earth's magnetic field. From the direction the needle points, you can determine the direction you're traveling, or you can determine what direction one object is from a second object.

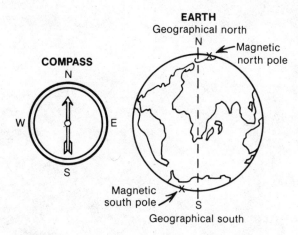

Scientists have discovered that, at all points on the Earth's surface, the north pole of a compass needle is attracted to and points toward the Earth's north magnetic pole. The north magnetic pole—so named because it is located in the Northern Hemisphere—is a point about 1,200 miles south of the north geographical pole (the northernmost point on the Earth). Similarly, the south pole of a compass needle is attracted to and points toward the Earth's south magnetic pole, a point located in Antarctica, about 1,200 miles north of the south geographical pole (the southernmost point on the Earth). Because scientists know that magnetic fields can be produced by electricity, they believe that the Earth's magnetic field is caused by electric currents within the Earth.

48. According to the passage, scientists believe that the Earth's magnetic field is caused by

(1) deposits of magnetic rock
(2) the development of the compass
(3) the force of gravity
(4) electric currents within the Earth
(5) the two magnetic poles

49. Which of the following people would have the *least* use for a compass?

(1) a mountain climber
(2) a mechanic
(3) an explorer
(4) a map maker
(5) a pilot

50. A hiker's compass is most apt to give an incorrect reading when the hiker

(1) is in a strong wind
(2) reaches the top of a high mountain
(3) walks along the shore of a large lake
(4) is in a rainstorm
(5) passes beneath electric power lines

51. Imagine that a person stands on the Earth's north geographic pole and looks at his compass. The north pole of the compass needle will

(1) point toward a place that's north of where he stands
(2) point toward a place that's south of where he stands
(3) freely rotate and not point in any particular direction
(4) point straight at his feet
(5) point in any direction that he faces

Questions 52 and 53 are based on the following information.

A lever is a simple tool that is used to help a person do some type of work. As shown in the drawings below, a lever is a rigid bar that is free to rotate about a fixed point called the fulcrum. The fulcrum is the only part of the lever that doesn't move. The object to be moved is called the load. The position on the lever where the person applies force (pushes or lifts) is called the effort. Depending on the relative positions of the fulcrum, load, and effort, each lever is placed in one of three classes. The first two classes of levers are shown below.

CLASSES OF LEVERS

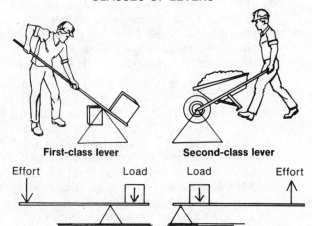

First-class lever   **Second-class lever**

Effort   Load   Load   Effort

Fulcrum   Fulcrum

In a first-class lever, the fulcrum is between the effort and the load.

In a second-class lever, the load is between the fulcrum and the effort.

52. A bottle opener is a familiar lever used to pry the cap off a bottle. Referring to the definitions above, how would you classify the bottle opener pictured below?

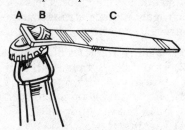

(1) as a first-class lever, with the fulcrum at point A
(2) as a second-class lever, with the fulcrum at point A
(3) as a second-class lever, with the fulcrum at point C
(4) as a first-class lever, with the fulcrum at point B
(5) as a second-class lever, with the fulcrum at point B

53. A double lever is a tool made by combining two levers of the same class. For example, the pair of pliers shown below is a double lever. Notice that in a double lever the object on which work is performed is considered the load. In the pliers, for example, the gripped nut is the load.

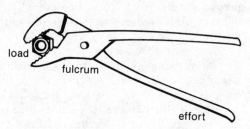

The nutcracker below is also a double lever. Which of the following correctly identifies the effort, fulcrum, and load?

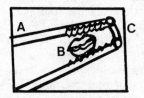

(1) A = effort, B = fulcrum, C = load
(2) A = effort, B = load, C = fulcrum
(3) A = load, B = fulcrum, C = effort
(4) A = fulcrum, B = load, C = effort
(5) A = fulcrum, B = effort, C = load

Questions 54–57 are based on the following passage.

One of the most controversial medical advances of the late twentieth century is the method of pregnancy known as surrogate motherhood. A surrogate mother is a woman who, on behalf of a couple (or a single person) desirous of a child, carries a fetus throughout pregnancy and birth. Then, immediately after delivery, the surrogate gives the child to the waiting couple.

A woman may become a surrogate mother by one of two methods. In the first method, she is artificially inseminated. A doctor uses a tube to place the man's sperm (sex cells) inside her uterus. She becomes pregnant when one of her own eggs becomes fertilized. In this type of pregnancy, the surrogate is actually the biological mother of the fetus she is carrying.

In the second method, a doctor implants a fertilized egg inside the surrogate mother's uterus. In this case the surrogate is not the biological mother of the fetus. The couple for whom she is carrying the fetus are the biological parents. The surrogate's only role is to provide the uterus in which the fetus grows until childbirth. For both methods, the surrogate is known as the birth mother because she actually carries and gives birth to the baby.

Most often, a surrogate mother is sought by a couple who, for some reason or another, are unable to have a child of their own. They choose this method of pregnancy because they desire that at least one or both of them be the biological parent of the child, even though a second woman carries the fetus. A surrogate mother may be hired, or she may be a friend or relative who volunteers her services.

Surrogate motherhood is controversial because it raises new types of issues concerned both with law and with human values. There are legal concerns about the rights of the couple, the rights of the surrogate mother, and the rights of the fetus or newborn baby. These rights are very hard to determine, especially in a situation in which either the couple or the surrogate wants to change any part of the contract or agreement concerning the child.

54. Which of the following is *not* a restatement of information presented in the passage?

(1) A surrogate mother is unable to have children of her own.

(2) A surrogate mother may be paid for her services.

(3) A surrogate mother may be the biological mother of the fetus she carries on behalf of others.

(4) A surrogate mother may be made pregnant by the implantation of a fertilized egg.

(5) A surrogate mother may not be the biological mother of the fetus she carries on behalf of others.

55. When a couple hires a woman to be a surrogate mother, risks are taken by everyone involved. From the possible situations listed below, choose the one that poses the *least* risk to the surrogate.

(1) The surrogate mother gives birth to a child with a birth defect, and the couple who hired her bring a lawsuit against her.

(2) The couple change their minds after the pregnancy is under way and decide that they don't want a baby.

(3) The couple refuse to pay the surrogate mother.

(4) The surrogate mother becomes emotionally attached to the baby and does not want to give the baby up.

(5) The child, born from a surrogate mother, may someday have difficulty adjusting to the facts surrounding his or her birth.

56. Which of the following could be a value of a couple who chooses to seek a surrogate mother arrangement? Surrogate motherhood is

(1) against the laws of nature

(2) too risky to the health of the surrogate

(3) a reasonable option for people who can't have children

(4) against the law

(5) not fair to either mother

57. Which of the opinions voiced below is *least likely* to be expressed by people who oppose the use of surrogate mothers?

(1) Pregnancy is risky to the woman giving birth, and it is not fair to place this risk on a surrogate mother.

(2) A surrogate mother will not provide necessary prenatal care since she doesn't intend to keep the child.

(3) People who are unable to have children of their own should choose adoption than rather using a surrogate mother.

(4) A surrogate mother should be paid at least the minimum hourly wage for every hour of pregnancy.

(5) Surrogate motherhood is not a natural process and should be banned.

Questions 58–61 refer to the information below.

Bread mold is the common fungus that is often seen growing on bread and other foods. To study the factors that influence the growth of this tiny plant, Kristen, a nutritionist, planned an experiment.

In her experiment Kristen wanted to find out if bread-mold spores (seeds) are air-borne (present in and carried by air). To investigate this question, Kristen toasted a piece of bread until it was crisp, and then she quickly placed it in a jar. She immediately sealed the jar with a tightly fitting lid. She then placed another piece of crisply toasted bread in a second jar. She did not place a lid on this second jar. She placed the two jars side by side on a table and observed them for three weeks. The results of her experiment are recorded in the following table.

Purpose of the experiment: To determine whether bread-mold spores are carried by air.

Observations at the End of Each Week

	1st week	2nd week	3rd week
Open Toast	No mold is observed.	Several spots of mold are observed on toast.	Mold covers much of the toast.
Enclosed Toast	No mold is observed.	No mold is observed.	Two spots of mold are observed on toast.

58. In her experiment, Kristen toasted the bread because toasting

(1) attracts bread-mold spores
(2) keeps bread from spoiling
(3) provides nutrients for bread-mold spores
(4) gives the bread a pleasant smell
(5) destroys bread-mold spores that may already be on the bread

59. The best summary of the information presented in the chart above is that

(1) bread mold forms on bread whether or not the bread is toasted
(2) bread mold forms on toast only when the toast is enclosed
(3) the rate of bread-mold growth on toast depends on exposure to fresh air, moisture, and temperature
(4) the rate of bread-mold growth on toast depends on the length of time the toast is exposed to fresh air
(5) bread mold forms on toast less quickly than it forms on bread that is not toasted

60. Which of the following is a hypothesis that is *not* supported by evidence presented on the chart?

    (1) Even a temporary exposure to air can result in bread becoming contaminated with airborne bread-mold spores.

    (2) Bread-mold spores grow better on bread that is not toasted because heat destroys certain nutrients.

    (3) More bread-mold spores grew on the open toast than the enclosed toast because the open toast had more exposure to bread-mold spores in the air.

    (4) Bread-mold spores can be made inactive and possibly destroyed by high temperatures.

    (5) By increasing the number of bread-mold spores on a piece of toast, you increase the amount of mold that actually grows.

61. Assuming that bread-mold spores are present in air, which of the following experiments would provide the best evidence concerning the effect of *moisture* on bread-mold growth?

    (1) Place one piece of fresh bread in a dry jar, and a second piece in a jar to which ten drops of water have been added. Seal both jars.

    (2) Place one piece of fresh bread in each of two dry jars. Seal one jar and leave the second jar open.

    (3) Place one piece of fresh bread in each of two dry jars. Add ten drops of water to each jar, and seal both jars.

    (4) Place two pieces of fresh bread in a single dry jar and leave the jar open for two hours. Then seal the jar.

    (5) Place one piece of fresh bread in each of two dry jars. Add ten drops of water to each jar and leave each jar open.

Questions 62 and 63 are based on the following information.

As part of a study of the causes and effects of lead pollution in the United States, the Environmental Protection Agency compiled the data shown in the graphs below.

GRAPH A: LEAD USED IN GASOLINE

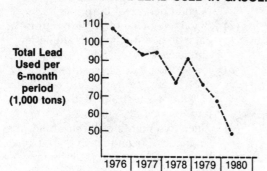

GRAPH B: AVERAGE BLOOD LEAD LEVEL IN AMERICAN ADULTS

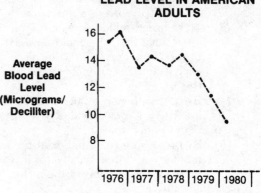

62. Which of the following is a conclusion that is supported directly by information in either of the graphs above?

   (1) Lead is a dangerous pollutant present in exhaust gases of cars that burn leaded (regular) gasoline.

   (2) By 1980, Americans were using less than half the yearly amount of gasoline that they had used in 1976.

   (3) Government regulations were responsible for the decrease in the amount of lead used in gasoline after 1976.

   (4) By 1980, the amount of lead pollution in the environment had been reduced to less than half of its 1976 value.

   (5) By 1980, the amount of lead used in gasoline had decreased to less than half its 1976 value.

63. Which of the following facts is needed in order to establish a cause-and-effect relationship between the two graphs above?

   A. Americans bought more unleaded gasoline in 1976 than in 1980.

   B. When leaded gasoline burns, particles of lead enter the atmosphere.

   C. Lead can enter the human bloodstream when a person breathes in air.

   (1) A only
   (2) B only
   (3) A and C only
   (4) B and C only
   (5) A, B, and C

Question 64 refers to the map below.

OCEAN CURRENTS OF THE WORLD

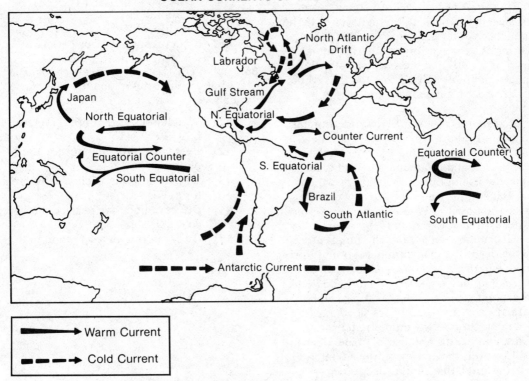

64. To which of the following studies would the map above be of *least* relevance?

(1) the study of ocean currents
(2) the science of weather prediction
(3) the study of volcanoes
(4) the study of aquatic animal migration
(5) the study of ocean navigation

Questions 65 and 66 are based on the following information.

Rhythms are patterns of behavior that take place periodically. Communities of living organisms exhibit daily, seasonal, and annual rhythms. An example of a daily rhythm is shown by hawks and owls. Hawks are diurnal animals and hunt only during the day, while owls are nocturnal animals and hunt only at night.

Migration is a seasonal rhythm. Animals migrate to find a warmer climate and new sources of food or to find a more suitable place to nest and produce their young. For example, ducks migrate at the start of winter from Canada to regions of warmer climate nearer the Equator. When the winter is over, the ducks return to Canada.

Hibernation, an annual rhythm, is a deep type of sleep that many animals go into during winter months. A true hibernating animal does not wake up during hibernation. Woodchucks and ground squirrels are true hibernators. Bears are not. Although bears sleep most of the winter, they do wake up often. Frogs, snakes, and lizards are also not true hibernators. However, they do spend their winters buried in mud, in a similar deep sleep.

65. Sleeping every afternoon is an example of

    (1) a daily rhythm
    (2) a seasonal rhythm
    (3) an annual rhythm
    (4) true hibernation
    (5) a nocturnal behavior pattern

66. Which of the following is a conclusion that can be drawn from the passage above?

    (1) Woodchucks go hunting more often in winter.
    (2) Bears sleep throughout the entire winter.
    (3) Salmon migrate each year in order to breed.
    (4) Ducks cannot live year-round in a cold climate.
    (5) Owls migrate only at night.

Use the chart below to determine the reading skills areas in which you need to do the most review. Circle any items that you got wrong and pay particular attention to areas where you missed half or more of the questions. The numbers in boldface are based on graphics.

Posttest Reading Skills Chart

Skill Area	Item Number	Review Pages	Number Correct
Comprehension	**1**, 4, 7, 8, 9, **11**, 13, 17, 20, 24, 35, 37, 42, 43, 54	14–30	_____ /15
Application	3, **6**, 19, 21, 23, 25, 28, 29, 30, 31, 32, 33, **34**, **39**, 40, 41, **52**, **53**, 65	31–41	_____ /19
Analysis	**2**, 10, **12**, 14, 18, 26, **36**, **38**, 44, 45, 47, 48, 50, 51, 55, **60**, **62**, **63**, 66	42–67	_____ /19
Evaluation	5, 15, 16, 22, 27, 46, 49, 56, 57, **58**, **59**, 61, **64**	68–91	_____ /13

If you got fewer than 44 items correct, go back and find the areas in which you had the most difficulty. Then, review those pages that you need additional work in.

Now, circle the same numbers for the items that you circled in the chart above. This will give you additional information about the science content areas in which you need the most review.

Posttest Content Areas Chart

Skill Area	Item Number	Review Pages	Number Correct
Plant and Animal Biology	16, 17, 18, 19, 23, 24, 25, 26, 27, 28, 29, 30, 31, 32, 33, 58, 59, 60, 61, 65, 66	92–121	_____ /21
Human Biology	35, 36, 37, 38, 42, 43, 44, 45, 46, 54, 55, 56, 57	122–51	_____ /13
Earth Science	1, 2, 11, 12, 13, 14, 15, 39, 48, 49, 50, 51, 64	152–83	_____ /13
Chemistry	7, 8, 9, 10, 41, 47, 62, 63	184–220	_____ /8
Physics	3, 4, 5, 6, 20, 21, 22, 34, 40, 52, 53	221–57	_____ /11

POSTTEST ANSWER KEY

1. **(4)** As shown on the graph, the surface layer is about 70°F, and the deep water is about 40°F. The thermocline is the transitional area between the two temperature regions.

2. **(2)** A volcano would be most disruptive because it would cause deep ocean water to boil, thus creating a region of hot water in what is normally a cold region of ocean. The other answer choices would do little to upset the normal pattern of ocean temperatures.

3. **(4)** Each of the other objects works by interacting with air resistance in some way, either by pushing against air or by having air push against it. Although a golf club swings through the air, air resistance does not make the club hit any harder.

4. **(2)** The passage states that blue light is scattered by air into the direction of your gaze. Thus, scattering changes the direction of movement of blue light.

5. **(2)** The passage states that scientists know how different colors of light are scattered by different types of gases in the Earth's atmosphere. Knowing the types of gases that make up the Martian atmosphere would enable a scientist to determine which color (or colors) of sunlight striking Mars would be scattered. This color would be the color of the sky as seen from Mars.

6. **(3)** The spheres carry like charges and will push away from each other. This follows the principle that like charges repel and unlike charges attract.

7. **(1)** The substances that are formed appear on the right-hand side of the chemical equation. Neither CH_4 nor CO_2 has a number preceding it, so you know that when one molecule of methane burns, only one molecule of CO_2 is formed.

8. **(4)** There are an equal number of oxygen atoms on each side of the equation. You can count them; you also know that this must be true if the equation is correct.

9. **(2)** Statement B implies that the number 35,000 is based on scientific evidence resulting from tests on engines using Syn 1.

10. **(3)** Statement A can't be supported by evidence, because the Syn 1 company can't know how its oil will compare to oil you use in the future. Statement D is also an opinion: the quality of stores where Syn 1 is sold is a matter of personal opinion.

11. **(5)** A full moon in indicated by the box at the lower right-hand side of the diagram. As you can see from looking at the moon in orbit, a full moon occurs only when the Earth is between the sun and the moon.

12. **(3)** Half of the moon's surface is lit by sunlight at any given point in its orbit. However, we see only part of this bright surface. As you can see from the diagram, most of the time, part of the side of the moon that's facing us is sunlit and part of it is dark. The moonlight that we see must be reflected sunlight.

13. **(2)** In the first paragraph, a fault is described as a collision boundary between two moving crustal plates.

14. **(4)** According to the passage, it is impossible to predict exactly where the next major quake will strike. San Francisco and Los Angeles are at equal risk.

15. **(2)** Weather conditions are not relevant in determining earthquake danger.

16. **(2)** A purebred results from inbreeding, the mating of nearly genetically identical animals. Thus, statements A and C must be true; B and D are incorrect.

17. **(3)** The passage states that hybrids are produced to create individuals with the desirable traits of each parent. None of the other answer choices is a correct restatement of information in the passage.

18. **(4)** Hybrids are produced when members of the same species mate—members that have distinct genetic differences. Only choice (4) names these two criteria.

19. **(4)** Each of the other choices is a result of breeding two organisms that are genetically very different. Answer (4) is an example of inbreeding, not hybridization.

20. **(4)** The passage refers to each form of potential energy as stored energy and to kinetic energy as energy of motion.

21. **(4)** A bathtub drain is designed to allow water to flow down through it, a use of stored gravitational energy. Boat oars make use of stored chemical energy (food energy) in the person rowing; a fireplace uses stored chemical energy in wood; a bicycle uses energy stored in the cyclist; an engine uses the stored energy in gas.

22. **(2)** The type of energy is not important. The relevant factors are availability, cost, safety, and feasability.

23. **(3)** A camel can go for a long period of time without drinking water. It does this by storing a supply of water within its own body, an ability that enables the camel to survive in the uncertain conditions of a desert.

24. **(1)** Animals give off carbon dioxide as a waste product of their breathing process.

25. **(1)** A huge forest fire both consumes a great amount of oxygen gas and releases a great amount of carbon dioxide gas. None of the other answer choices would greatly affect the oxygen–carbon dioxide balance.

26. **(5)** When ammonia is broken down before it is converted into nitrates, the nitrogen cycle is interrupted. Nitrates are necessary for plant growth.

27. **(3)** The types of crops previously grown would have the least effect on a new crop.

28. **(4)** A chameleon lays an amniote egg and has scaly, horny skin—common characteristics of reptiles. The chameleon is a small lizard.

29. **(5)** Bat offspring are nourished from the glands of the mother bat, a type of feeding that is an identifying characteristic of mammals.

30. **(2)** A salamander is an amphibian and must return to the water to reproduce. As implied in the description, adult salamanders live on land.

31. **(4)** A killdeer flies and lays eggs, two of the main identifying characteristics of birds. Some insects also fly and lay eggs, but *insect* is not given as an answer choice.

32. **(5)** Although it lives only in water, the whale gives birth to live young and then nourishes the newborn from the glands of the mother. Whales are mammals.

33. **(1)** Because the seahorse lives only in water and lays eggs, you know it's a type of fish.

34. **(3)** The stored energy is greatest when the passenger car is at its highest point.

35. **(3)** As the third circle graph shows, type O is by far the most common blood type of American Indians. No other blood type is even a close second for this ethnic group.

36. **(1)** As seen on each circle graph, O is the most common, followed by A, B, and AB, for all three ethnic groups.

37. **(3)** Look for *B* in the *Blood Type* column. If you follow the row for type B, you see that type B can donate blood only to type B or type AB.

38. **(4)** Only O can give blood to all of the other types, while only AB can receive blood from all of the other types.

39. **(2)** You'd expect that a room in which the air is stagnant (not moving) would have a temperature distribution such as that shown in graph b: the lower temperature air would be near the floor and the higher temperature air near the ceiling, with a smooth transition region in between.

40. **(2)** Only the sail on the sailboat is not an example of an object that has something to do with either gas being added to a closed container or an enclosed gas being heated.

41. **(4)** The guitar string stops moving because energy changes from one form to another. Each of the other answer choices deals with *matter* changing from one form to another.

42. **(4)** Answer (4) is a correct restatement of information contained in the second paragraph of the passage. None of the other alternatives is correct.

43. **(5)** A transfusion of Rh-positive blood to an Rh-negative patient could be made in an emergency situation as long as the recipient did not have Rh-positive antibodies in his or her blood. None of the other answers is relevant to the danger that this type of transfusion may involve.

44. **(2)** Discovery of the Rh-factor problem has led to medical treatment of affected babies. It has not resulted in a cure available for a woman's first pregnancy, any change in how people choose mates, or a better understanding of birth control.

45. **(4)** When Rh-positive blood is introduced into the body of an Rh-negative person, Rh-positive antibodies form.

46. **(4)** The doctor will want to check the father's blood to see if he is Rh positive. If he is, the doctor will want to be prepared to take steps to protect the fetus throughout pregnancy and birth.

47. **(4)** By comparing the chemical formula $CaCO_3$ with the formula CaO, you can see that one C atom and 2 O atoms are given off. Therefore, CO_2 is the gas that is given off.

48. **(4)** The last paragraph of the passage states that scientists believe that the Earth's magnetic field is caused by electric currents within the Earth.

49. **(2)** Of the people listed, a mechanic would have the least concern about the accuracy of directions. Each of the others would need to have an accurate compass.

50. **(5)** Because the passage states that magnetic fields can be produced by electricity, it is reasonable (and correct) to conclude that strong magnetic fields may surround electric power lines. These fields interfere with the proper working of a compass.

51. **(2)** According to the passage and illustration, when you stand on the north geographical pole, every other point on Earth is south of you, including the north magnetic pole.

52. **(2)** The fulcrum is at point A, the point that doesn't move. Point B is the load because the edge of the cap is lifted up. Point C, the handle, is the effort—the point where force is applied. The relative positions of these three points make this a second-class lever.

53. **(2)** The effort is the place where you apply force. As with the pliers, the gripped object is the load. The fixed point is the fulcrum.

54. **(1)** Choice (1) is false, since some surrogate mothers bear children. When a woman is artificially inseminated, the fetus grows from one of her eggs. All of the other answer choices are true and are restatements of information presented in the passage.

55. **(5)** Only choice (5) is not a direct risk to the surrogate. This is a potential problem that the parents who raise the child may face.

56. **(3)** People who seek a surrogate-mother arrangement are likely to believe that they are making a reasonable choice.

57. **(4)** People who oppose the use of surrogate mothers do so for all reasons except answer (4). Choice (4) expresses opposition to payment amounts but not to surrogate motherhood itself.

58. **(5)** To see if bread-mold spores come from air, Kristen had to first eliminate any spores that might be present on the bread she used. She toasted the bread to kill or deactivate any spores on it.

59. **(4)** Only choice (4) is a summary of information obtained from the chart. Choice (2) is false. The other choices may also be true, but the chart itself does not provide any supporting evidence.

60. **(2)** Only choice (2) is a hypothesis for which no supporting evidence is available on the chart. The chart says nothing about untoasted bread.

61. **(1)** Only choice (1) gives evidence in which moisture is the only variable that differs when comparing one bread sample with the other.

62. **(5)** Graph A shows this decline. Answer choices (1), (3), and (4) are true, but no information about exhaust gases, government regulations, or forms of lead pollution (other than lead used in gasoline) is given in either graph. Answer (2) is not true and cannot be inferred as true from either graph.

63. **(4)** Both statements B and C are needed to establish a cause-and-effect relationship between the two graphs. The graphs show a decline in the average amount of lead in Americans' blood at the same time that the usage of lead in gasoline declined. Knowing B, you can reasonably conclude that less lead in gas results in less lead in the atmosphere. Knowing C, you can reasonably conclude that less lead in the atmosphere results in less lead in human blood.

64. **(3)** Ocean currents are not likely to have much bearing on volcanic activity.

65. **(1)** An activity that takes place every day is a daily rhythm.

66. **(4)** Ducks go south for the winter, so it is reasonable to conclude that they could not live year-round in a cold climate. The passage says nothing about the migration of salmon or owls, so choices (3) and (5) are wrong.

ANSWER KEY

CHAPTER 1: COMPREHENDING SCIENCE MATERIALS

Exercise 1
pages 16–17
1. (2) Answers (1) and (3) are both mentioned, but they are details.
2. (3) All three paragraphs discuss how scientists are trying to find life on distant planets.

Exercise 2
pages 17–18
1. (4) The recycling of used oil is mentioned in both the first and third paragraphs.
2. (3) Throughout the passage, the author stresses that recycling old oil is something you can do that will benefit the environment.

Exercise 3
page 20
1. (1) Paper is represented by the largest piece of the circle.
2. (3) Only answer choices (2) and (3) relate to information found on the graph, and choice (3) is the only fact that supports the author's argument.

Exercise 4
page 22
Only numbers 1 and 3 should be checked.

Exercise 5
page 23
1. (4) Answer (4) is the only detail actually given in the passage. Answer (1) is not true, and (2) is an opinion.
2. (3) Only rain is mentioned as the way that pesticides enter groundwater.

Exercise 6
page 25
1. A transparent object lets most of the light pass through it. Only a small part of the light is reflected or absorbed. Examples include glass and water.
2. An opaque object allows no light to pass through it. Light is either absorbed, reflected, or both. Examples include wood and metal.

Exercise 7
pages 25–26
1. (4) According to the drawing, precipitation includes "snow, rain, hail, etc." Each of these falls to Earth.

2. (5) On the drawing, the word *evaporation* is used with forms of moisture that are returning to the atmosphere (shown by arrows pointing upward).
3. (3) The best answer choice is (3) because it includes all of the processes described by the other answer choices.

Exercise 8
page 27
1. The author thinks quite highly of robots.
2. The author implies that a robot costs less than an employee.
3. You can infer that the work done by a robot is as good as or better than work done by a regular employee.
4. You can infer that the author is an owner. Assembly-line workers are not enthusiastic about losing their jobs to robots.

Exercise 9
pages 27-28
1. (4) The author thinks that the books are based on "questionable research" and are making "health nuts" a fortune.
2. (2) The author says that the mice research "suggests" that middle-aged or older people ought to seek advice about exercise. Thus, answer (2) is implied.
3. (3) The author's attitude about exercise is certainly negative, which leads the reader to infer answer (3).

Exercise 10
page 30
1. (1) Although not a data point, the point on the line above 20 minutes corresponds to a temperature almost midway between 40° and 60°. The best answer would be 48°.
2. (4) The point on the data line directly to the right of 35°F lies above the 40-minute point.
3. (3) At 50 minutes, the water is partially, but not completely, frozen.

CHAPTER 2: APPLYING SCIENCE CONCEPTS
Exercise 1
page 32
2, 4, 5 Numbers 1 and 3 are not inherited traits.

Exercise 2
page 33
1, 2, 4 Numbers 3 and 5 relate to heat but not to expansion or contraction.

Exercise 3
pages 33-34
(3) Because the tailbone has no known use, it is considered a vestigial organ. Each other organ mentioned has a use of some kind, although the use may be limited.

Exercise 4
pages 35-36
1. (5) The relationship is commensal because the beetles nutritionally benefit but do not harm the ants.
2. (3) The relationship is parasitic because the fungus harms the chestnut tree as it takes nutrients from it.
3. (2) The relationship is saprophytic because the bacteria take nutrients from the remains of dead organisms.
4. (1) The relationship is predator-prey because the lioness kills and eats another organism.
5. (4) The relationship is mutualistic because both fungus and algae benefit from living together as a lichen.

Exercise 5
pages 37-38
1. (3) You would need to know the purpose of animal migrations in order to answer the question correctly.
2. (3) The Rocky Mountains are far from the ocean, so the tide would not affect them.
3. (1) Choice (1) is possible, while choices (2) and (3) are rare occurrences.

Exercise 6
page 38
1. (2) The nuclear waste issue is considered to be one of the most important issues facing the nuclear industry today. It is frequently discussed on TV and in newspapers.
2. (4) Reducing the amount of money spent on acid rain research only prolongs the problem; it does not help reduce it.

Exercise 7
page 40

1. 10:00 A.M.
   San Francisco time is three hours earlier than New York time.
2. forward
   New York time is later than San Francisco time.
3. wide awake
   When it's 10 P.M. in New York, it's only 7 P.M. in San Francisco.

Exercise 8
page 41

1. (3) Molars are used for the hard chewing required to soften adequately a piece of cut steak.
2. (1) Incisors are used for biting things off food held outside the mouth.
3. (2) Most people automatically try to bite a piece of string with their canine teeth.

CHAPTER 3: ANALYZING SCIENCE MATERIALS

Exercise 1
pages 43–44

1. o
2. f
3. h
4. f
5. o
6. h
7. f

Exercise 2
page 44

Answers may vary.

1. *Fact:* One possible answer is that a home computer can perform thousands of calculations each second.
2. *Hypothesis:* One possible answer is that, based on what is already known about computers, scientists believe that the human mind stores and sorts information in the same way a computer does.
3. *Opinion:* One possible answer is that a thinking computer would be a great benefit to our society.

Exercise 3
pages 45–46

1. (3) Only answer (3) is a fact. Answers (1) and (2) are predictions, and (4) and (5) are not correct.
2. (5) Only answer (5) is a hypothesis. Answers (1) and (3) are facts, and answers (2) and (4) are opinions.
3. (2) There is evidence available to support each of the other choices. Only (2) is a personal belief that is not supported by fact.

Exercise 4
pages 49–50

1. (2) Only answer choice (2) is supported by the graph. Of the specific causes named, the cancer bar is second in height only to the heart disease bar.
2. (1) Only (1) is an opinion that can't be proven. Each of the other answer choices is a fact.
3. (4) Only answer choice (4) is a reasonable explanation of an observed fact.

Exercise 5
page 51

Answers may vary.

1. The writer assumes that life exists on one or more other planets.
2. The astronaut assumes that unmanned spacecraft can't do an adequate job and that some information will be obtained through space travel.
3. Rhoda assumes that cold water will freeze more quickly than warm or hot water.
4. People assume that these drugs work and that there will be no serious side effects.
5. Doctors assume that there is always a chance that a drug may harm a developing fetus.
6. Astrologers assume that the positions of stars and planets can tell us something about human beings.

Exercise 6
page 52

1, 4 Both of these statements would need to be true if Jerry is correct. Statements 2 and 3 are simply facts, and 5 is irrelevant.

Exercise 7
pages 52–53

1. **(2)** People who demand an end to nuclear power plants do so because they assume that someone will listen to their demands. Only (2) mentions this possibility.
2. **(3)** To support nuclear power, a person would have to believe that a safe disposal method for radioactive waste will someday be invented.

Exercise 8
page 55

1. **(3)** The manufacturers of Goodgrow Fertilizer want you to think that the plants are identical in every way, except in height and in the type of fertilizer that was used.
2. **(4)** You can most easily answer this question by eliminating those choices that are assumptions Goodgrow wants you to make. These unstated assumptions are given as answer choices (1), (2), (3), and (5).

Exercise 9
page 57

1. c
2. e
3. b
4. a
5. d

Exercise 10
page 58

1. An increase in temperature could result in the evaporation of the Earth's oceans.
2. A decrease in temperature could result in the freezing of the Earth's oceans.

Exercise 11
pages 58–59

1. **(5)** Of the answer choices, only the death of tropical forests is a direct effect of an ice age. Answer (2) is not an effect—it is part of the definition of what an ice age is.
2. **(2)** Only answer (2) is a cause that could have brought about the end of the Mesozoic era. Each of the other answers is related to the Mesozoic era, but none of these answers is a cause.
3. **(4)** According to the passage, dinosaurs died because of the death of the tropical forests, the lush vegetation that was their food supply.

Exercise 12
page 60

1. heat, pressure, and chemical change
2. heat
3. erosion and cementation

Exercise 13
pages 60–61

1. **(3)** The purpose of a solar panel is to capture sunlight energy and use it as needed to heat a building.
2. **(1)** As shown in the drawing, the heat exchanger warms the air that passes next to it.

Exercise 14
page 63

Only choice 1 should be checked.

Exercise 15
pages 63–64

1. **(3)** Of the choices given, only answer (3) is a general rule that is both practical and reasonable.
2. **(5)** Only answer (5) is a conclusion that follows directly from the observation and your knowledge that a burning candle consumes oxygen.

Exercise 16
page 66

1. *moderate breeze*
   By looking in the *What Happens* column, you can see that both types of gales would be too strong for children to play in.
2. *gale*
   During a gale, tree branches break.
3. *strong gale*
   34 m.p.h. + 20 m.p.h. = 54 m.p.h. A 54 m.p.h. wind would be within the range of a strong gale.

Exercise 17
page 67

1. **(3)** The comparative size of the Earth is found in the column that gives the diameter (distance across) of each planet.
2. **(5)** Hydrogen and helium are the elements out of which the four largest planets are made.

CHAPTER 4: EVALUATING SCIENCE MATERIALS

Exercise 1
page 70

2, 5 All the other choices relate to smoking but not to the health risks involved.

Exercise 2
pages 70-71

1. **(3)** Only answer (3) mentions a legal definition of being too drunk to drive.
2. **(4)** Any car could have a burned out headlight, regardless of whether or not the driver was drunk.
3. **(2)** You determine that light, the faster of the two, will reach you more quickly.
4. **(4)** The cause of lightning has nothing to do with the distance and speed of both light and sound, those things related to the "rule of thumb."

Exercise 3
page 72

1. from north to south
2. from west to east
3. **(3)** the prediction of volcanic eruptions

Exercise 4
page 73

1. **(4)** Capturing fish and sieving beaks would be found on birds that obtain food from water sources.
2. **(1)** Both insect-eating and tearing beaks are used by birds for attacking small land animals.
3. **(5)** The brain size of a bird has nothing to do with its beak structure.

Exercise 5
pages 74-75

1. **(3)** Two animals that eat the same foods often must live in different parts of a forest.
2. **(2)** You need to know whether diesel exhaust produces more pollution, not whether it is smellier or more expensive.

Exercise 6
pages 75-76

1. **(5)** If Brenda's hypothesis were correct, all parts of the Earth would experience winter at the same time. As you may know, it is the tilt of the Earth's axis, not distance from the sun, that determines seasons on different parts of the Earth.
2. **(2)** Just because the United States produces a surplus of food does not mean that everyone gets his or her fair share of the food.
3. **(4)** Gasoline will float on water only if the two liquids are not miscible in each other and if water has a greater density than gasoline.
4. **(5)** For alcohol to float on oil, alcohol and oil can't be miscible in each other, and the density of alcohol must be less than that of oil.

Exercise 7
page 78

1, 4 Gold is listed as a metal, so 2 is not true. Choices 3 and 5 are also false.

Exercise 8
page 79

1. **(4)** Only choice (4) is true for both drawings A and B.
2. **(5)** The teeter-totter will balance only when the weight of each child is the same. To determine if this is the case, you need to know the weight of each child.

Exercise 9
page 81

1. Betty must choose between her religious values and the value she places on having children.
2. Jay must choose between his political values and the value he places on his job.
3. Wilma must choose between the value she places on a clean environment and the value she places on saving money.

Exercise 10
pages 81-82

1. **(3)** To sacrifice a baboon in the hope of saving a child, a person must value an infant's life much more than the life of a baboon.
2. **(1)** Only choice (1) represents a reasonable answer to this question, which addresses the issue of suffering caused to animals by medical research.
3. **(2)** Only answer (2) mentions the issue of comparative intelligence.

Exercise 11
page 84

1. **(2)** The other choices do not describe *positive* aspects of genetic engineering.
2. **(3)** The artist seems concerned about the possible dangers of some types of scientific research.
3. **(1)** The private company would be a proponent of genetic engineering. With only the information given, it would be impossible to determine the attitudes of the politicians.

Exercise 12
pages 85–86

1. **(3)** The drawings are meant to emphasize that much money is spent for space-based weapons and not enough is being spent to solve social problems.
2. **(5)** By the drawings, the artist shows his concern about how tax money is being spent.
3. **(1)** Answer choice (1) acknowledges the artist's concern but says in effect that the defense of the United States is a must, even if it means cutting back on government aid to the poor.

Exercise 13
page 88

1. **a.** identify a problem
   b. collect information
   c. form a hypothesis
   d. perform experiments
   e. draw conclusions
2. to have a second group of plants with which to make a comparison as the treated plants grew
3. If only one plant grew in each planter, it would not be possible to establish a reliable pattern of differences.

Exercise 14
page 89

1. **(5)** Choice (5) is the best because it describes the use of both a control group and an experimental group. Choices (1) and (2) do not use different-size cages for each group of mice. Therefore, in these two designs no comparative information could be obtained.

2. **(3)** Answer choice (3) is the best. If he gets the same results with new groups of mice, he can be pretty sure that his hypothesis is correct. Using the same number of mice ensures that crowding will occur again in the smaller cage.
3. **(1)** The most relevant evidence would come from studies of people who live in crowded conditions similar to those of the crowded mice.

Exercise 15
pages 90–91

1. **(3)** The brick and the paper clip fall at the same rate, as do the rock and the paper clip.
2. **(4)** Although the leaf and the paper clip are about the same weight, the leaf has a much larger surface. The difference in amount of surface might account for the difference in rate of falling.
3. **(5)** Wanda must drop two very light objects: one that has a small surface (the spoon) and one that has a large surface (the paper).
4. **(4)** Since the moon has no air, it also must have no air resistance. However, unlike the space shuttle, the moon does have gravity.

CHAPTER 5: PLANT AND ANIMAL BIOLOGY
Exercise 1: Overview of Plant and Animal Biology
page 93

1. d
2. c
3. a
4. e
5. b

Exercise 2: Plant and Animal Biology
pages 93–95

Comprehension

1. **(3)** The two paragraphs point out a variety of life forms living their daily lives.

Analysis

2. **(1)** While it's true that frogs eat insects, it is only an opinion that frogs are more important to humans than are worms.

3. **(5)** The meat in the control jar must be kept away from flies for the experiment to give conclusive results.

4. **(4)** Choice (3) is incorrect because the meat will rot whether inside or outside the jar. The cloth keeps flies from landing on the meat and laying eggs, so (4) is correct.

Evaluation

5. **(2)** Redi needed to start the experiment with meat that did not already contain fly eggs, or his experiment would have failed.

Exercise 3: The Life Cycle
page 96
1. growth
2. decline
3. beginning
4. death
5. maturity

Exercise 4: Living Things
page 97
Comprehension
1. **(5)** This is stated directly in the passage.

Analysis
2. **(2)** Animals that are slow to respond to stimuli that warn of danger are not likely to live long.

Evaluation
3. **(4)** Only answer (4) deals with the instinct for survival, an important difference between an animal and a puddle.

Exercise 5: Flowering Plants
page 100
1. a. The roots anchor the plant and obtain water and minerals from the soil.
   b. The stem holds up the leaves and transports water to them.
   c. The leaves carry on photosynthesis (food production).
   d. The flower contains the reproductive structures.
2. Your answer should include any two: bees, butterflies, hummingbirds.
3. a. T
   b. F
   c. F

Exercise 6: Plant Responses
pages 100–101
Application
1. **(2)** The Venus's-flytrap responds to an insect's touch, an example of touch response.
2. **(5)** The best answer is circadian rhythm. These flowers open and close in twenty-four-hour cycles.
3. **(3)** The roots grow in the direction of gravity, an example of positive geotropism.
4. **(1)** The sunflower moves to follow the sun, an example of phototropism.

Exercise 7: Animal Defenses
page 103
1. a. (2)
   b. (5)
   c. (3)
   d. (1)
   e. (4)
2. Animals' defenses help them hide from natural predators.

Exercise 8: Social Insects
pages 104–105
Comprehension
1. **(1)** Only choice (1) accurately sums up the main idea of the passage. Choices (2), (3), and (5) are only details, and (4) is not true.

Analysis
2. **(4)** If a hive is attacked, the worker bees sting the aggressor and then die. In this case, the bear is the aggressor.

Evaluation
3. **(3)** Choice (3) is true and is unlike any human social group, even a military unit. All the other choices are true of both humans and insects.

Writing Activity 2
page 105
Answers will vary, but you should include examples such as the following:
- Squirrels tease dogs and cats by chattering at them from the top branch of a tree.
- Dogs bark or jump up on the door when they want to be let outside.

Exercise 9: Cell Structure
page 107
1. d
2. a
3. e
4. c
5. b

Exercise 10: Cell Functions
pages 107–108
Comprehension
1. (5) Cell walls are not found in animal cells.
2. (2) According to the passage, chromosomes, which contain hereditary information, are formed from chromatin during cell division.

Application
3. (3) It is chloroplasts that are used by green plants for photosynthesis.

Exercise 11: The Structure of Organisms
page 109
1. F
2. T
3. F
4. T
5. T

Exercise 12: Cell Specialization
page 110
Comprehension
1. (4) All organisms start life as a single cell.

Evaluation
2. (5) Only the type of cell will tell the cell's function. Choice (4) is not correct because an organ contains many types of tissues.

Writing Activity 3
page 110
Your response might include points such as the following:

Yes	No
• I like knowing that I could have such a positive effect on someone else's life.	• It would be too traumatic for my family and friends.
• My life might someday depend on getting a transplant, so I should be willing to donate, too.	• My religion forbids the removal of organs after death.

Exercise 13: Chromosomes and Genes
pages 112–13
1. heredity
2. chromatin, nucleus
3. gene
4. two
5. chromosomes

Exercise 14: The Mechanism of Heredity
pages 113–15
Comprehension
1. (4) Only choice (4) is a correct summary of information given in the passage. Choice (1) is true, but it is a detail.

Application
2. (2) Of the various pairs, only choice (2) is a pair of animals that aren't similar in body shape and behavior.

Evaluation
3. (1) Identical twins have the same genetic makeup. If they were put in different environments, it would be easier to determine which traits are inherited and which are not.

Analysis
4. (4) All plants with at least one T gene are tall. Therefore, the T gene is dominant.
5. (4) Taking the four possible combinations of the two gene sets Tt and Tt, you get TT, Tt, Tt, and tt. Notice that we've written the capital T before the small t. You could also write Tt as tT.

Exercise 15: Ecosystems
page 116
1. c
2. e
3. b
4. a
5. d

Exercise 16: Communities of Living Things
pages 117–18
Analysis
1. (2) With a limited food source, many frogs would die. And, with the death of its predator—the frog—the grasshopper population would increase.
2. (4) Population increases only when more organisms are born each year than die.

Evaluation
3. (5) Each of answers (1) through (4) will directly affect the bass in Waldo Lake.

Exercise 17: Darwin's Theory
pages 120–21
Comprehension
1. (2) Choice (2) is a summary of Darwin's theory. Choices (1) and (3) are not true. Choice (4) is a detail.

Analysis

2. **(4)** If the land animals are scarce, being able to capture water animals would be the most useful survival trait.

Evaluation

3. **(1)** A beak is most useful for capturing food, so choice (1) is correct.

Evaluation

4. **(5)** Only choice (5) deals with how organisms may change over long periods of time, the main idea of Darwin's theory of evolution.

Application

5. **(1)** Only choice (1) is a trait that an animal might have some control over. By jumping a lot, a frog might strengthen its legs.

Evaluation

6. **(4)** If there was not much vegetation close to the ground, a giraffe would need to hunt high in trees for vegetation.

Writing Activity 4
page 121

Answers will vary, but you could include some of the following points:

Yes	No
• Even if rain forests offer no cure for cancer or no new energy source, they are a rare natural asset that should be saved.	• There are more urgent problems facing us, such as world hunger and discrimination.
• Every species on Earth has the right to exist.	• We need timber and cleared land more than we need rain forests.

CHAPTER 6: HUMAN BIOLOGY
Exercise 1: Overview of Human Biology
pages 123–24

1. a. body structure and function
   b. *Homo sapiens*
2. a. similarities in the structure of organs
   b. similarities in chemical makeup

Exercise 2: Evolution
pages 124–25
Comprehension

1. **(5)** Humans can create clothes, shelter, and other things that help them survive in harsh environments. Answer choice (3) is also a correct statement, but it is not a summary of the first two paragraphs.

Application

2. **(2)** Primates can walk erect on two legs. The gorilla is the only animal listed that fits this description.

Analysis

3. **(4)** Since Darwin believed that all organisms evolve, it is most reasonable that he would conclude answer choice (4).

Evaluation

4. **(3)** Only answer choice (3) deals with evidence that possibly links the early history of humans with the early history of apes.

Writing Activity 1
page 125

Answers will vary, but your list could include the following points:

Pro	Con
• We can't do without the medical knowledge gained through animal experimentation.	• Animal experimentation is cruel and should be stopped.
• I feel for the animals, but I also think a human life is more important than an animal's life.	• Experimenting with animals is unfair, since animals can't speak up for their rights or, in a lab, fight back.

Exercise 3: The Human Brain
page 128

1. two
2. left, right
3. neurons

Exercise 4: Brain Functions
page 128
Comprehension

1. **(3)** According to the reading selection, these nerve fibers are believed to allow the two halves of the brain to communicate.

Application

2. **(5)** Answer choice (5) is correct because it is the left half of the brain that controls the right side of the body.

Evaluation

3. (2)   Maddie can use statement A; some
          people are extremely intelligent, yet
          their brains are no larger than other
          people's brains. She can use statement
          C; humans are smarter than
          elephants.

Exercise 5: A Long and Healthy Life
page 130
1. T
2. T
3. F
4. T

Exercise 6: Aging and Life Span
pages 131–32
Comprehension
1. (1)   The passage states that half the deaths
          in the U.S. each year are caused by
          heart and blood vessel disease.

Analysis
2. (2)   Answer (4) is not true because poverty
          is also a source of stress. Answers (1)
          and (3) are not relevant, and (5) is false.

Comprehension
3. (1)   Increased average income is not men-
          tioned in the passage, nor is it necessar-
          ily related to life expectancy.

Evaluation
4. (4)   The amount of money spent on food is
          not important to know. It's the type of
          food that's purchased that is important.

Analysis
5. (3)   This conclusion is most reasonable when
          you consider that only the underfed
          mice lived beyond average life
          expectancy.

Evaluation
6. (2)   The time of day that the mice ate is not
          important. The researcher is interested,
          though, in the quantity of food eaten
          and the causes of death.

Writing Activity 3
page 133
Your lists could include some of the following
points:

Concerns
- financial worries
- illness or pain
- family living far
  away

Benefits
- retirement
- grandchildren
- wisdom

Exercise 7: Nutrition
page 134
1. b
2. e
3. d
4. a
5. c

Exercise 8: Diet and Exercise
pages 135–36
Comprehension
1. (5)   Excess calories are stored as body fat.

Application
2. (3)   Of the professions listed, the accountant
          is apt to get less exercise than the peo-
          ple in answer choices (2), (4), and (5).
          The accountant also will not need the
          calories required by the pregnant
          woman, who needs extra calories for the
          growth of the fetus.

Analysis
3. (4)   Exercise uses up energy (food calories).
          Thus, the more you exercise, the more
          food calories that are used up and not
          stored as body fat.

Evaluation
4. (3)   Answer choice (3) is not relevant be-
          cause it does not include height, an im-
          portant comparison factor.

Comprehension
5. (2)   This information is given in the chart.
6. (4)   This information is given in the chart.

Exercise 9: Body Structure and Movement
page 139
1. T
2. F
3. F
4. T
5. F

Exercise 10: Muscles and the Nervous System
pages 140–41
Comprehension
1. (1)   The purpose of the nervous system is to
          carry messages from one part of the
          body to another. In this way it acts as a
          communication network.

Application
2. (5)   Breathing occurs naturally and without
          conscious control.

Analysis

3. **(4)** An injury to the spinal cord in the lower back would affect all nerves impulses that try to travel to and from all lower points on the body, namely the legs.
4. **(2)** The nerve impulse must be sent from the girl's hand to her brain before she feels any pain. Then a nerve impulse is sent back to her hand, so her muscles contract and she pulls her hand away.

Evaluation

5. **(3)** Of the answer choices given, only choice (3) is related to the production of body heat as discussed in the reading selection.

Exercise 11: Eating and Breathing
page 145

1. d
2. a
3. b
4. e
5. c

Exercise 12: The Circulatory and Digestive Systems
pages 145–46
Comprehension

1. **(1)** According to the passage, the epiglottis performs this protective function.
2. **(5)** The circulatory system transports and delivers nutrients and oxygen to the body cells and waste carbon dioxide gas to the lungs.

Analysis

3. **(2)** Choice (2) is always true. Answer choices (1), (3), (4), and (5) may be true, but they would not cause an extra burden to be placed on an overweight person's heart.

Evaluation

4. **(4)** Answer choices (1), (2), (3), and (5) are all true, but choice (4) is neither true nor false. Choice (4) is an opinion based only on human values.

Writing Activity 4
page 146

Answers will vary, but your response could include the following points:

Yes	No
• In order to make an informed choice about sex, teenagers need to know the facts. They need to learn the facts from reliable sources such as parents or doctors—not from other teenagers.	• Discussing sex only puts ideas into children's heads—ideas that could get them into trouble.

Exercise 13: Reproduction and Human Genetics
pages 148–49

1. F
2. T
3. T
4. F
5. T

Exercise 14: Pregnancy and Prenatal Care
pages 149–51
Comprehension

1. **(1)** Identical twins form from one fertilized egg, not two.
2. **(4)** The female egg cell has twenty-three unpaired chromosomes compared to forty-six chromosomes (twenty-three pairs) found in all other cells.

Analysis

3. **(5)** The mother-to-be should avoid all types of chemicals, including those such as paint that can be accidentally inhaled.
4. **(4)** If a woman finds out she's pregnant, it would be best for her to discontinue social drinking.

Comprehension

5. **(3)** Since sickle-cell anemia is passed on genetically, it is not contagious.

Analysis

6. **(3)** Since any of the four gene combinations shown beneath the children is equally likely to occur, there are two chances in four (or 50 percent probability) that a child will be an NS person.

Analysis

7. **(2)** As shown in Diagram B, there is one chance in four (or 25 percent probability) that this couple will have a child with sickle-cell anemia (SS).

CHAPTER 7: EARTH SCIENCE
Exercise 1: Overview of Earth Science
page 153
1. oceanographer
2. astronomer
3. paleontologist
4. geologist
5. meteorologist

Exercise 2: Studying the Earth
pages 154–55
Comprehension
1. (3) According to the passage, the Earth undergoes many changes, both natural changes and those caused by people.

Analysis
2. (1) Only statement A is a hypothesis. Statement B is a fact, C is an opinion, and D is a prediction.
3. (2) Only statement B is a fact. Statement C is an opinion, A is a hypothesis, and D is a prediction.

Evaluation
4. (5) An environmental geologist would be most interested in toxic waste dumps because these dumps directly affect the safety of the environment.

Exercise 3: The Earth in Space
page 157
1. a. (4)   2. a. Mercury
   b. (3)   b. third
   c. (5)   c. Pluto
   d. (1)   d. 6 trillion miles
   e. (2)   e. 100 billion

Exercise 4: The Solar System
page 158
Comprehension
1. (4) According to the article, Copernicus had the correct idea that the sun is at the center of a system of orbiting planets.

Evaluation
2. (3) Planets do not give off their own light, but the sunlight striking the planets enables us to see them. Distance from the sun and surface temperature are not relevant to our ability to see the planets.

3. (5) Both statements A and D give you reason to think that the sun orbits the Earth. Statements B and C are true but not relevant.

Writing Activity 1
page 159
Answers will vary, but you could have used some of the following points:

Manned Flights
- The human perspective is necessary.
- Some technical activities can be performed only by humans.

Unmanned Flights
- Unmanned flights are safer.
- Unmanned flights are just as effective as manned flights.

Exercise 5: Seasons on Earth
page 160
1. a. T   c. F
   b. F   d. T
2. a. twenty-four hours
   b. one year (365 days)

Exercise 6: The Earth's Rotation
page 161
Application
1. (1) February is the hottest of the months listed. Remember, since the seasons are opposite, February in Brazil is like August in the United States.

Comprehension
2. (2) As shown on the diagram, Paris is eight time zones earlier than Seattle. Eight hours before 6:00 A.M. Saturday is 10:00 P.M. Friday.

Analysis
3. (4) The flight takes five hours, and an extra three hours is "lost" because of time zone changes. Thus, the flight reaches New York City at 4:00 P.M. (8:00 A.M. + 8 hours).

Exercise 7: Structure of the Earth
pages 163–64
1. a. 71, 29
   b. continents
   c. oceans
   d. crust
   e. mantle, outer core, inner core
2. a. a hypothetical supercontinent that no longer exists
   b. the movement of continents along the Earth's surface
3. earthquakes, volcanoes

Exercise 8: Plate Tectonics
pages 164–65
Comprehension
1. (2) Plate tectonics refers to the movement of rigid plates on the Earth's surface.
Analysis
2. (4) Of the answer choices given, only (4) is a hypothesis that attempts to explain the shapes of the continents.
Evaluation
3. (2) Of the answer choices given, only (2) involves something (rain) not relevant to volcanic activity.

Writing Activity 2
page 165
Answers will vary, but some possible reasons for evacuation and possible problems are listed below.

Reasons	Problems
• Lives would be saved.	• Tax money would be wasted on people who were needlessly evacuated.
• Some people might be able to save valuable possessions.	• Factories, stores, and businesses would lose money because of the temporary shutdown.

Exercise 9: Map Symbols
page 167
1. b
2. c
3. d
4. f
5. a
6. e

Exercise 10: Reading a Topographical Map
page 167
Comprehension
1. (2) According to the contour line readings, Eagle Ridge is over 3,100 feet high, the highest elevation shown.
Application
2. (3) The close contour lines that represent a steep slope appear on the west (left) side of Black Mountain.

Exercise 11: The Earth's Atmosphere
pages 169–70
1. the layer of gases (air) that surrounds the Earth
2. Ozone absorbs harmful ultraviolet rays.
3. carbon dioxide gas
4. 46 percent

Exercise 12: Layers of the Atmosphere
pages 170–71
Application
1. (1) The troposphere extends to an altitude of about eight miles and, therefore, contains the cirrus clouds.
2. (5) The shuttle must first pass through the top layer of atmosphere called the *thermosphere*.
3. (4) The ionosphere is the layer that affects long-distance radio reception.
4. (3) The mesosphere is the layer above the stratosphere, which is the ozone layer.
5. (2) The damage is caused in the stratosphere, which is the layer containing ozone.

Exercise 13: The Earth's Weather
page 172
1. a. (4)   d. (1)
   b. (5)   e. (2)
   c. (3)
2. a. clear, pleasant weather
   b. wet or stormy weather

Exercise 14: Weather Forecasting
pages 173–75
Comprehension
1. (2) Air pollution level is a part of weather reports in some cities, but it is not mentioned in the reading selection.
Application
2. (4) Like northern Canada, Antarctica is very cold.
Comprehension
3. (3) According to the definitions on map symbols, an isotherm connects places with the same temperature.
Analysis
4. (5) The map shows winter conditions in the United States. December is the best answer.

Exercise 15: The Changing Earth
page 177
1. rock fragments and organic materials
2. By burrowing, they allow air and moisture to seep into the ground.
3. Weathering (the breaking of rock) occurs before erosion (the movement of broken rock).

Exercise 16: Weathering and Erosion
pages 178–79
Application
1. **(4)** Ocean waves are a type of water erosion.
2. **(5)** Gravity causes rocks to fall as a landslide.
3. **(2)** When rock is changed by an acid, chemical weathering is occurring.
4. **(1)** Freezing water breaks granite by the process of physical weathering.
5. **(3)** In a desert, wind blows piles of sand from one place to another.

Analysis
6. **(5)** Arranged in order, the steps show how a river with a slight bend causes the bend to increase and then get cut off to form the oxbow lake.

Exercise 17: The Earth's Past
page 182
1. 4 to 5 billion years
2. Any three of these: solid rock, caves, tar beds, ice
3. Cenozoic

Exercise 18: Rock Layers
pages 182–83
Analysis
1. **(3)** Coal is formed from the remains of a tropical forest and limestone from the remains of ocean life.

Application
2. **(5)** Of the answer choices given, only the sea worm is a form of ocean life, the types of fossils found in limestone.
3. **(3)** Of the animals listed, the extinct camel is the one most likely found in a desert, the most probable explanation of the sandstone.

Analysis
4. **(2)** The variety of types of layers indicates that answer choice (2) is the best answer.

CHAPTER 8: CHEMISTRY
Exercise 1: Overview of Chemistry
page 185
1. d
2. e
3. b
4. a
5. c

Exercise 2: Studying Chemistry
pages 185–86
Comprehension
1. **(3)** According to the essay, salicylic acid, the basic ingredient of aspirin, was used in its natural form (as found in willow bark) by the American Indians.

Analysis
2. **(5)** Only statements B and C can be supported by facts. Statement A is a personal opinion that can't be proven true or false.
3. **(1)** There is no way to prove which science is the most difficult to learn.

Writing Activity 1
page 186
Your response could include one of the following arguments.
- The company should pay for victims' hospital expenses and evacuation.
- The company should not be held responsible.

Exercise 3: The Atomic Theory of Matter
page 188
1. a. elements
   b. protons, neutrons, electrons
   c. neutron
2. a. F
   b. F
   c. T
   d. T

Exercise 4: The Elements
pages 188–89
Comprehension
1. **(2)** Oxygen makes up 65% of average body weight, and hydrogen makes up 10%, for a combined total of 75% (65% + 10% = 75%).

Evaluation

2. **(5)** Carbon is listed as the second most abundant element in the first table, but is not listed at all among the nine specific elements shown in the second table.

Exercise 5: Protons, Neutrons, and Electrons
page 193

1. **a.** atomic number
   b. protons, neutrons
2. **a.** 11
   b. 12
   c. 11

Exercise 6: The Periodic Table
page 193
Comprehension

1. **(3)** The periodic table shows that atoms are listed by atomic number, the number of protons in the atom's nucleus.

Application

2. **(3)** According to the essay, elements that are listed in the same column have the same number of electrons in their outermost shells. In the periodic table, magnesium is listed in the same column as calcium.

Analysis

3. **(2)** Elements that are listed in the same row have the same number of shells. Reading the table from left to right, you can see that oxygen and lithium are both in the second row.

Exercise 7: Chemical Formulas
pages 194–95

1. **a.** two
   b. five
   c. six

2. C_4H_{10}

Exercise 8: Elements in Combination
page 195
Application

1. **(5)** The *2* in front stands for two molecules, while the subscript that follows an atom's symbol shows the number of atoms. Therefore, $2Fe_2O_3$ is the correct way to show two molecules of Fe_2O_3.

2. **(2)** The notation C_6 means that there are six atoms of carbon in the molecule. H_{12} indicates twelve atoms of hydrogen; O_6 indicates six atoms of oxygen.

Exercise 9: Chemical Bonding
page 197

1. **a.** (3)
   b. (4)
   c. (1)
   d. (2)
2. ionic bond: a bond formed when an electron transfers from one atom to another
   covalent bond: a bond formed when one or more electrons are shared between two atoms

Exercise 10: Different Combinations of Elements
pages 198–99
Comprehension

1. **(2)** Both unconsciousness and death are mentioned as effects associated with breathing concentrated carbon monoxide.

Analysis

2. **(4)** All answers will contribute to worker safety, but safe ventilation is of immediate importance to all employees because of the danger of carbon monoxide gas from car exhaust fumes.

3. **(2)** Answer (2) ensures that you minimize your breathing of carbon dioxide gas within an enclosed area.

Evaluation

4. **(3)** You can reasonably assume that light-headedness or dizziness may be the first effect felt by someone breathing too much carbon monoxide—a hypothesis that, along with the essay, supports conclusion (3).

Writing Activity 2
page 199

Your response might include the following points.
• Chemical weapons can continue to make people sick long after a war is over.
• Chemicals are unfair because they are invisible. There's no clear enemy to fight against.

Exercise 11: Phases of Matter
page 201

1. boiling point
2. freezing point
3. 32 or 0; 212 or 100

Exercise 12: Freezing Point
pages 202-203
Comprehension

1. **(3)** Find the point on the 3-gallon system line that is directly to the right of −15°F on the vertical axis. This point lies directly above 5 qt. on the horizontal axis.
2. **(2)** Protection to 0° takes about 5 qt., while protection to −20° takes about 7 qt. The answer is found by subtraction: 7 qt. − 5 qt. = 2 qt.
3. **(5)** No specific information is given for temperatures above 10°F or below −35°F.

Analysis

4. **(1)** The two graphed lines tell you that the larger system requires more antifreeze for every level of protection.

Exercise 13: Physical and Chemical Changes
page 204

1. physical change: a change in which a substance's appearance changes but those properties that enable you to identify it remain the same
   chemical change: a change in which a substance actually changes into other substances
2. **a.** chemical
   b. physical
   c. chemical
   d. physical

Exercise 14: Observing Physical Changes
pages 204-205
Analysis

1. **(2)** The room temperature determines whether thirty minutes is long enough for all the ice cream to warm to its melting temperature. If the room is cold, the ice cream may melt more slowly.
2. **(5)** Statement C is true because melting an ice cube can be reversed by simply refreezing the water, whereas sanding a board cannot be reversed. Statement D is true because melting ice is a change of phase, and sanding results in a change of shape of an object.

Exercise 15: Chemical Reactions
page 206

1. **a.** chemical equation
   b. reactants, products
2. **a.** one
   b. twelve
   c. twelve

Exercise 16: Chemical Reactions in a Greenhouse
page 207
Application

1. **(2)** As shown on the right side of the equation, six molecules of water (H_2O) appear as a product.

Analysis

2. **(2)** According to the equation, water is used to produce the glucose that plants use for energy.

Evaluation

3. **(5)** Because plants use carbon dioxide to produce the glucose needed for growth, placing more of it in the air is thought by some growers to speed plant growth.

Exercise 17: Solutions
page 208

1. d
2. c
3. b
4. a

Exercise 18: Types of Solutions
page 209
Application

1. **(4)** As mentioned in the essay, a carbonated soft drink consists of a gas dissolved in a liquid.
2. **(1)** Paint and paint thinner are both liquids.
3. **(2)** Punch mix is a solid, and water is a liquid.

Exercise 19: The Chemistry of Life
page 211

1. **a.** carbon dioxide, water
   b. carbon
2. organic chemistry

Exercise 20: Types of Fats
pages 211-12
Comprehension

1. **(1)** As seen on the graph, safflower oil contains the largest amount of unsaturated fat and also the least amount of saturated fat. Thus, safflower oil is the answer.
2. **(4)** Only olive oil has bars of equal height for both types of fat.

Analysis

3. **(3)** Statement C refers to a chemical ingredient, a substance that can be tested for. Statement A may or may not be true, but there's no test that can tell. Statement B is simply an opinion.

Exercise 21: Hydrocarbons
page 213

1. a compound that is composed of only hydrogen and carbon
2. a hydrocarbon containing a large number of carbon atoms

Exercise 22: Products That Contain Hydrocarbons
pages 213-14
Comprehension

1. **(3)** Methane would not be considered a polymer because it has only 1 carbon atom. Statements (1), (2), (4), and (5) are true for all three fuels mentioned.
2. **(4)** Gasoline, at 45%, is the main petroleum product and is represented on the graph by the largest part of the circle.

Analysis

3. **(3)** Transportation fuels include gasoline (45%), diesel fuel (7%), and jet fuel (7%). 45% + 7% + 7% = 59%.

Exercise 23: Pros and Cons of Plastic
page 216

1. strength, versatility, durability
2. any three: seabirds, seals, sea lions, turtles

Exercise 24: An Environmental Concern
page 216
Comprehension

1. **(4)** Its resistance to weathering and decay makes plastic difficult to dispose of, and this is the reason for the environmental concern.

Analysis

2. **(3)** Method A leads to ocean pollution, and method C leads to air pollution even if the burning is done far from land.

Exercise 25: The Greenhouse Effect
page 219

1. greenhouses
2. Carbon dioxide acts as a heat-trapping agent.

Exercise 26: Consequences of the Greenhouse Effect
pages 219-20
Application

1. **(2)** Like a nursery greenhouse, a car lets sunlight in but does not allow the trapped heat to escape easily.

Analysis

2. **(5)** Only answer (5) is a cause of the greenhouse effect. Answers (1) and (4) are both results.

Evaluation

3. **(3)** The protection of polar bears is not related to the greenhouse effect. Each of the other answers is.
4. **(1)** Because all hydrocarbon fuels contribute to the greenhouse effect, the best answer is (1). Choices (2) and (3) are partial solutions but not as complete as (1). Choice (4) wouldn't work, and (5) probably wouldn't help.

Writing Activity 3
page 220
Your response could include the following points:

Positive	Negative
• If chemical pollution continues at its present rate in *any* country, the existence of life on this planet is at risk.	• It would be difficult, if not impossible, to regulate every coal producer in the world.
• A global campaign would encourage feelings of world unity.	• Developing countries would resent regulation that slows their progress.

CHAPTER 9: PHYSICS

Exercise 1: Overview of Physics
page 222

1. d
2. a
3. b
4. c

Exercise 2: The Science of Energy
pages 222–23

Analysis

1. **(3)** Answers (1), (2), (4), and (5) are facts related to energy use, but only answer (3) is given in the essay as a *cause* of increased energy use.
2. **(4)** The essay mentions that physics research often leads to new consumer products, a fact that supports answer (4). Answers (1) and (3) are false. Answers (2) and (5) are not true in all cases.

Comprehension

3. **(5)** Adding the fossil fuel percents gives 30.2 + 28.5 + 30.8 = 89.5 percent or about 90 percent.

Writing Activity 1
page 223

Your response could include the following points:

Positive
- Computers enable workers to get their work done faster.

- Mistakes are easier to correct on a computer.

Negative
- Some people are intimidated by a computer's technology.
- Deadlines can be missed if a computer goes down.

Exercise 3: Newton's Laws of Motion
pages 225–26

1. **a.** force: any push or pull that can affect either an object in motion or an object at rest
   b. inertia: an object's natural resistance to any change in its motion
2. **a.** 3   **c.** 1
   b. 2   **d.** 2

Exercise 4: Properties of Motion
pages 226–27

Application

1. **(1)** According to the discussion of Newton's first law, the fact that a force is needed in order to stop a moving object (such as a car without brakes) is the result of that object's inertia.
2. **(3)** The sprinkler rotates because of a reaction force felt by the sprinkler nozzles from the pressure of the escaping water. Reaction force is explained by Newton's third law.

Analysis

3. **(5)** Oil would allow the sprinkler head to rotate more easily and thus react to the water by rotating more quickly. Increasing the water flow would also increase the reaction force felt by the sprinkler nozzles.
4. **(3)** As you can calculate from the graph, an object's speed increases by 32 feet per second during each second of fall.

Exercise 5: The Law of Conservation of Energy
page 229

1. constant
2. kinetic energy, potential energy
3. Friction

Exercise 6: Energy and Motion
pages 230–31

Application

1. **(2)** The energy is partly kinetic and partly potential only at point B, where the ball is halfway between its highest point (all potential energy) and lowest point (all kinetic energy).

Analysis

2. **(3)** The ball will have the greatest amount of force at its point of maximum kinetic energy, point C—its lowest point.

Evaluation

3. **(5)** The energy that was in the ball is not lost during impact. It is transferred to the building, breaking the building apart and creating sound and heat.

Exercise 7: Expansion and Contraction
page 232
1. **T** When a solid is heated, its molecules move faster and it expands.
2. **F** As the gas loses heat, its molecules move more slowly and it contracts.
3. **T** As the temperature rises, the gas gains heat energy. The molecules move faster and push harder on the inside of the tire, causing the pressure to increase.
4. **F** As water cools, it contracts.

Exercise 8: The Nature of Heat
pages 232–34
Analysis
1. (2) Heat always flows from the hotter object (the iron) to the colder object (the water) until both objects reach the same temperature.
2. (5) Since heat causes matter to expand, the metal beams expand during times of high temperature. The gaps provide room for this expansion.

Comprehension
3. (2) Locating *body temperature* on the diagram, you can see that the correct reading is 37°C or 98.6°F.
4. (4) Since 37°C is normal body temperature, 38°C is a slight fever. Choices (2) and (3) represent normal temperatures. Choice (1) is too low, and (5) is much too high.

Evaluation
5. (2) Because of the seriousness of a high fever, it is best to try to reduce the fever with a damp cloth and to seek immediate medical advice.

Exercise 9: Water Waves and Sound Waves
page 236
1. **F**
2. **T**
3. **T**
4. **T**

Exercise 10: Frequency and Hearing
pages 237–38
Analysis
1. (2) As shown in the table, a dog can hear frequencies as low as 15 cps, while a human's lower limit is 20 cps.
2. (3) Grasshoppers can "speak" at frequencies as high as 100,000 cps but can hear only at frequencies as high as 15,000. No other animal listed has this unusual ability.

Evaluation
3. (3) The table shows that most animals can hear at both lower and higher frequencies than those at which they can "speak." The main exception is the grasshopper.

Exercise 11: Light Waves
pages 239–40
1. a. vacuum
   b. wavelength
2. a. F
   b. T
   c. F
   d. T

Exercise 12: Properties of Waves
pages 240–41
Application
1. (4) The sound waves must diffract—move around barriers like doorways and corners—in order to reach your ears.
2. (3) The light waves cross a boundary when passing through the oil. When light waves refract, the light is separated out into a spectrum of colors.
3. (2) The echoes are simply sound waves reflecting off the alley and the surrounding buildings.
4. (5) Emilio bobs up and down each time the crest of a new wave reaches him.

Exercise 13: Electricity
page 243
1. d
2. c
3. e
4. b
5. a
6. a. static electricty, electric current
   b. conductor

Exercise 14: Electric Circuits
page 244
Application
1. (5) Statement B is false because electrons always flow away from the negative side of a battery. Statement C is false because a break in a circuit will stop the current flow to all points in that circuit: both light and bell turn off.

Analysis

2. (2) Only by opening switch b can you break the circuit that contains light 1 while, at the same time, not breaking the separate circuit that contains light 2.

Exercise 15: Superconductivity
page 246

1. e
2. d
3. a
4. b
5. c

Exercise 16: Superconductor Research
pages 246–47
Comprehension

1. (4) According to the passage, the main feature of superconductors is that they do not produce heat when electric current passes through them.

Analysis

2. (5) Only (5) is a possible cause of superconductivity. Answers (1) and (2) are simply observed properties of superconductivity, not causes. Nothing in the passage would lead you to infer that either (3) or (4) is correct.

Analysis

3. (4) Although it is certainly true that utility companies will save money, consumers will share in the savings only if the utility companies pass these savings along. Consumers probably will continue to use the same amount of energy, and they will not neccesarily switch to electric heating from gas or oil.

Evaluation

4. (2) Choice (2) identifies a value often known as greed! Unfortunately, this is what actually happens when scientists around the country race to develop new products.

Exercise 17: Magnetism
page 248

1. T   3. T
2. F   4. F

Exercise 18: Types of Magnetic Materials
pages 248–49
Application

1. (3) The thumbtacks are strongly attracted by the magnet.
2. (2) Lodestone is found in the earth, so it is naturally magnetic.

Comprehension

3. (5) Weak repulsion is classified as diamagnetic.

Application

4. (1) Since helium shows no reaction to a magnet, it is classified as nonmagnetic.
5. (4) Slight attraction is classified as paramagnetic.

Exercise 19: Radioactivity
page 251

1. alpha particles, beta particles, gamma rays
2. half-life

Exercise 20: Half-life
pages 251–52
Comprehension

1. (5) Radioactive elements decay constantly.
2. (4) Find the point on the curve that lies directly above the "3 days" point on the horizontal axis. From this point, follow the dotted line across to the answer on the vertical axis: about 125 nuclei remain after three days.

Exercise 21: Nuclear Power
page 253

1. *fission:* splitting a nucleus by bombarding it with other particles
2. *chain reaction:* the production of nuclear energy by the controlled fission of nuclei
3. *nuclear reactor:* a device in which controlled chain reactions are carried out
4. *nuclear fusion:* joining together two atomic nuclei

Exercise 22: Nuclear Energy
page 254
Comprehension

1. (3) In both nuclear and coal plants, steam is used to turn the turbine, which turns the electric generator.
2. (5) According to the article, U-235 is a type of fuel used in nuclear fission.

Analysis

3. **(2)** Only (2) is a statement about the future. Choices (1), (3), and (4) are facts, and (5) is an opinion.

Writing Activity 2
page 254

Your response could include one of the following points:

Pro-Nuclear	**Anti-Nuclear**
• If we stop producing nuclear weapons, our political enemies may have an advantage over us.	• If we don't stop producing nuclear weapons, we may destroy all life on Earth.

Exercise 23: Forms of Energy
page 257

1. uncontrolled
2. controlled
3. controlled
4. uncontrolled
5. controlled

Exercise 24: Our Energy Future
page 257
Comprehension

1. **(2)** According to the article, the cost of solar cell electricity is very high.

Analysis

2. **(4)** Technical problems and excessive cost are the most frequently given reasons that many energy sources are not yet widely used.

Evaluation

3. **(2)** Natural disasters may have a slight impact on energy production, but all the other choices are more relevant.